THINKING POPULAR CULTURE

Tara Brabazon has ushered cultural studies out of the drawing room and prodded it back onto the streets, where it matters more than ever.

Justin O'Connor, Queensland University of Technology, Australia

Brabazon is a 'war writer', grappling not with the culture wars but with war itself, including the wars within. She offers a cultural studies appropriate to the period between 9/11 and the present. Her elegiac essays range widely. Brilliant Brabazon is an antidote to the Bush 'war presidency' and its dispiriting denouement. She makes cultural studies matter again.

Ben Agger, University of Texas at Arlington, USA

Tara Brabazon has written a beautiful, passionate, and political book about popular culture in which the learning of pleasure is matched by the pleasure of learning, critique, and civic engagement. One cannot think about politics without engaging popular culture as a powerful educational force, and Thinking Popular Culture *is one of the best books available to confront this crucial question with great insight, enormous courage, and sense of social responsibility.*

Henry Giroux, McMaster University, Canada

Dedicated to my dancing mother Doris, my fashionable father Kevin and my husband Steve, the Levon Helm of Cultural Studies.

A special dedication must go to the 10,000+ students in three countries who have shared their education with me since 1992. Through war, terrorism, darkness and fear, you have shown grace, intelligence, humour and empathy. Whatever distance separates us, I cherish the moments of thinking and dancing, laughing and writing.

Finally, thanks to the Popular Culture Collective for support, advice and sharing a kind and respectful international community.

Thinking Popular Culture
War, Terrorism and Writing

TARA BRABAZON
University of Brighton, UK

ASHGATE

Published by
Ashgate Publishing Ltd
Wey Court East
Union Road
Farnham
Surrey, GU9 7PT
England

Ashgate Publishing Company
Suite 420
101 Cherry Street
Burlington, VT 05401-4405
USA

www.ashgate.com

British Library Cataloguing in Publication Data
Brabazon, Tara
  Thinking popular culture : terrorism, war and writing
  1. Popular culture
  I. Title
  306

Library of Congress Cataloging-in-Publication Data
Brabazon, Tara.
  Thinking popular culture : war, terrorism and writing / by Tara Brabazon.
      p. cm.
  Includes index.
  ISBN 978-0-7546-7529-7
1. Popular culture. 2. Terrorism in mass media. 3. War in mass media. 4. Mass media and public opinion. 5. Digital media. I. Title.

  HM621.B73 2008
  306.0917'521--dc22

                                                                    2008028449

ISBN 978 0 7546 7529 7

Printed and bound in Great Britain by
MPG Books Ltd, Bodmin, Cornwall.

Contents

VISION

Introduction

Interventions in/denial

Like most stories of writing, this tale begins with reading. Irvine Welsh is a famous writer, one of the select few whose name is larger on the dust jacket of books than the title. He is also aggitatively creative: he has built new vocabularies and graphologies, transforming how words appear on the page. But I did not realize the scale of his importance, relevance and generosity until I read his foreword to Paul Vasili's *The First Black Footballer* where he outlines the social costs of a ruling class dominating the voices and attitudes of a time, spewing out values and ideas that create a narrow and damaging view of history and culture.

> The point is that while a well-funded cultural system exists to spew out ruling-class culture, any culture, art and history promoted outside of this system relies largely on concerned maverick groups or individuals. The society is only 'liberal' or 'pluralist' to the extent that it tolerates those different voices which are generally let in to spice up the mainstream only when it becomes intolerably bland. In the meantime, we lose so much of our culture.[1]

Welsh's support for this book was crucial. Vasili had crafted an important project of historical recovery. He rebuilt the life of Arthur Wharton, the 'first' black British footballer. Such a valuable manuscript rarely attracts an audience, with sports fans drawn to season reviews and hagiographies. Irvine Welsh's name on the cover granted the book a wide audience. He used the space in his foreword to enact a precise and pointed attack on those in power and the political apparatus they use to keep it. He recognized that the powerful, the white, the ruling class take what they want from disempowered lives and experiences to freshen up the marketing of popular culture, but tolerates little sharp critique or resistance. The ignorance of black history in supposedly quintessential 'British' sports is merely one symptom of a blind ignorance of difference and the fear of change and criticism.

At a time where university 'research' is defined as that which corporations, pharmaceutical companies and conservative governments pay us to do, those of us who think, read, write and create have some choices to make. For me, becoming a McDonald's Professor of Nutrition or the Body Shop Professor of Alternative Therapies holds little appeal. It is Irvine Welsh – and writers like him – who crash through the mediocre, the meaningless and the banal. Through his non-fiction even more than his fiction, he reminds us about class and its consequences on people's lives.

> Inequalities in society are what the rich reward themselves with. And these inequalities not only have to be maintained but justified.[2]

> What we really need is freedom *from* choice.[3]

In a time when choosing a mobile phone ring tone is a 'political' statement about identity, Irvine Welsh's attack on choice and inequality is more accurate and incisor sharp than has emerged from political parties in years. At some point in the last two decades, most citizens in post-industrial nations made a decision that choice (in shopping centres) was more important than equality (in society).[4] Welsh reminds readers that there are other ways of thinking, being and writing.

The power and passion in Welsh's work emanates from non-fiction, rather than his fiction. But how is his writing to be categorized: political diatribe, literary journalism, ficto-criticism, auto-ethnography? Many of these labels are destructive, involving journalists and critics who cannot write putting labels on those who can. Publishers are mindful to keep their fiction and non-fiction lists as separate as skin after a post-wax Brazilian. Those who write between categories and move between fashion and the archive, university and community are living in the wrong time for publishing and politics.

Irvine Welsh gave many of us the permission to write, think and create, even though we were not born into the right class, the right country or had the accent, name or university degree that was meant to create the network to permit publishing and critical review. Instead of reeling off famous literary 'influences,' he stated that:

> I was never a great reader of fiction, that's the problem that I had. People make the assumption that if you work in some medium a lot of your references come from that medium as well. I think the biggest practical influence I had was through working for the council.[5]

Welsh's statement is courageous and important. He confirms that writing melts from many contexts and environments. Now, as we jolt and rumble through the 2000s, our political and social systems are suffocating in their intensity, ripped by war, 'natural' disasters and celebrity makeovers. Popular culture has a fluidity to match these difficult changes. With postmodernism living on vapours and multiculturalism in crisis, we now have problems in understanding how to grasp and negotiate difference. The speed of change is tracked by rapid labeling and periodization. A post-9/11 world flowed into a post-7/7 world. Each act of terrorism squashed older theories of time, history and politics. Instead of more numbers, we need more intricate explanations for why young men choose to fill a backpack with explosives, to kill those going about their work or leisure. There is a cold wind biting through our pleasures, laughter and hope. The darkness of the present is not enlightened through the rose-coloured illuminations of the past. Nostalgia is an anti-political formation. Yet by summoning a past with a plan, a future can be made of our choosing. While direct and violent action is justified in the name of a 'War on Terror', a much more distinct, considered and careful war on ideas is necessary. *Thinking Popular Culture* is part of this project of persuasion, dialogue, argument and exchange.[6]

Instead of this more difficult mission, writers, scholars and critical thinkers have often turned away from their responsibilities. Judith Butler confronted these losses – this crisis – of dissent and debate in her potent collection of essays, *Precarious Life*.

> It was my sense in the fall of 2001 that the United States was missing an opportunity to redefine itself as part of a global community when, instead, it heightened nationalist discourse, extended surveillance mechanisms, suspended constitutional rights, and developed forms of explicit and implicit censorship. These events led public intellectuals to waver in their public commitment to principles of justice and prompted journalists to take leave of the time-honored tradition of investigative journalism.[7]

While the film makers Michael Moore[8] and Robert Greenwood, and the intellectuals Howard Zinn[9] and Noam Chomsky,[10] have shown great courage in these difficult times, the impact of Fox News and the closing of international news bureaus[11] has resulted in self-appointed 'experts' replacing expertise. Web 2.0 has meant anyone with an opinion and a particular type of literacy has a chance to present their words, video and pictures. This blog, wiki, Google, Flickr, MySpace, Facebook, YouTube discourse has enabled a confusion of democracy with digitization,[12] and social justice with libertarianism. There is a reason for this displacement of thoughtful, researched argument with random, emotive blogging. Terrorized grief has justified a loss of thought and dissent,[13] rather than an opportunity to reconsider and reevaluate older topographies of power and economics. The limits to what can be said, seen, heard or thought are determined through the suffocating labels that have been placed on dissenters: foreigners, asylum seekers, terrorists, unpatriotic, un-American, un-British, un-Canadian, un-Australian. The use of such terms represses the recognition that all deaths are equivalent, that the mourning and grief suffered by 'foreigners' are as dense and destructive as those of 'citizens'.

In this environment, John Carey titled his book with a provocative question: *What Good Are the Arts?* He acknowledged that there are groups in the culture who gain power and privilege by affirming particular artists and performers as disconnected from the grimy world of commerce, sleaze and sex. Carey realized that 'the arts have traditionally excluded certain kinds of people as well as certain kinds of experience'.[14] He probes the value of – and in – 'the arts' and asks for explicit criteria through which importance, relevance and significance are determined. The focus of my book – on popular culture and not 'art' – signifies a project of activism, intervention and change.[15] The ranking and judging of experience and emotion is not only illogical but the residue of past inequalities in the present. Our time necessitates a confrontational, active (re)interpretation of such categories and assumptions. We can learn from the wars, fights and courage of the past. George Orwell, from the crucible of a fight against Nazism, arched back into history to acknowledge a fellow campaigner for justice and equality.

> When one reads any strongly individual piece of writing, one has the impression of seeing a face somewhere behind the page. It is not necessarily the actual face of the writer … Well, in the case of Dickens I see a face that is not quite the face of Dickens's photographs, though it resembles it. It is the face of a man of about forty, with a small beard and a high colour. He is laughing, with a touch of anger in his laughter, but no triumph, no malignity. It is the face of a man who is always fighting against something, but who fights in the open and is not frightened, the face of a man who is generously angry – in other words, of a nineteenth-century liberal, a free intelligence, a type hated with equal hatred by all the smelly little orthodoxies which are now contending for our souls.[16]

Dickens was a soldier in the war of ideas, as was Orwell. They were not always right and they were not always politically expedient, but they had the courage to fight and be wrong.

Academic writing and writers – particularly when their topic is popular culture – have even greater difficulty creating the space and courage to fight against orthodoxies. Split between well-researched monographs that few will publish and fewer will read and a textbook market that many will read and no one will understand, there is nothing left to wager with the devil at the literary crossroads. Yet surprises do emerge, and these edgy and disturbing books not only have to fight publishers, referees, editors, copyeditors and marketers, but also reviewers. Sometimes and somehow these words survive. One example of an academic critic misjudging and misinterpreting an innovative and important

4

book emerged from David Birch's review in the acclaimed journal *Cultural Studies*.

> This can mean, as is the case with Iain Chambers's book, that the final product is unnecessarily simplistic, theoretically confused, too broad in its sweep through the subject and/or time, and methodically uncertain in direction and execution. No amount of high-status academic appropriations and referencing (to Barthes or Lyotard) or unspecified quotations (from Nietzsche, Artaud or Breton) is likely to help – particularly in Chambers, where referencing is carried out in a haphazard and idiosyncratic way. People, concepts and terms should not act simply as markers to other disciplines and ways of thinking, but should be a fully necessary and integral part of an interdisciplinarity required for understanding a book's argument and position.[17]

The book being discussed is Iain Chambers' *Urban Rhythms: Pop Music and Popular Culture*. It went on to become the indispensable research foundation for soundscapes, urbanity and pop. It is the book of the field. This early review failed to grasp the difference between innovative scholarship and a derivative and dull restatement of earlier originality. Instead, Birch argued that 'primary data can often stand best without comment'.[18] This mode of Rankean empiricism, where facts can be denuded of interpretation, is dangerous in all historical periods, but in a time of xenophobia, terrorism, war and public relations, 'the primary data' is difficult to capture, isolate or categorize. Chambers' *Urban Rhythms* survived this review. How many radical, difficult and important books lose their audience through such mis-readings?

George W. Bush described himself as a war president.[19] The status of both 'the war' and 'the presidency' was debatable and must not be left to stand 'without comment'. He left a legacy for a generation of writers after the conclusion of his presidency. All of us are war writers. We sculpt and craft our sentences through the punctuation of tanks and missiles, flags and coffins. For those of us who write about popular culture, such a context is even more damaging. It is not a time to talk about home decorating and dancing, macramé and makeovers. A dense – but productive – guilt must be part of the context for pop writers in this era. Where we place this shame – for writing rather than shooting – is important. During the First World War, there is an apocryphal story that two earnest middle class ladies entered Oxford to recruit for the British army. Discovering a young man reading Thucydides on a park bench, one well-dressed matron asked, 'And what are *you* doing to save Western civilization, young man?' The young don only temporarily looked up from his book to reply, 'Madam, I *am* Western civilization.'[20]

Such academic confidence in our own time of war is misplaced. The finest political – and popular – writers like bell hooks and Hanif Kureishi have confronted the injustices of race and religion through screen and education. In acknowledging the pain and potential of difference, these fine writers – to restate Kureishi's book title – have connected 'the word' and 'the bomb'. While – like Welsh – a great writer of fiction, it is Kureishi's non-fiction that has found its time and purpose. After writing two pivotal articles in *The Guardian*, he published a slim but evocative book, *The Word and the Bomb*. The title itself is noteworthy. His writing is not only sharp but has bladed the platitudes and simple justifications for war, activating complex histories of difference.

> In the post-war period, race – and now religion – have become subjects around which we discuss what is most important to us as individuals and as a society, and what scares us about others. Race is a reason to think about free speech and 'hate' speech; about integration, or what we have to be in order for society to work, and about the notion of the 'stranger'. We use the idea of race to think about education, and what we assume our children should know; about national identity; whether we need an identity at all, and what such an idea means; about sexuality, and the sexual attitudes and powers we ascribe to others, as well as our place in the world as a nation, and what our values are. We think, too, through the often mystifying topic of multiculturalism, about how mixed and mixed-up we are, so much so that we find it disconcerting for others to be multiple, and even worse, for us to be so, too.[21]

Our difficulty in 'mixing' confirms how 'mixed up we are'. This war against terror/ism is not a question of representation, but survival. The goal now is to increase the debate and increase our struggle over ideas. Those of us who work in media and cultural studies have a task. Through the 1980s and 1990s discussions of 'theory' – often mislabeled as poststructuralism or postmodernity – disconnected the approach to study from an object of study. Research in popular culture in particular was buried in abstractions of resistance, hegemony or ideology. The consequences of this debate are visible in our postgraduate programmes to this day: the (safe) attention to method too often overwrites and neutralizes the tough discussion of ideas and how they connect to social and political change. This book is founded on the necessity to build a rational, secular thinking popular culture that contributes to the society from which it emerges.

Thinking Popular Culture was written after September 11. Not only was this a period of pensive questioning about the consequences of terrorism and the war used to fight it, but a time of powerful dissent in unusual forms and places, such as the rebirth of the popular documentary which used alternative methods of distribution through DVD.[22] Perhaps described as 'the Michael Moore effect' and extended through Robert Greenwald's triology of *Unconstitutional*, *OutFoxed* and *Uncovered*, these films provided alternative voices and views about democracy and civilization. Greenwald revealed the motivation for his film making.

> I'm proud to be part of these three films. I hope you will enjoy them. I hope you will be affected by them. But most importantly I hope that you will take what they say, what they talk about, and then go out and take action to have the kind of country and the kind of world that we want for ourselves and for our children.[23]

The idea that these important projects and ideas have operated outside of the mainstream television stations and cinema complexes shows that popular resistance can emerge in a way that slices through the flattening of expertise and a shrinking of debate. This intellectual work, in the best Gramscian tradition, summons alternative ideas and punches them out into society. Good sense becomes common sense.

Thinking Popular Culture is motivated by these films, alongside 40 years of media and cultural studies. Writers such as Raymond Williams, Stuart Hall, Henry Giroux, Iain Chambers and Henry Jenkins[24] have not only questioned cultural value but the political shards and debates in our daily lives. The media-tions of the self, through screen and sound, teach us about identity and community, exclusion and belonging. The richness of their research is a motivation to continue their work. The tragedy is that media studies is suffering vitriolic attacks from journalists. Janet Street-Porter, in particular, has been dismissive and small-minded in her criticism. She stated that, 'I would never employ anyone with any qualifications in media studies: they are useless.'[25] This book – no book – cannot counter such a blanket assault on a particular approach to writing, research and scholarship, but it can catch a spark of the energy and dynamism that this approach offers in moments of social and political threat.

Thinking Popular Culture is inspired by the courage of media studies researchers, writers like Irvine Welsh and Hanif Kureishi and the suite of documentary film makers who challenge the status quo, agitate the powerful and reveal the lies. My task is to explore popular culture that matters, that probes the assumptions of war, whiteness, Christianity, masculinity and progress. John Gray argued that 'the suicide warriors who attacked Washington and New York on September 11, 2001 did more than kill thousands of civilians and demolish the World Trade Center. They destroyed the West's ruling myth.'[26] Wars are times when the ideologies that are often buried in clichés of business as usual are dusted off to justify premodern violence and gothic retribution. Questioning such a project, and unimpressed by neo-evangelical 'celebrations' of burgeoning new media, I remain interested in new writing and new ideas on all media. Carefully selected slices of culture are captured in the following pages, to assess their impact in furthering change and critique. The chapters vary in length but chatter amongst themselves: *The Office* playfully mocks the serious documentary film making of *No Direction Home*. Johnny Cash soberly questions Christianity while the Pet Shop Boys march through fundamentalism. Louis Vuitton's leather is sliced up by Boy London. Live 8 is silenced by the bombs of 7/7. The writing in this book is drawn to those parts of the cultural landscape that are not only pulled to the 9/11 political magnet, but offer (just) a moment of hesitation and resistance through this attraction. The four sections – Think, Design, Sonic and Vision – are touch pads to key into the commitments and confusions of 'war writing' during a war that was declared outside of the parameters of the international community and, like the best soap operas, never seems to end.

It is the correct time for such a book to emerge. In the political silences and suffocations since September 11, popular culture has been a concertina crushed by the dual pressures of market forces and militarism. Now that the leaders in the Coalition of the Willing when the Twin Towers fell have also fallen from grace, it is important to write the cultural history spanning from 2001 to 2008. Commencing with that ashen September day and concluding in the year Bush limped from his presidency, we untangle the popular culture from the politics. Through Big Brother, text messaging, the iPod 'revolution', Web 2.0 and user-generated content, it is necessary to pick the scab of popular culture to reveal the scars of war. Although unpalatable and perhaps incorrect, Andrew Keen's critique of our contemporary age should be considered.

> What kind of media ecosystem is best to encourage, nurture and reward talent? … I don't think this digital narcissism is it. People want to broadcast themselves rather than listen to what others are saying. I'm nostalgic for the world I grew up in where there was a clear distinction between author and audience. It's hard to be good at what you're doing. In the same way that not everyone should be doctors or teachers or astronauts, not everyone should be an author. Most people do not have anything interesting to say.[27]

While Keen's ruthless judgment of others is provocative, he offers a starting point for debate. Instead of assuming that all social networking sites, blogs and YouTube videos are intrinsically of value and building democracy, Keen is carrying forward an antiquated notion of cultural value. Nostalgia can be a counter-productive political force, and also anti-popular culture. At its best, pop occupies its present. This book neither celebrates the new nor validates the old, but explores the cycles and relationships in the history of popular culture.

There is anger in these pages and hostility at hypocrisy. But there is also a commemoration of courage. Popular culture moves. It is flighty, promiscuous and dangerous. It does not abide by the artificial and overloaded boundaries of race and nation, exclusion zones and border protection. While evocative postcolonial theory has signposted this fragmentation, its maxims and ideas are rarely mobilized within popular discourse. Homi Bhabha does not have the public profile of Julie Burchill. Etienne Balibar is not as recognizable a name as Irvine Welsh. Such statements make no judgment about quality, but influence. Popular culture can summon, shape and change subjectivities. It can be compliant, conservative or resistive. This book is drawn to the transgressive – to the interventionary – to pop that thinks, attacks and disturbs. Popular culture teaches us about how to be a man or a woman, young or old, black or white. It fills the empty spaces of our knowledge with content and aspirations. Pop is a contingent formation, triggering concurrent racialization, commodification and hybridization. While Islamaphobia is the grammar of current affairs and news broadcasting, there are also spaces to write and think differently. Young Muslim men, hooded and on public transport, have a greater role than the script that has been written for them as a threat to 'civilization'. The focus on terrorism means that the costs of the resultant xenophobia and racism are underplayed and silenced to ensure national security. Paul Gilroy confirmed that:

> Multicultural society seems to have been abandoned at birth. Judged unviable and left to fend for itself, its death by neglect is being loudly proclaimed on all sides. The corpse is now being laid to rest amid the multiple anxieties of the 'war on terror'.[28]

Multiculturalism has been mashed through the historic clash of civilizations and religions. Terrorism exists, but we must ask each day how our actions, language and interpretation of events provoke either destructive prejudice or effective recalibrations of societal injustice. The tension between governance and inequality too often triggers a 'tick the box' culture. Are we disabled? Are we Muslim? Are we gay? Life, identity, conflict and experience flit around such boxes. When differences are essentialized and multiculturalism is celebrated not questioned, nationalism becomes the default model for social inclusion.

Cultural diversity and differences are threats to closed and 'safe' national unity, but like all challenges, they productively unsettle commonsense and the patterns of our 'normal' lives. In rebranding identity and demanding critical thought – not blogged opinion or wiki editing – some popular culture raises critique from within consensus. Axiomatic answers about religion, family, motherhood, fatherhood, race and multiculturalism are no longer enough to understand the context and truths of our lives. We require more knowledge, more reading, more debate and more cultural resources to ensure not only social inclusion, but social justice. Through wars and elections, it has been a bland pop cultural decade. My mood has matched women's hemlines: uneven and frayed. Paris Hilton and Nicole Richie giggled through a simple life, only reinforcing the class injustices that no one – seemingly – wishes to mention anymore. We are more interested in fuel prices and interest rates than the redistribution of wealth in our societies. I am not sure when mascara choice became more important than education, but we need to see a lot more women speaking about politics, sport and the economy rather than makeovers, fitness and cosmetics.

Occasionally, popular culture can intervene, critique and shred accepted and acceptable behaviour. Perhaps the power of popular culture during the presidency of George W. Bush was that numerous alternative Americas – away from a War on Terror or hawkish neo-conservatism – were constructed and projected.[29] It was a Woody Guthrie America of dissent, alternatives and consciousness, and his popular cultural children have continued his legacy. The brilliant and defiant Margaret Cho, who is not only a stand-up comedian but philosopher and atheist prophet, is an American who thinks critically about being American.

> People think too simplistically nowadays. They need only sound bites to sustain them. This is why the news anchors on the Fox network always scion and then repeat catchphrases, to manipulate and brainwash the masses. The ease with which the message is heard and assimilated is the key to Fox's success, and ultimately may lead to the demise of democracy itself. Isn't that sad? That stupidity alone might take America down?[30]

Smart popular culture is a great remedy for dumb public culture. Cho has chosen to stay and fight. Another fine fighter is Jon Stewart. Best known for *The Daily Show*, a 'comedy' programme spoofing news and politics,[31] and his book *America*,[32] he also destroyed CNN's *Crossfire* while appearing on it.[33] His explanation for enacting this self-critique (from within) captures the power of interventionary popular culture.

> Thomas Goetz: It was also a powerful critique of television that people agreed with. It was good television.

> Jon Stewart: Boy, I never want to be part of something called 'good television'. I can tell you that with certainty. That is not a comfortable place to be. But you know what it was? It was a person not playing the role that is prescribed to them under normal circumstances.[34]

Stewart has captured the pivotal definition of *Thinking Popular Culture*. It is knowing the rules of the dominant culture, understanding the limitations of media and genre, but still transgressing and challenging dominant people and ideas from within. Stewart is building and facilitating news literacy in a time of

Fox News and tabloidization. While offering his attack from cable channels, he shreds television from within television.

> Stewart: Tomorrow is perhaps one of the most important days of your life, and yet you have chosen to spend the night before with me. Senator, as a host I am delighted. As a citizen I am frightened. Your response?
>
> Clinton: It is pretty pathetic.[35]

Ignoring the burden of representation in being an educated, intelligent, affluent white man, he offers critiques of both modernity and tradition, tabloidization and politics.

Thinking Popular Culture is a war book, yet it is not a review of Al Qaeda strategies. It is not implicated in Francis Fukuyama's jump away from the neo-conservative road.[36] It does not have the piquant grandeur of John Gray's theories of modernity.[37] Instead, it is a book about war and popular culture, and war in popular culture. Most importantly, it is a reminder to those political leaders who dismiss pop as trash or rubbish[38] that there is movement in rhythm, energy bolting out of a screen and a switch blade jutting from the crease of design. If there is a characteristic of this new century, then it is a lack of imagination, a lack of dissent, an inability to ask the difficult questions of those in power, and to maintain a focus long enough to obtain an answer. The popular culture revealed in these pages is courageous: singers, designers, writers, film makers and thinkers who slice through contradictions and paradoxes with humour and determination. May we learn from their example and use the word, the song and the screen, rather than the bomb.

THINK

Google is white bread for the mind

Ten years ago, the best-seller lists were filled with books about sex. Correction. Relationships. Mars and Venus peppered our personal lives. Self-help gurus skipped around talk show circuits with grace and limitless confidence. Now that sex gets in the way of shopping and relationships are replaced with social networking sites, new gurus pump up the wonders of digitization, exhibiting the enthusiasm of eight-year-olds managing Attention Deficit Disorder without Ritalin.

We live in a post-Marxist, post-feminist, post-postmodern, post-post-postcolonial age. With everything in the post, there are few theories of change. Instead, we describe crisis. Locked in the digitized echo chamber of Google, small events and micro-traumas resonate with too great a sonic impact. As a result, the scale and spectrum, tone and texture, of the analogue and digitized world becomes flattened, shrunk, Google ranked on popularity, packaged and sold. Because Google page ranks sites on the basis of popularity, it is reasonably easy to influence the algorithms that display and order results. Called Search Engine Optimization (SEO),[1] all users must monitor not only the content of the sites returned but also the (lack of) diversity and rationale for the ranking.

Instead of thinking while searching, we are like seagulls swooping down for chips in a beachfront carpark. We have no idea how the chip got there or the dangers involved in eating it. The aim is to fly in, grab a tasty morsel before our less competitive friends find it and swoosh out as quickly as possible before anyone sees us. Any parallels with our contemporary university system are purely accidental.

Reading, writing and publishing have also changed in this seagull culture. The focus is on micro-events of insignificance that are puffed into an historical revelation of biblical importance. Bookshelves are filled with tipping points[2] and wisdom of crowds.[3] Chris Anderson's *The Long Tail*[4] captures an argument so simple it can be conveyed through the title. He investigated Amazon, eBay and online music retailers to show how 'endless choice' is creating 'unlimited demand'. He argues that the focus on best-sellers is misguided and the internet has changed 'everything'. Technological determinism is fused with neoliberalism, where the market promises endless growth and choice. There is no questioning of whether choice – in and of itself – is valuable, or at what point (a tipping point?), consumerism presents a nasty bill rather than a welcome dividend. When do the waste, environmental damage, banality and stupidity create permanent and unredeemable harm?

It is fascinating how many of these books look inward to other Web 2.0 hyped-up sources as evidence for their arguments rather than outward to analogue history. For example, in *The Long Tail*, Anderson states:

> ten years ago, people complained that there was a lot of junk on the Internet, and sure enough, any casual surf quickly confirmed that. Then along came search engines to help pull some signal from the noise, and finally Google, which taps the wisdom of the crowd itself and turns a mass of incoherence into the closest thing to an oracle the world has ever seen.[5]

An oracle? In a secular society, we look for gods and demons on the internet and everlasting life under the surgeon's knife. For Anderson to transform an algorithm into an oracle not only shows the success of the Enlightenment's vision of science, truth and progress, but that Web 2.0 lacks a secular agenda and rationale for being. In most Google searches, Wikipedia's entry is offered as the first returned site. This is not a long tail service. It is a ruthless ranking of popularity. Also, the sponsored links hover near the cursor at the top of the page for the accidental misreading of the ranking. Marinating in the irrelevant, pointless and silly presents a bill for education and citizenship. Scanning book titles replaces reading books. Google searches replace research.

My favourite subtitle in this oeuvre is Malcolm Gladwell's *Blink: The Power of Thinking Without Thinking*.[6] This phrase embodies a celebration of experience and feeling, rather than rationality and argument. The morphology of these digitized histories is as predictable as watching the life of that chip on the seaside. Wherever the history commences, with the Arpanet, CERN, Microsoft, Google, the iPod or Web 2.0, the male writer offering his tale invariable confirms that one particular hardware or software innovation changed 'everything'. As a result of this supposed revolution in technology, *everything* is online. *Everyone* is online. Social relationships are managed through social networking sites. Commerce is e-commerce. Teaching is now replaced with facilitating. We have seen this relanguaging in the past. I am old enough to remember when we used to have librarians. Now we have information managers and resource centre administrators. The dark tragedy of our age is that at the very point where we need leadership from librarians and teachers to negotiate our way through an information-thick – rather than rich – age, managerial and administrative decisions change our designation, function and purpose.

Reflective histories – let alone historiographies – of technology, information or education rarely trouble these digitally hyped-up writers and administrators. Jeff Gomez's *Print is Dead*[7] is the archetype of this new pathology in publishing. He describes his goal as to create 'a tidy one-stop shopping experience for the future of the book debate'.[8] His problem is that eBooks failed. In fact, it was a catastrophic disaster. But he did not blame publishers or young people, the group he calls 'digital natives'[9] for this failure. The morphology of the digital folktale cannot allow actual facts to disturb the clean narrative. Instead, he described those who still read print on paper as 'slightly hysterical',[10] 'pretentious'[11] and 'self important'.[12] While confident in the labelling of others, no media literacy theory or information management literature is cited anywhere in *Print is Dead*. Better scholarship emerges when probing how different media platforms activate diverse styles of reading.[13] Scrolling through a screen is effective for some research modes. Movements through print on paper are useful for other projects. The configuration of an artificial choice between books or eBooks, paper or screen, is an inaccurate rendering of current readership practices and ignorant of a palette of fascinating and emerging literacy scholarship.

There are so many – too many – writers offering simple answers to complex questions about platform migration and cultural value. Will Richardson's *Blogs, Wikis, Podcasts and Other Powerful Web Tools for Classrooms* confirms that 'resistance is futile' and describes himself as being 'an internationally known "evangelist" for Web 2.0 platforms'.[14] This language is important. In an era of thinking without thinking and evangelists whose faith is placed in a software application rather than teaching quality, we – who believe in thinking while thinking and argue against fighting fundamentalism with other fundamentalisms – need to deliver a patch to the present. This patch will not solve Vista's myriad incompatibilities, but will anchor our Googling seagull culture to an intricate and complex history of media and popular culture that moves between, not through, analogue and digital environments.

The last decade has generated two magnetic poles that have pulled cultural and political forces towards them: September 11 and Google. The accelerated history written since 2001 has configured shallow and compressed narratives about modernity, nationalism, multiculturalism, education and identity. Google has been the ideal mechanism to locate facts without context for a digitized constituency who have gained just enough literacies to pass through an education system testing competency rather than expertise and skills rather than knowledge. When framed by a context of fear, where foreigners are everywhere and borders must be patrolled, the safe screen of Google ranks and superficial surfing beckons. The combination of digitization and a war on terrorism is writing a fast history that churns out plenty of information, but little time for reflection and few interpretative tools. Some have labelled and diagnosed this problem with a(n appropriately) soundbite phrase. Andrew Keen, in the flawed but expansive book, *The Cult of the Amateur*, has questioned the cost of a loss of expertise.[15] I have monitored the 'Google Effect'[16] and *The University of Google*.[17] But my concern in this chapter – and throughout *Thinking Popular Culture* – is that as more attention has been granted to the hyped-up promises of technology, the less scholarly focus has been placed on popular culture.

Popular cultural studies has died,[18] as internet studies and web-related research and teaching has increased. While not as publicized as the closing of the Birmingham Centre for Contemporary Cultural Studies, the Manchester Institute for Popular Culture at the Manchester Metropolitan University, that great beacon for so many of us who studied popular culture around the world in the late 1980s and 1990s, closed in 2006. Its three directors through its history left the project in different ways. Derek Wynne died in 2002 while playing football. Justin O'Connor took his projects on city imaging and urban regeneration to the University of Leeds as their Professor of Cultural Industries and then on to the Faculty of Creative Industries at the University of Technology in Queensland, Australia. The first director, Steve Redhead, is the Professor of Sport and Media Cultures at the University of Brighton. Significantly, none of the living ex-directors of the MIPC still flag popular culture in their work.

In a time where Google is white bread for the mind, providing tasty morsels of information without intellectual context or attention to literacy, one part of the *Thinking Popular Culture* project is to bring back dangerous, strange, inspiring and challenging popular culture to publishers, journals, universities and classrooms. Luckily, from the ashes of the MIPC's published works, two underutilized guides remain to help me through this journey. This chapter remembers, reclaims and logs an important article that had a bumpy journey through publishers and editorial boards and has been practically ignored since it was written. It is 15 years since Jon Savage and Simon Frith published 'Pearls and swine: intellectuals and the mass media'. The article first appeared in the MIPC Working Papers in Popular Cultural Studies and later the *New Left Review*,[19] after being rejected by the *London Review of Books*. It also appeared in Steve Redhead's *The Clubcultures Reader*,[20] a collection of the best seminars delivered in the MIPC. Significantly, Google Scholar only reports 15 citations since 1993 and most of these citations are from scholars outside the United Kingdom.[21]

The article was shaped by quite immediate social forces. Jim McGuigan had published *Cultural Populism*,[22] where he argued that the study of popular culture had been over-run by academics celebrating – uncritically, he argued – particular fandoms as 'resistive' to 'dominant culture'. For McGuigan, this was a form of left-wing populism. John Fiske[23] and Henry Jenkins[24] were framed as particular targets, but many cultural studies academics were implicated in the discussion. McGuigan's critique was so successful that there was little space left to offer intelligent commentary about popular culture. Fiske later retired from the academy with his extraordinary legacy in the United States of America and Australia underwritten and under-recognized. Jenkins moved his 'celebrations' to Web 2.0, where his textual poaching could be rebranded as participatory culture.[25] Frith and Savage, while logging McGuigan's concern, also questioned the right-wing populism of the journalists associated with style journalism, including the now closed *Face* magazine and *The Modern Review*. Toby Young and Julie Burchill offered what Frith and Savage believed was an anti-intellectual expression of enthusiasm for popular culture, becoming cheerleaders for the market economy and foreshadowing the flattening of expertise that would predominate the Web 2.0 world. Experience replaced expertise and street credibility became more important than academic credentials.

Frith and Savage – operating in this crunched space between right- and left-wing populism and trying to value the study of popular culture through Jim McGuigan's blistering and effective critique – tried to craft a way forward for scholars, journalists, fans and citizens. It is a pathway few have taken. Digitization, terrorism, anti-intellectualism, celebrity culture, vocationalism and the marketization of universities have transformed popular cultural scholars into punch drunk researchers that are labelled luddites, dumbed down or strange. Through these challenges, Frith and Savage created inspiring work that is worth revision. They realized that, 'for both academics arguing about the curriculum and journalists arguing about the arts pages, what is at issue is "popular culture" – how we should think about it, how we should study it, how we should value it'.[26] They locate 'a crisis of critical language',[27] in finding and moderating the space between high theory and the high street.

How popular culture is written about and taught must capture, challenge and channel passion and energy, but also find a way to express this dynamism while establishing critical distance from it. Because this discussion of popular cultural value slipped away in the celebration of digitized connectivity, the debate that most worried Frith and Savage – between journalists and academics – has been marginalized. Both groups have suffered through the flattening of expertise through user-generated content and this digitized culture of equivalence. The resultant flattened normality perpetuated through English culture, which Frith and Savage describe as 'domestic, heterosexual, suburban, middle-class',[28] then overdetermines the abnormal, the different and the defiant. They believe 'the cultural question becomes where, precisely, do these [different] people live? The political question is how to keep them there – out of sight at the margins.'[29] Gay men only gain visibility when they put the light into light entertainment. University academics are only used as cheap talking heads when documentary film makers have run out of micro-celebrities promoting their next book or fitness DVD. Inner cities only exist for crime and hooded teenagers. Rural environments are only needed as an origin to work out food miles to the suburbs. Digitization has increased the invisibility of these marginalized groups. In analogue life we meet diverse groups in exercise classes, in shopping centres and on the street. But the digitized screen is ruthless. It is a social guillotine. Those with literacy, equipment and context can live and play on the screen. Those who were outside of Web 1.0 only have the injustice reinforced and increased through Web 2.0. For all Facebook's social connectivity, of news feeds of trivia and uploaded photographs of 'friends' dancing and drinking, analogue poverty and injustice amid the Morlocks does not touch digitized, connected, 'collaborating' Eloi.[30]

The digital screen has kept the different, foreigners and the outsiders at the margin more than Frith and Savage could have imagined in 1993. They argue that dichotomies of ordinary versus elite, journalist versus academic and conservative versus progressive have stifled the study of popular culture. When digital versus analogue is woven through these binaries, the result is uncomfortable silence. There is no space to differentiate within popular culture, to value parts of it differently. For media and cultural studies academics, either we validate the rulings of the arts establishment or become a cheerleader for *American Idol*. We need to build an interpretative matrix and information scaffold through which we can once more add depth, complexity and an analytical framework to all media, art and culture. This will ensure that a *Daily Telegraph* opera critic cannot abuse Paul Potts as being 'a karaoke crooner'[31] while ignoring the distinguished history of singers such as Mario Lanza, Howard Keel and Jane Powell, who moved arias from opera houses and into cinemas and the family home through the twentieth century. It will also mean that xenophobic, racist, homophobic, sexist or simply banal popular culture can be placed in context, rather than automatically celebrated or ignored. All culture requires more history, debate and discussion. In this way, we can both acknowledge and translate the past of media and cultural studies into a workable paradigm in our present. Rather than sighing about dumbing down or the decline of academic and journalistic standards, we can think, create, interpret and debate not the value of culture – the what and how of the aesthetic – but the why of culture, its purpose and function.

Stuart Hall famously remarked that he is only interested in popular culture because it is a site of struggle between dominant and subordinate groups. Without that struggle, he 'doesn't give a damn about it'.[32] Actually, in moving hegemonic models from Gramsci to Poulantzas and beyond the war of position, writers and researchers also need to explore the role of popular culture – particularly digitally convergent culture – in *undermining* struggle through a flattening of debate. While Hall rightly spent his career critiquing the binary of high and popular culture, very few of the critics that went on to be inspired through postmodern and poststructuralist theorizing predicted what would happen when the grand narratives – the expansive explanations of life, history and identity – were cut away. The flattening created conformity, not struggle and the platform migration from analogue to digital meant that so many of the multi-sensory, multiliterate and complex analogue texts have not been digitized and are invisible in the Google ranking.

I always teach my students to find and probe what is not being talked about, what questions are not being asked. There is a rationale for my imperative: what is absent from the history of ideas is often more important than what is present. Google PageRank makes asking these questions difficult. The problem is made worse because Wikipedia actively removes original research,[33] demands a neutral tone[34] and deploys metadata to lift its profile through Google searches.[35] We do not live in a time where commonsense and neutrality is the pathway to truth, let alone equality. Intervention is necessary and required. It is not a question of perpetuating Savage and Frith's dichotomies in terms of arguing in favour of – or against – market forces. Creative industries debates have taken scholars, policy makers and students beyond Althusserian-inflected studies of the state.[36] It is significant that the theorist of choice for fashionable academics at the moment is Bourdieu. Compared to Althusser,[37] Poulantzas[38] or even Foucault,[39] Bourdieu offers simple concepts like cultural capital that are elegantly presented, but not grittily difficult. Basically, Bourdieu is Althusser for hippies: weak views, well written and strongly held.[40] Frith and Savage demanded more of academics. The maxim that they bequeathed us from this extraordinary essay is that:

> the great failing of our age is the idea, received wisdom from right to left, upmarket and downmarket, that to be popular you have to be populist, which means an uncritical acceptance of an agenda set by market forces.[41]

My task, and I hope to share this goal with many readers of this book, is to open out the space for dangerous, difficult popular culture, to neither accept market forces nor deny market forces, but barge through safe, secure suburban life and into a new way of living through difference, rather than denying it. This is the *Thinking Popular Culture* project. The first stage in this research is historical reclamation, remembering and valuing the Thinking Pop of the analogue age, ensuring that it is intellectually migrated into our post-September 11 environment. But there must also be space to contextualize and research specific nodes of popular culture that provoke or act defiantly against the simplicities of celebrity culture. It is sociology and history that has been lost from digitization. In the bubbling, exciting environment of the present, supposedly everyone is online and using mobile phones and social networking sites. Even more seriously, there is a disturbing assumption that online collaboration is synonymous with democracy.[42] Actually, a few careful studies from the PEW Internet and American Life Project[43] and OfCom[44] show that there are extraordinary differences in how diverse groups use media platforms. Until the sociology and history of the World Wide Web start to hold a more distinguished place and role in debates about democracy and cultural value, then assumptions about 'everyone' will ensure that some of the most fascinating discussions about analogue and digital media are not even commenced.

Researchers in media and cultural studies have a responsibility to probe, push and understand the contemporary popular cultural landscape and temper present enthusiasm with past realities. A series of tripartite questions provide the spine for this inquiry.

Who is online?
Who is not online?
What are the consequences of this digital exclusion?

What platforms are being used by specific groups? Why?
What platforms are not being used by specific groups? Why?
What are the consequences of different deployment of media resources?

What materials and sources are captured in the online environment?
What materials and sources are not captured in the online environment?
What are the consequences of not digitally migrating particular sources of information?

What functions, roles and aims are best activated in analogue environments?
What functions, roles and aims are best activated in digital environments?
What methods and strategies can be developed to create a movement between – not through – analogue and digital environments?

There is enough research involved in answering these questions to keep scholars, writers and journalists busy for a lifetime. But they all distil to one question from Lenin – Vladimir Illich, not John (Lennon). What is to be done?[45] Currently, I have two ways to answer this question. One way is to agitate the relationship between research and popular culture. The other is to reframe our link between teaching and popular culture. These two tasks form the final two parts of this chapter.

Taking flight: (Analogue) Byrds in the digital age

The Byrds are an important research topic to demonstrate the potential of a rejuvenated popular cultural studies. They are also a site to apply the shape of digital research raised in this chapter.[46] Like most long-lived popular culture, a study of this band is useful to track and trace changes to music, recording, audiences and technology. The series of tripartite questions about online and offline research offered on the preceding page can be applied most effectively to historic pop, offering sources to track the pathways from unpopular to popular culture and back to popular memory. The role of the past, history and nostalgia can also be mapped while monitoring the digital interventions in analogue popular culture, determining what has been migrated and what has been lost. Influential popular culture moves between the analogue and digital, and can hook deeply into our identity and narrate experience. In the case of Roger McGuinn, founder of The Byrds and a man who can list one of his achievements as creating a new way of playing guitar, fans and scholars can also explore when the compression, transferability and repeatability of digitization is of value, and when the preciousness of the analogue – the transitory, ephemeral, ambiguous – serves scholars and citizens well.

The Byrds generally, and Roger McGuinn specifically, were a cultural, social and musicological translator between Bob Dylan and The Beatles, and genre translators between folk and rock, folk rock and psychedelia, folk rock and country, folk rock and progressive rock. The best example of this capacity as cultural translators is their first single, 'Mr Tambourine Man'. While currently the best known version of this song is Bob Dylan's original, particularly after Martin Scorsese's *No Direction Home*,[47] it is important to remember that Dylan's entry into popular culture, rather than folk culture, came through covers of his material by Peter, Paul and Mary,[48] but most significantly through The Byrds.

Bob Dylan's long acoustic 'Mr Tambourine Man' of five and a half minutes in two four time with multiple verses and an understated chorus, was replaced by The Byrds' 4/4 time signature, electrified instruments, compression into two and a half minutes, and featuring few verses and many choruses. There are many reasons why this translation of 'Mr Tambourine Man' was and is so extraordinary. The first is the change in tempo. The movement to four four time created a space for innovative instrumentation. While the famous wrecking crew at Columbia Records[49] built the bedrock of the original track, Roger McGuinn was the only member of The Byrds to play on the single. What he accomplished – in terms of guitar technique – places him alongside Jimi Hendrix and Eric Clapton in the ranks of guitarists who changed how subsequent players pluck and strum the strings. Roger McGuinn's innovations were to both the right hand technique of finger picking and left hand chord construction. That scale of originality is rare. Robbie Robertson of The Band was inventive with the left hand through the creation of new finger shapes that stylized chords, returning guitar picking patterns to American roots music which was part of the early project on *Big Pink* and the self-titled 'Brown' album. Robertson's decision to de-emphasize the guitar during the period of 'Rock God' guitarists like Clapton created space for Levon Helm's innovative drum patterns, accent and voice, best captured on 'The Weight'[50] and 'Up on Cripple Creek'.[51] The great innovators in picking technique remain Eric Clapton and Jimi Hendrix for speed, dexterity and control over tone. 'Layla'[52] and 'All Along the Watchtower'[53] capture the volume and energy of their expertise.

Roger McGuinn stands alone because of his innovative techniques with both the left and right hand. He also gains points for degree of difficulty. The Rickenbacker 12-string guitar is, in mechanical terms, one of the most complicated guitars to play.[54] While the low action – particularly when compared to the Fender Telecaster – permits easy barre chords and rapid movement around the fretboard, the tight packing of strings makes it almost impossible for men in particular to either chord cleanly or to finger pick, because there is little separation between the strings. Either in spite of, or because of, these difficulties, the 12-string Rickenbacker is the sound of The Byrds. In fact, the 'jingle jangle'[55] guitar is a sonic metonymy for the 1960s. Roger McGuinn, playing the 12-string Rickenbacker, is the perfect melding of a guitarist's technique and the guitar's capabilities. He connected the blues 12-string acoustic guitar of Leadbelly with the style commenced by George Harrison on his 12-string Rickenbacker in *A Hard Day's Night*. McGuinn, having learnt the five-string banjo and the rolling pick style associated with roots and country music, was able to combine both a flat pick, held between thumb and first finger, with metal finger picks on the third and fourth fingers. In other words, he picked and strummed the strings of a 12-string using the fast-picking skills he honed while playing banjo. The ringing arpeggios are what causes the 'jingle jangle' sound. This sonic intervention has entered popular culture as the sound of the 1960s, and has fetishized this odd, difficult and distinctive guitar for musicians, fans and collectors.[56]

To manage the closely packed strings, McGuinn also changed his left hand technique through the finger arrangement of chords. As an example, he used two rather than three fingers to hold an A chord. That configuration then freed up the remaining fingers to add hammer-ons and pull offs to the basic chord shape. The combination of banjo picking and new chord formations ensured that, in the movement from two four to four four time signatures, the

Rickenbacker guitar line appears to fill out the available sonic space. In the case of 'Mr Tambourine Man', the result was two and a half minutes of sonic silk.

While The Byrds later brought jazz atonalities and sitar drones to popular music through 'Eight Miles High' and captured and developed country rock through the 1968 album *Sweetheart of the Rodeo*, their popular cultural sun was setting as the 1960s progressed. Fascinating scholarly work emerges at the point where popular culture becomes unpopular culture. For The Byrds and McGuinn, it was 1970–71. There is an appropriateness to the fact that the band that created the sixties sound only just survived the decade.

However – and importantly for the *Thinking Popular Culture* project – another Roger McGuinn story commences through this movement from popular culture to post-pop, and it involves the internet. McGuinn continues to play live concerts as both an individual and in different band line-ups, some involving the former Byrds, Bob Dylan or – in one of the most unusual – in the late 1980s with Crowded House in a combination they called ByrdHouse.[57] Significantly, and unlike Dylan, McGuinn has never butchered his early material. He performs 'Mr Tambourine Man', 'Turn Turn Turn', 'Eight Miles High' and 'My Back Pages' as the audience wishes to hear it, in concert after concert, year after year, as an analogue memory of the 1960s.[58]

While his analogue history of musical innovation on guitar ceased with the 1960s, his digital history of music innovation began in 1994, when he started to record traditional folk and folk artists and upload the results. He formed the Folk Den[59] in November 1995 and has continued to release a different folk song each month to download for free. This was before MP3s, the iPod and podcasting. As each of these disruptive software[60] and hardware platforms emerged, he improved and widened the project.

After The Byrds, McGuinn has continued this role as translator, deploying digitization as a way to archive the analogue. He uses podcasts to create a new space for old folk and old folkies that has died in the corporatized – and threatened – radio and music industries. There is probably less space for folk-oriented music on commercial radio than at any point since the early 1960s. But the long tail of podcasting is able to create a space for diverse genres.[61] McGuinn recognized the potential of digital music, compression and the web years before other musicians. He blogs, promotes his music and tours, and used the capacity of e-commerce a decade before Radiohead supposedly invented a new way of selling music online with *In Rainbows*.[62]

McGuinn has also remained politically active, particularly in speaking about digitization and popular music. In 2000, he testified before the Senate Judiciary Committee hearing on downloading music[63] and offered oral testimony for the history of the relationship between performers and record companies. While the record companies have justified their attacks on downloaders because it starves the artists of revenues, McGuinn reported that The Byrds had received no royalties for their hit singles. For 'Mr Tambourine Man' and 'Turn Turn Turn', they only ever received their advances. These were split five ways, with each Byrd receiving a few thousand dollars. Even for his 1989 solo CD *Back from Rio* for Arista Records, which sold 500,000 copies worldwide, he received only a modest advance and no royalties. He confirmed for the Committee that, 'even though I've recorded over twenty-five records, I cannot support my family on record royalties alone'.[64] He compared this situation to his online sales with MP3.com, where he receives 50 per cent of royalties. MP3.com absorbs all packaging and distribution costs when the songs are released as a CD.[65] McGuinn has received thousands of dollars from these folk recordings. Also, *Treasures from the Folk Den* was nominated in 2002 for the Grammy in the Best Traditional Folk Album category. That success has allowed him to continue to release a monthly track through a free podcast from *The Folk Den*, which is now downloadable from iTunes.

Significantly, like most early technological innovators, McGuinn had assumed that his projects would be freely available to all. However, Jim Musselman from Appleseed Recordings reminded him that not everyone had a computer or was online.[66] Appleseed is an interesting project in itself, without the involvement of McGuinn. They describe their goal as 'sowing the seeds of social justice through music'.[67] Appropriately, they provided a way for McGuinn's online innovations to gain a distribution mechanism for those communities without access to a stable internet connection or the literacy to find and download sonic files. Musselman suggested they make new recordings of Folk Den songs with some inspirational folk musicians from the 1950s and early 1960s. While McGuinn did not go to the Appalachians to record songs, he went to the houses of Pete Seeger, Tommy Makem, Judy Collins, Odetta and Joan Baez. He used a computer with multi-track software, Cool Edit Pro.[68] So at the moment that his musical innovation – in terms of technique – is not leading the industry, his technological, political and historical innovations are at their height.

McGuinn had been the early adopter of musical technologies, but as with The Byrds more generally in a post-Scorsese Dylan history, his innovations are underwritten, under-recognized and under-researched. The absence of Roger McGuinn in the refereed scholarship is remarkable, and while there are some strong books on The Byrds, his digital innovations and interventions have not been mentioned or cited. Like a digitized Alan Lomax, he not only preserves old folk songs, traditions and voices but creates and records new music for new platforms. He is also a teacher of these new ideas, releasing some of the most inspirational instructional DVDs on how to play a basic folk guitar,[69] a 12-

string guitar[70] and home recording.[71] Just as McGuinn was the sonic translator between Dylan and The Beatles, Leadbelly and Harrison, he is still translating between the analogue and the digital, acting as corporeal archive, preserving a sonic moment of the 1960s for past and future listeners.[72]

For those of us who have the great opportunity to teach and write for a living, the McGuinn story is an inspiration. It captures the best of what Edward Said, in his posthumously published book, described as late style.[73] Said was interested in tracking the late work of Beethoven, Mozart and Strauss in particular. Technical competency in form – with words, music or paintbrush – creates opportunities for incredible innovation in content. The mastery of technique, when based on experience, shapes an aptitude for resistance and refusal. McGuinn's late style offers a model for melding innovation and preservation, change and continuity.

Teaching pop

If Web 2.0 is to become more than a brand or marketing device, then those of us interested in education, equality and creating quality popular culture must infuse it with content. Roger McGuinn's story is motivating. My hope in response is that Web 2.0 will signify that we have entered a period of mature discussion rather than confusion, blame and shame. I want this phrase to signify that the web is complex, intricate, large and open for analogue plug-ins. To create a socially just Web 2.0, we require an honest recognition of what tasks, topics and functions are best served through a digitized screen, and when it is appropriate and necessary to snap shut the laptop to enter the analogue world of ephemerality, tangibility and ambiguity.

Complaining about the digital nonsense online is like abusing Fred Astaire because he was a better dancer than singer. It misses the point. We are far better to locate and diagnose the problem – the flattening of expertise in digital environments – and then systematically and carefully improve the quality of the scholarly material that is available online. This is incredibly important because since the turn of the twenty-first century, two parallel developments have emerged. Libraries are reducing their subscriptions to print-based journals at the very point that publishers such as Routledge, Sage and Berg have acquired most of the highly ranked journals, aggregated them and sold them at a high price to universities and the academics who have given their research and writing for free. More recently, some publishers have decided to no longer provide a free copy of the journal or offprints to the writer of the article, requiring them to buy (back) their own published ideas.

Researchers, writers, activists and citizens can complain about this corporate restriction of scholarship, or we can actually do something. Online open access journals are an opportunity for academics to intervene in this corporatized knowledge system. Writers and researchers can assist these journals by offering our better articles, rather than out-takes and offcuts to these editors. We can also referee for these journals. Examples of academics that have courageously answered this challenge and require our support include Ben Agger's *Fast Capitalism*,[74] Gerry Coulter's *International Journal of Baudrillard Studies*,[75] Paul Stortz's *History of Intellectual Culture*[76] and Samar Habib's *Nebula*.[77] In assisting these editors to improve the quality, range and influence of these journals, the flattening and compression of expertise in the online environment will transform. Surfers, through gateways such as Google Scholar,[78] the Directory of Open Access Journals[79] or the Public Knowledge Project,[80] will be able to find refereed scholarship that is not restricted or sold by commercial publishers.

Those of us who teach and write in media and cultural studies have a task. Through the 1980s and 1990s research in popular culture in particular was buried in abstractions. Theory – capital T – became the intellectual home of the clever, but disconnected. By the late 1980s, it was up to Angela McRobbie to ask of cultural studies: 'Why do it? What's the point? Who is it for?'

> But what has worried me recently in Cultural Studies is when the theoretical detours become literary and textual excursions and when I begin to lose a sense of why the object of study is constituted as the object of study in the first place. Why do it? What is the point? Who is it for? On my first reading of many of the papers [at this conference] I was gripped by panic. Where have I been for the last five years? Much of this kind of Cultural Studies does not at all tally with what I teach, with what I find useful in understanding the everyday world and everyday culture around me.[81]

If radical and disruptive humanities research is to survive, then the first few decades of the 2000s must be focused on reconnecting the object of study and a rationale for study. In this way, *Thinking Popular Culture* contributes to the culture from which it emerges.

There has never been a more exciting time to be working in, with and through the media. There has never been a more important time to create an informed political culture. But in an age where 'everything' is available online and everyone is online, why invest in formal education, why attend underfunded universities to be taught by marginalized academics? How do teachers and writers maintain the enthusiasm to connect and create an excitement for learning? The best of popular culture, as exemplified by Roger McGuinn, must leave us with a feeling of awe. If popular culture is taught well to undergraduates, then it is inspirational and motivational. As shown by McGuinn, studying pop is also surprising. It provides a site of translation between where our students are and where we want them to be.

The question is how to create a Learning Pop from a Thinking Pop. Throughout the history of universities and formal education, popular culture has been intentionally and actively excluded. The strength of teaching the popular, to summon Stanley Aronowitz and Henry Giroux's phrase, is that it creates 'a language of possibility'.[82] Following their challenge, the goal of my teaching and writing life is to transform popular culture, not into a static object for an investigation, but into the matrix of an educational dialogue about the pathways from information to knowledge. Google is part of popular culture, not disconnected from it. Within this model, there is no separation of 'old' and 'new' media. Instead, this recognition confirms that a socially just, intellectually rigorous and democratic citizenry must spend time selecting an appropriate media in the correct context, rather than allowing a search engine to supersede critical thinking.

Some literacies are more important than others. Those in power claim their books, media, technological platforms and language as quality and part of educational curricula, while discrediting the rest. Those operating outside of these values and choices may resist, or their literacies and texts may be lost to history. Yet struggle does not always result in resistance. Audiences, consumers, citizens – all of us – seek out environments in which we are comfortable, and understand the language, signs and codes. Rarely do we gravitate to those images and ideas that make us uncomfortable or that we do not understand. The electronic revolution that Google has continued has made possible the reproduction, ranking and dissemination of a particular set of cultural symbols, but also the careful filtering and selection of a digital environment to ensure that the empowered users of the web are comfortable and unchallenged. The popularity of Google keeps the compliant complicit and the complicit compliant. The best example of this dismissal of any critique of the digitally literate emerges when anyone abuses, laughs at or discredits blogging. Once in the world of blogging, our literacies are blunted and accustomed to minutia, opinion and unchecked data. When critiqued, the default position of bloggers is to affirm their freedom of speech.[83] Actually, they have confused freedom to blog with freedom of speech, ignoring the freedom of speech of those without a stable system of telephony, let alone broadband.

In such a model, media studies is not a trivial elective to a serious academic programme of study, but the pivotal discursive translator between ways of learning and ways of living. After the post-compulsory school years, there are too many assumptions that students can manage and coordinate multiple literacies, from oral conversations to reading advanced theory, writing analytical prose, referencing, interpreting diagrams and working through a diverse sonic and visual palette. The integration of student's popular culture into the curriculum allows them to feel comfortable in their textual environment, while being challenged to develop new analytical skills. If both the texts and literacies are foreign, then our students for whom a university is disconnected from the experiences of their family and friends are further alienated from the curriculum. Actually the point of pop – and the agenda of media and cultural studies – challenges the imperatives and goals of teachers as much as students. Popular culture, when integrated into education and teacher training, prepares schools and universities for managing diversity.

Popping education

The gift of education is understanding, awareness and consciousness and it pays dividends in the long term. The outcomes of a university education cannot be listed like the outcomes of a business model, through shareholder dividends. In being humble to the scholars who preceded us, in moderating our experiences to truly hear and contextualize the words of others, we see ourselves as part of a society, a community on a thinking journey to feel more.

I had the great privilege of being appointed to a professorship at 37 years of age. It is an important number. Those of us who are fans of Marianne Faithful know that it is the year when we know we won't ride through Paris in a sports car with the warm wind in our hair.[84] When I first heard this song in my teens, I thought – like we all do – that being 37 was one step away from death. But it has been extraordinary to be of this age, in this age, of popular cultural history. I was 17 when acid house jacked through musical history and 21 when techno jumped over genre and rhythm. Those of us who shared that time – those sounds and feelings – felt like we were at the centre of the world. But then, life got serious for so many of us. After tutoring and occasional lectures in my early twenties, I gained my first full-time academic appointment at 24. The only problem was that I had to leave my home and migrate to New Zealand to take this post. I left family, friends, the dancing and the rhythms to be a grown up. The work was hard, almost as tough as Wellington's winds. Then to keep in work at the end of my contract, I moved to Rockhampton, Australia's 'Beef Capital', where tropical rain punctuated the day and beer kegs never seemed to empty at night. I made it back home again to Perth, the capital at the western edge of Australia, for a few years, but it was to be a transitory homecoming.

The well-deep tragedy of leaving my home and my country again for another academic post in the United Kingdom remains disorienting and upsetting. Migrants always mourn the loss of what our alternative lives could have been.

But after September 11, migrants became foreigners and a source of threat, violence, fear and loathing. The loss of family and friends for a second time is worse in an era of xenophobia because I am a migrant living in a country whose newspapers excrete anti-immigration bile on a weekly basis[85] and a Professor of Media Studies, the discipline that is blamed for dumbing down, declining educational standards and the fall in literacy.

As a foreigner, as a migrant, as a woman and as a Professor of Media Studies, there is one truth that guides me in this international journey through popular culture and the academy. Societies and their citizens are judged, not by the wealth of their most successful businessmen, but by the treatment of those people who stumble or are challenged physically, socially, culturally or economically. Instead of understanding and solving social injustice, easy options and choices are our new normality. Libraries are underfunded, but that is acceptable because there is Google. Commercial publishers are aggregating journals and raising costs, but that is acceptable because there are freely available blogs and Wikipedia. Teaching staff are overstretched, but online education can solve these troubles by removing students from our campuses. These are digital medications for analogue problems. But what sort of medicine is it? Palliative care for dying public institutions? Administered sedatives so that political progressives can sleep through the losses and weathering of citizenship? Amphetamines to accelerate the speed of change so that we do not feel the emotional costs of the loss through the cold thrust of 'the new', rather than the careful consideration of 'the useful'?

We need better solutions for our students, our staff and our society than digitized opiates. It is 50 years since Raymond Williams published his essay 'Culture is ordinary'.[86] In this essay, he reminded us of unpopular culture and even more unpopular politics. While many progressive critics shake their heads in disgust at what Williams or George Orwell or E.P. Thompson might think of contemporary culture if they were still alive, I always carry with me Thompson's commentary about one of his classes. He was worried that a whole term would pass without a good solid row between the students.[87] Throughout *Thinking Popular Culture*, I bring forward the row, the debate about big ideas and issues, while also remembering the gift of a thoughtful media education in difficult times.

Stop crying – start thinking. Putting the punch back into pop

Popular culture, at its breast-enhancing best, is claustrophobic in its disappointments. Nice girls with strong abdominal muscles and weak politics are hurting feminism as much as the ears. With voices so frail, they could not pull a skin off a rice pudding, let alone reveal inconsistencies in the patriarchy. Their naivety, while carefully groomed, makes them as sharp as a wet cornflake. Paris Hilton went to prison, cried, was released from prison, cried, went back to prison, cried, was released from prison, cried, and then appeared on television to continue the promotion of her most famous microproduct: herself. Meanwhile her ex-best friend Nicole Richie uses boggle sunglasses/face masks to hide all emotion behind the tinting. Perhaps they are merely shielding her from the bright light of the refrigerator. Britney Spears and Amy Winehouse have transformed rehab into a revolving door, living car crash lives of smeared eye liner, drugs, big hair, no hair, marriage, divorce and challenges with underwear.[1] Much of the post-1945 era featured bad boys like the Rat Pack and the Brat Pack. Now the bad girls have taken over the tabloidized sex, drugs and fast cars. Now though, the hair is bigger and the shoes more expensive.

What exists under the tattoos, below the beehives and behind these sunglasses? What emotions are being hidden? Too much of popular culture in the 2000s has been safe, punctuated by grating canned laughter. Men have become like drapes: the thicker the better. Tom Cruise is the embodiment of this principle. When he tested the springs of Oprah's couch, the pop world changed. The cultural history of the twenty-first century will be written in terms of Before Tom Jumped (BTJ) and After Tom Jumped (ATJ). For all to see, our level of stupidity and investment in the banal became so ridiculous that even the most judicious of celebrity watcher had to look away from the facile ugliness. The beautiful Dorian Tom of *Risky Business* finally showed us the portrait in his attic. We can never forget what we have seen ATJ.

We have been prepared for this destruction of the dream factory. All over the world, *Big Brothers* were telecast, but unlike the Orwellian vision, they removed the irony and fear. We are all complicit in this invasion of the private sphere. The more complicated and frightening that war, surveillance and poverty has become, the more underwear is revealed above women's hipsters-vaginasters. Women are spending too much time pulling their tops down and trousers up. There are other things we should be doing. Let the arse cleavage show for a moment. Think about why scholars and citizens should be angered by the crap that passes for culture. Ponder what – precisely – we are going to do about it. While makeover programmes offer to make us ten years younger, we must re-make the last decade, not in terms of wrinkles and collagen but the lines, folds and shadows of politics and popular culture.

After September 11, the televisual domination of cooking, shopping, gardening and makeover programmes has been implicated in a political system where the United Nations is sidelined, a Coalition is willing to 'liberate' a sovereign nation and news journalism is hopelessly conflated with infotainment and uninformed interpretative commentary. While our minds are filled with pulling up our trousers, buying sun-dried tomatoes, building water features in our garden and giggling at cosmetic surgery blunders, there has been an acidic corrosion of thinking, questioning and critique. Kalamata olives will not create peace in the Middle East. The *Backyard Blitz* team will not makeover downtown Baghdad. *Ready, Steady, Cook* will not lend their culinary skills to the population of Fallujah.

It is becoming increasingly difficult to determine where lifestyle programming stops and current affairs begin. Why is there so much crying on television? Personal tragedies, captured through a voyeuristic lens, have replaced an investigative journalism which fights corruption or political mediocrity. If it happened now, Watergate would still refer to a hotel, not the downfall of a president. A prime-time slot does not pass without seeing some flaked out, freaked out screamer crying about a personal injustice, generally involving a credit card or dodgy customer service. Meanwhile the social, economic and political organization of the world is decaying, which requires more debate and considered attention than shoddy car dealerships, home improvements, dieting disappointments or television tie-ins. Blokey empathy and feminine sympathy about the newest (raw meat and cold spinach) diet is making me nervous. Peeling away the spin is tough: a cross pollination of nonsense is infusing the media. *American Idol*'s losers pop up in shopping centres. *Survivors* are reborn as talk show hosts. Finding a place outside of mediocrity – or even a position from which to judge mediocrity – is becoming tougher. Just to recap: Bono is a singer in a 1980s rock band. He is not the head of the United Nations. Clearly, much is going on behind Bono's sunglasses. He even called Tony Blair and Gordon Brown 'the John and Paul of the global development stage'.[2] I am uncertain about whether to shake my head at his brown nosing or marvel at his metaphor, but I am certain that John Lennon would not be impressed hearing his name used in vain. Blair may have left office, but the consequences of his decisions not only *in* politics but *for* popular culture require some careful attention.

To put the problem another way: why, as the (post) Iraq war became more violent, did television become more stupid? In his 2004 book *Understanding Celebrity*, Graeme Turner enacted a courageous intellectual, political and social service. He refuted the intrinsic 'democracy'[3] of reality television.[4] In an extension of his argument, he showed the consequences of marginalizing talent and ability in favour of a desire for fame.

> Much of the participation in reality TV is aimed at a certain kind of recognition of the self. Even though the contestants on Idol may be competing for the chance to be a successful singer, we frequently find them arguing their case to the judges in terms of their essential selves – their intrinsic star quality – rather than in terms of their musical skills or abilities. *American Idol*'s notorious William Hung, for instance, attempted to impress the judges by pointing out that he had never had any training in singing or dancing – as if this was an argument in his favour. If celebrity is understood as a natural attribute of the self, rather than a mode of production and consumption, then of course it was.[5]

This fascination with the miniature, minor and irrelevant has kept popular culture small and safe. At its best, pop is playful *and* dangerous, funny *and* serious. Celebrating the grassroots democracy of reality television programmes, delighting in the ability of get-a-life-and-switch-that-bloody-phone-off-SMSers voting housemates/renovators/singers/ice skaters/pole dancers/strippers into pseudo-celebrity oblivion means that we have vacated discussions of the 'work and life balance' to the Men's Movement, Dr Phil and neo-conservatives. We have resisted critiquing the drivel that fills night-time programming. *Friends* was never funny, and that was years before Brad left Jen for Angelina.[6] And I laugh *at* Samantha in *Sex in the City* – not with her. A generation of feminist theorists has continued the flawed argument of the 1960s' sexual 'revolution'.[7] Sexual intercourse is not intrinsically 'freeing' for women. Perhaps sex is simply sex, not the basis of liberation, and half a century after the 1960s, campaigners for social justice require new methods for debate and challenge. Having sex is different from having rights.

In an era of the post – postmodern, postcolonial, postindustrial and postfordist – the certainties of origins and endpoints, narratives and their resolutions, disappear as rapidly as weapons of mass destruction. In such a moment, the most radical of acts is to laugh at the establishment, ridiculing their pomp, confidence and hypocrisy. The key is, through this ironic humour, to maintain the tether between laughter, popular culture and politics. Probably the last great hope for television is comedy. *The Office* is one of the finest satires ever made, continuing the genre's fascination with dysfunctional men on the skids. Similarly, the Australian comedy *Kath and Kim* – instead of rewriting the workplace – remoulded suburbia. These attacks on reality television and situation comedy genres have created a space for the edgy, innovative and achingly funny. *Little Britain* blurred work and private life, confirming that all of us are in drag. We are all proclaiming – metaphorically – that we are the only gay in the village, while there are communities of strangeness, pleasure and difference that encircle us. *Gavin and Stacey* reminds little England of the long-term scars of colonization in Great Britain, with the Welsh being the basis – not of xenophobic stereotypes – but gentle emotion and commentaries on family.

These alt-comedies capture the unpredictability of contemporary pop culture. We learn to laugh again at those in power. If we had giggled and scorned the stridency of Margaret Thatcher, the mock-sporting mateship of John Howard and the linguistic inelegance of George W. Bush, then we would not be in the mess we are now. At such times of terrorism and war, we must never confuse reality with reality television, or crying with critique. We must laugh with a purpose.

Coalition of the guilty

It was a pretty usual Australian Christmas: too much food, too much booze and an endless tapestry of heat. Barbecue-burnt sausages, garlic bread and cheesecake were washed down with sticky wine. Families – in all their complexity and difficulties – enfolded us. Once more, I heard too much Abba and talked to (too many) relatives about shoe shopping and Christmas tree decorations. This quietness and repetition has a comfort to it. Both my parents are living and I am aware that there will be a Christmas dinner where I will not share shredded sausages with an intact familial unit. When we reach a certain age, every moment of happiness is undercut by an unsettling awareness that it will not last.

On returning to my suburban home on Boxing Day and expecting a lazy day watching Adam Gilchrist and the lads dominate the second cricket test of the summer, by mid-afternoon my benign channel switching became more urgent. It appeared that enormous waves – named first a Seaquake and then a Tsunami – had destroyed the coastlines of South East Asia. Loss of life was indeterminate at the start, but slowly – over two weeks – built to 150,000 deaths. As the months progressed, we would know that a quarter of a million people died on that dreadful day and its aftermath.

The television uptake in mid-afternoon Western Australia on Boxing Day was startling. The first satellite television news channel to commence reportage was BBC World. Their wide radio network of global journalists began submitting stories. We heard (about) the Tsunami before we saw it. Within 30 minutes, CNN activated its mesh of reporters with satellite phones, sending grainy and jolted images back to a shocked audience. Sky News followed. Fox News did not bother cutting into its pre-programmed Christmas footage about brave soldiers, patriotic civilians and the distribution of American flags to the military forces in Iraq.

The story built through the following days. CNN generated subtle, emotionally attuned investigative journalism. Mike Chinoy, the Channel's (now former) Senior Asia Correspondent, coordinated an integrated coverage within the region. Fox News moved very little from its patriotic coverage of Iraq. The metaphors from the inked well of terrorism had little resonance in this new environment. The South East Asian region features many religions, languages and social differences. The crisp terrorism-inflected determination of 'foreigners' did not function through the grief, mourning, death and disease. President Bush did not speak on the disaster for three days after the event. As Margaret Cho confirmed:

> He is by far the most embarrassing president in history. Never fails to embarrass. After the Tsunami, he didn't really help the victims out very much. I mean, why should he? They don't have oil. All they have is batik, and he don't look cute in a sarong. So he put together the Tsunami Taskforce Relief Force, headed by Jeb Bush, which is like sending Danni Minogue.[1]

In such a context, what could Fox News offer? The answer was continued coverage of Iraq where – supposedly – the ideological order was clear and predictable.

The odd and awkward convergence of terrorism, Iraq War II and the Tsunami in the immediate media coverage was uncomfortable. 'Ground zero'[2] and 'waves of mass destruction'[3] were used too often to describe the passage of the seaquake. Through this journalistic inappropriateness, there were concrete political reasons for this overlay of ideas and events. Community borders that exclude foreigners have calcified after the events of September 11. The emotional responses to those burning buildings means that it has been difficult to subsequently and critically evaluate how these events have been represented. Three thousand people lost their lives on that day. But 250,000 lost their lives in the Bosnia conflict, and up to one million people were killed in 1994 during the genocide in Rwanda. Each day, 24,000 people die from malnutrition and 30,000 children under five die from preventable causes.[4] Such a scale of death places the Tsunami into a context beyond the Twin Towers.

In the lead up to September 2001, foreign stories occupied half the media time they did in 1989. This lack of global content created an inward and nationalist focus on nightly news broadcasts. Jennifer Lawson, a Washington, DC-based independent producer, offered a rationale for this situation.

> We as a nation were so surprised by what happened with 9/11. Had we known more about how others view us and our policies, I don't think we would have been so surprised. We get very little coverage from Indonesia or the Philippines, and almost no backgrounders, even though there are links to al Qaeda-type organizations. The news is always crisis-oriented, and then it drops off the radar screen. Even our coverage of Afghanistan dropped off.[5]

Fox News Channel solved the problem of few foreign bureaus by reducing non-American news stories and the literacies to understand them. They spend little time on international material and stress domestic news. The station chose to be different from CNN or BBC World by promoting a patriotic and narrow performance of Americanness. Their programme style is colloquial, ideological and anchor heavy.

The consequence of this cultural shift is that few public figures speak in full sentences. A detailed argument is redundant. Slogans become facts. Ponder these phrases that have entered our vocabulary:

Weapons of mass destruction
Coalition of the Willing
Evil doers
Pacific Solution

Regime change
Axis of Evil
Asylum seekers
War against terror

Ideologies are carried through these phrases so that alternative trajectories are silenced. What was the Australian problem that caused a 'Pacific Solution'? If there is an Axis of Evil, is there a parallel Axis of Good? What was the Coalition willing to do? Technological change has increased the speed through which 'news' is proliferated, often encouraging unchecked rumour and gossip to overwrite and decentre journalistic standards of ethics and reporting. Clichés swarm informed commentary. The reduction in time between information availability and the creation of a news narrative triggers a 'rip and read' mentality.

In such an accelerated information environment, a pre-emptive war on Iraq was not only waged but justified. This sound bite culture has a major impact on the calibre of political debate. In 1968, the political sound bite was 43 seconds, which reduced to 9.8 seconds in 1988 and seven seconds by 1996.[6] The speed at which ideas are expressed, and the truncated vocabulary utilized to express complicated ideas, makes it difficult to encourage researched, theorized interpretations and intellectual rigour. This accelerated culture[7] creates an impetus for accelerated literacy. There is not time to move – with reflexivity – from speed reading to deep thinking.

The closing of foreign news bureaus by Fox News and the focus on the United States at a time of war on terrorism has created a space that separates journalism and politics. These gaps in media reportage were revealed in the days after the Tsunami when amateur tourist video replaced professional photographic journalism. User-generated content masked the loss of international expertise and coverage caused by the withdrawal of journalists and photographers. The foundations, audience and literacies for MySpace and

YouTube were in place. Once this acceptance of grainy amateur footage from the Tsunami was demonstrated by the web and televisual audiences, it was a short path to Saddam Hussein's YouTube execution. These institutional challenges in media representation shadowed the transformation of military alliances. In the panicked days after the Boxing Day disaster, a 'Donor Group'[8] was summoned by the United States, Australian, Japanese and Indian governments to coordinate relief. This coalition continued the Iraq War trend in underplaying the United Nations' role in managing global relations. Former Prime Minister Howard chose to operate outside the UN in his donation and loan of one billion dollars to the Indonesian government in the wake of the quake. Actually, the international community did not need to construct a new matrix of aid coordination. It already exists. It is called the United Nations.

For Christian-dominated countries, Christmas is meant to be a time when – after the excessive shopping and wrapping – there is time to celebrate with family and friends. But as 2004 expired, the contrast of what we had and what others had lost was achingly obvious. The scale of this disaster was medieval it its intensity, sheering the shiny surfaces of modernity glossed by news networks. The uneven distribution of wealth, facilities, health care and running water has always existed. This tragedy only made such disparities stark in the televisual gaze.

Tragically, the subsequent years were no better than 2004. The earthquake in Pakistan threw millions into homelessness. The image of families living in makeshift tents through two brittle winters confirmed that the world really did not change after the Tsunami. Those tents remained through 2006 and the global tragedies relentlessly plodded on, being matched with genocidal intensity by the events in Darfur. The invisibility of a world beyond Calais continues. There has been a cost to 'them' by focusing on 'us'. The cost of the War on Terror has been the implicit – and often explicit – construction of some citizens of the world as being simply expendable. Rarely is such a difference noted or reported. Occasional letter writers reel in horror at the compartmentalization of humanity into tiers.

> I found the Comment piece on Iraq last week genuinely shocking. Why? Because, although it was deemed important to tell us of the loss of 175 British and nearly 4,000 US soldiers, and to mention that the cost to the Treasury is at least £1.7bn, you nowhere gave a figure, or even a possible range of figures, for the number of dead Iraqi civilians.[9]

The poor, the black, the invaded and the dispossessed are suffering through not only a genocide of neglect, but a precise and methodical stripping of humanity. We must arch beyond individual ambition, national xenophobia and celebratory militarism. We must demand greater complexity, interpretation and debate from our news broadcasters. We must shatter a terrorism of the mind and coalitions of the guilty. If anything positive emerges through the Tsunami or the disasters that followed, it must be a renewed commitment that – regardless of our race or religion – we have a responsibility to learn from others, care for differences and demand extreme truth rather than extreme makeover programmes.

I am Australian. That means that I live a paradox. A little pocket of Europe has been trapped in the Asian and Pacific region. This paradox can be a productive one, translating between the expectations and assumptions of colonization, civilization and history. Australians are a coastal people. We have much in common with our regional Asian neighbours. These similarities require recognition and respect. Australians – as the translators of geographical paradoxes – should be tough enough to demand better journalism and global thinking. Unfortunately, Australia is also the birthplace of Rupert Murdoch. Intriguingly, he relinquished this origin and allegiance to become an American citizen and increase the scale of his media empire. There is a lesson there.

The eighth deadly sin

Like most of the academic community, the gap between summer holidays and the start of a new semester is a wild ride of curriculum preparation: finding the freshest research, writing lectures, fighting administrators who prefer statistics to scholarship and ensuring that (almost) every contingency and trauma that can befall any wide-eyed 18-year-old student, short of crack addiction and binge drinking, has a solution or at least a strategy to help.

In 2006, I taught a new course, the last course I taught in Australia before moving to the United Kingdom. Titled *Creative Industries*, it tried to offer the best combination of policy and politics, assessment and analysis, commentary and critique. A problem that has emerged in many of these courses around the world is that academics become evangelical cheerleaders for the market economy, rather than cautious and concerned scholars questioning the low wages and casualized labour that are 'accepted' as part of the creative sector. I wanted to ensure that students thought deeply about what happens to our identity when one group's work transforms into another group's leisure. The course seemed strong, meaty and provocative, but we can never assess our success and failure until the first lecture on the first day.

In my digital journey through work, leisure and lifestyle to find current reading material for students, I discovered Daniel Ben-Ami's essay from *Spiked*. The title grabbed my interest: 'Why people hate fat Americans'.[1] He investigates the metaphors of fatness, which transform overeating into a more general symptom for over-consumption. Ben-Ami offers a strong corrective of consumption as 'a problem'. He affirms that nutritionists have become the new preachers, with 'health' morphing into a justification for repression and restriction. Eating is clearly much better than sex, and (bloody) nutritionists are the cardinals of calories. Gluttony is restated as a deadly sin.

Ben-Ami's argument has made me think about restraint. I attended a Catholic school, so repression and restriction are as natural to me as sensible shoes and big knickers. But he has realized that much of the world is *both* anti-American and fanatical about obesity because excessive consumption is seen to be the only safe debate left in a xenophobic and terrorized time. Instead of actually discussing the redistribution of wealth, there is an acceptance that the current form of capitalism and the market economy is beyond discussion or reproach. In other words, the progressives have 'lost' the economy so we 'fight' over culture. Journalists and researchers talk too much about shopping and not enough about how the goods stocked in the store are actually produced.

Certainly something odd is happening to consumerism, and it is not simply a displacement of economic injustice. I have been watching people's behaviour in shops for the last few years. I have seen shrill hostility at cashiers, crazy frustration if sales items featured in a catalogue are not available on the shelves, and pseudo post-coital release after the satiation of a purchase. The smile of customers as they walk away from the cashier is like a cow who has just chewed the best chaff. It is not the excess and waste that has pricked my shopping skin. Ben-Ami's critique of consumerism is correct. What worries me is the emotional investment in the capitalist exchange of goods. In our social system, we all have the right to spend, spend, spend – and when the credit card is full, get another card and – spend, spend, spend some more. The problem is not in the purchase. The problem is when the purchase is marinated in feelings of pride, love, confusion, fear and self-loathing. Save emotion for the people in our lives. A discounted toaster or sparkly shoes do not deserve to be invested with passion.

In the orgy of Christmas gift-giving, Boxing Day returns and post-Christmas sales, I often wonder when – precisely – shopping became a competitive sport. Like a moth drawn to a flickering Body Shop candle, the act of accumulation – the thrill of the chase – is performance art for the 2000s. Dada had the Cabaret Voltaire. We have catalogue shopping. I think it was Oprah who first made me conscious that a nice day at the suburban shopping centre had become something more disturbing. Each year, Oprah hosts a show titled 'My favorite things'. She then proceeds, for an hour, to feature products she enjoys, and at the end of each infomercial the entire audience receives the goods. This process goes on for product after product. Yet whether Oprah features lipstick or a DVD player, the audience of (almost all) women reaches a height of shrill excitement beyond love, beyond sex, beyond orgasm. They cry and wail like they are in the presence of a deity, rather than a bra and knickers set. Looking at their wide-eyed expressions and hearing their medieval shrieks, even I wonder why women were given the vote. If this is the state of femininity, then it is time for that sex change operation.

It is not the excess that worries me, well not much. This is not the medieval moment of the book where I blather on about the necessity for frugality and frigidity. It is too late – about 40 years too late – for an inquisition, a poker in the eye or the arse, to warn against the dangers of buying yet another mint green scatter cushion or adding more burgundy throw rugs to a room that already appears to have the colour coordination of a technicolour vomit. There can be no return to the simple life of monochrome, monotony and monogamy. Even that phrase – 'the simple life' – has been appropriated by Nicole Richie and Paris Hilton, the former best friends, the simulacrum celebrities who did little except diet, shop and wear enormous sunglasses. My dream – actually my revenge narrative nightmare – is to interview Paris Hilton and ask her what book she is reading at the moment and what she believes is the most effective method for handling religious fundamentalism. This will be a challenge, as her customary answer to all questions – 'that's hot' – does not fit too well. In my Generation Xer old age, I am becoming frequently intolerant of those who do not read. These times demand a large library and handbags filled with books, not small dogs whose only practical use is to fire up a barbecue.

We cannot structure our lives around avoiding the seven deadly sins, whether gluttony or sloth, greed or wrath, lust, envy or pride. If people want to shop, then let them shop. If people want to earn as much money as quickly as possible, not caring about the consequences to others or the environment, then let them go. If people want to lie on the lounge suite, eat ice cream and watch a programme spinning the latest diet revolution, then let them spoon Ben and Jerry's into their nostrils if it makes them forget that current affairs used to be about interpretative journalism rather than calorie counting.

No, it is too late to preach that the seven deadly sins actually hurt us. Those who are vain and greedy are successful. Those who are angry get their way. The lustful have a date on Saturday night rather than wistfully hoping that an internet introduction service might create a happy ending. The slothful are at least getting enough sleep, compared to the over-worked, over-scheduled and desperate minions who populate our open planned offices. The gluttonous are the stars of day-time television and the biggest winners on *The Biggest Loser*. Those who sin win.

Really, our focus needs to be on what I believe is the eighth deadly sin: stupidity. With all the stress on food and shopping, our minds are cluttered and confused. All of us must push and probe ourselves to read and think beyond our limits. Comfortable living creates compliant thinking. We need gluttony of the mind: stuffing our brain with ideas, not our stomachs with ice cream.

When Paris became a celebrity, not a city

The cultural landscape is split between the wicked, loud and shabby slappers of pop and the virtuous, silent, staunch defenders of high culture. This latter world is a place where the peaceful, serene and chaste modernists protect the masses from being seduced by the flashy, loud and tacky slags of popular culture. But like sand through the hourglass, the days of this particular life have ceased, and just like every good soap opera, we have to ask what is going on now, and what will happen next. Certainly something strange has warped popular culture in the last five years. Magazines have been leading the way in this trashy trajectory. They puff out our daily lives and open up our desiring selves, teaching us how to have sex, how to have a family, how to have sex without having a family and how to spend and spend and spend. Citizens become happy little consumers.

This is an era of explosive development in new magazines. Men's titles are expanding and the publications aimed at women are even more highly articulated into distinct markets. We also have a boom in fitness, health and technology magazines, promoting anything from iPods to iyengar yoga. Magazines are highly postmodern cultural forms, revelling in surfaces, welcoming differences and marinating in myriad ephemeral and fashionable possibilities. They also operate pedagogically – teaching us about the rules of love, romance and makeup. We learn how to be women and the importance of accessorizing, pedicures and styling mousse. We learn about being a man and the necessity for washboard abs, staying single, and why using moisturizer – or the more blokey name of 'face protector' – is not girly, but a necessary accoutrement to modern masculinity.

The wider project of magazines is to conflate femininity, disappointment and consumerism. The point is to transform women's bodies into an incomplete, uncomfortable and occasionally dangerous DIY project that requires constant maintenance and a heavy duty waxing gun. Hair must be removed. Exercise must be done. Heels must be worn. Food must be avoided. But in our shopping-fixated society, women simply cannot consume any more. We cannot buy any more perfume, clothes, shoes or handbags with an Audrey Hepburn motif. I own so much nail polish that I could not use it in ten lifetimes, even if I painted my entire feet – not just the toenails – with the ever-expanding palette of new season's hues. That is why men's magazines have leaped in number and range. Men are the new women, and must be taught how to consume: to buy clothes, watches, exquisite food, expensive alcohol and even stupid exercise equipment.

Beyond this transformation of masculinity, the other innovation during the last five years has been an increase in celebrity-based magazines with titles like *Heat* and *Famous*. There has always been an interest in 'stars', but these 'soft' news stories have now permeated all levels of journalism. Termed tabloidization, this movement tracks the shift from politics to crime-based stories, daily news to promotional and publicity stunts, and a shift from a discussion of social issues to a voyeuristic fascination with celebrity profiles. Images are more important than words. Put bluntly, this is a journalistic journey from news to entertainment. While theorists such as Kevin Glynn locate the 'popular power' and 'transformation' of culture through tabloidization,[1] other writers such as S. Elizabeth Bird are more considered in their analysis.

> I do believe readers use the tabloids in resistive, playful and creative ways, but I am skeptical about how that translated into real, progressive change. Just as often, tabloids maintain dominant ideologies.[2]

Bird's corrective is important. Reading does not align with understanding and consciousness does not inevitably create change. Even more disturbingly, the circulation of banality and the flattening of expertise means that the media literacy required to differentiate between the important and the trivial is weathered. The premise of tabloidization is that 'we' want to know about Posh and Becks, Geri's diets and Britney's revolving door relationships. It appears that a whole generation has lost its surname. Perhaps this is the greatest definition of fame. One name is big enough to capture this micro-sized, consumerable life.

I realized a few years ago when comparing men's and women's magazines that women were incorrectly blaming 'the media' or 'men' for their obsession with weight and dieting. The women featured in men's magazines are larger in size than the inverted mops in frocks on celebrity-fixated covers. In other words, women purchase publications featuring skinny chicks. Whenever women buy magazines featuring praying mantis people with a chin so sharp that it could slice salami, then we are implicated in our own disempowerment.

Do not blame men – they like bigger women. Blame ourselves. Look at some recent celebrity magazine covers. One week, editors 'worry' about drastic dieting and the beautiful Kate Hudson 'forced' to lose 30 kilos. In the next issue, the weird Mary-Kate who – besides having a strange name – has decided to wear a dress showing she's a few sweets short in the lolly jar. So what is happening here? Perhaps women are displacing body fears onto celebrities. More likely, I think there is a desire for ordinary women to revel in the fact that these perfect specimens also have bad hair days, own dodgy track suit pants and can eat a whole box of chocolates in one sitting. This is revenge with a kick.

There are reasons for this displaced fascination with fame. After the death of Princess Diana, there was a void in women's magazines. Suddenly a new range of celebrities were required to fill the pages. In collapsing the boundaries between news and entertainment – news and advertising – tabloidization also tracks a movement to more conservative politics as newsprint captures events and ideas that – really – do not matter. Ellis Cashmore realized that 'in a properly run world, celebrities would entertain us and politicians would govern us. In today's world there's a different protocol, one that has melted such divisions of labour.'[3] Magazines are part of this 'melting' process, enmeshing the social and the economic in an unpredictable and often destructive fashion. Women can be made whole – made complete – with one more pair of shoes or one more handbag with too little space for stuff and too many logos for show.

The credit cards that fuel the fashion industry, and the consumer debt that results from them, display not only an abeyance or deficiency of funds, but a gulf between the expectation of needs and the capacity to pay for them. Credit cards also mask inequalities and create a complex muddling of rich and poor. With a massive growth in dependency culture through credit cards, the connection between autonomy and consumption only lasts until the arrival of the next bank statement. Through 2008, the credit squeeze, the credit crunch and the global collapse of banking networks showed that finally the international credit card bill was overdue. Celebrity culture, hyper-consumerism and tabloidization mean that we frequently forget what we need to remember, and remember what we need to forget. Until Paris as a noun, name and description again captures a city not a celebrity, we should be worried.

Free wiki (but what is the cost?)

There is an addictive quality to Wikipedia. After a few minutes of clicking between Peter Andre, spray-on tan, Jordan (sorry, Katie Price) and breast implants, I no longer feel the need to read magazines. Tabloidization has moved from our news agencies to online 'encyclopedias'. A world of sleaze, crime, sex and violence is revealed, and that is just the page on Heather Mills. From Mucca to Macca, the most Ritalin-starved nine-year-old could fill hours of fun bouncing from link to link and search to search.

The Wikipedian pretence for 'neutrality' of approach[1] not only blocks originality from scholarship and research,[2] but features a high proportion of journalistic articles as references. This shifting mode of citation is no surprise. In a Web 2.0 age, bloggers are the new journalists, and journalists are the new academics. In Wikipedia-land, scholarly, original research is redundant, inconvenient and deleted as unsubstantiated content.

While writing an academic article, I realized – suddenly – how theories of originality, scholarship and argument were subtly marginalized through Wikipedia. During my research for a book chapter,[3] I visited Wikiworld to see how the collaborative encyclopedia presented the 'Virginia Tech shootings' in comparison to peer-reviewed analysis. Significantly, I was redirected from the 'Virginia Tech shootings' to the 'Virginia Tech massacre'.[4] *Shooting* and *massacre* do not hold the same connotation, but capture the fickle nature of Wikipedia's supposed neutrality.

In a *Guardian* article (journalists are the new academics, remember) Gary Younge described Wikipedia as 'a comprehensive if fallible online research tool'. Comprehensive and fallible are two odd words to use in relation to research, or indeed in relation to each other. There are many critiques of Wikipedia, including the vandalism[5] that is possible when using a software application where 'anyone' can edit text. However, adding *bumtitbottom* to Katie Price's entry is not serious and easy to correct, probably easier to correct than her *bumtitbottom* cosmetic surgery. More insidious is the 'consensus' approach that is presented as a truth, with collaboration valued over expertise.

My greatest concern with Wikipedia is a lack of expertise and judgment when determining significance. Occasionally articles are deleted for their profound stupidity, but the problem is that 'editing' in Wikiworld means the enlargement rather than reduction of entries. So as a scholarly experiment, I assembled ten topics to compare – not vandalism, factual errors, interpretation or originality – but Wikipedia's internal credibility and capacity to rank and judge relevance and importance.[6] Or put another way, I probed why information is not the same as knowledge and why re/searchers need to sometimes question 'the wisdom of crowds'.

Here are ten Wikipedia searches, and their results.[7]

1. The entry for 'Klingon' is longer than 'Latin'.
2. The entry for Franz Ferdinand (the band) is longer than the entry for Franz Ferdinand (the man whose assassination started the First World War).
3. The entry on Obi-Wan Kenobi (Jedi Knight) is nearly double the length of the entry on E.P. Thompson (historian and CND activist).
4. The entry on Elvis Presley is longer than the entry on Karl Marx.
5. Dolly Parton's entry is twice as long as Leadbelly's.
6. Abba's entry is longer than Woody Guthrie's.
7. The Eurovision Song Contest has a longer entry than rock 'n' roll.
8. 'Wikipedia' has a longer entry than 'library'.
9. The entry for 'user-generated content' is longer than the entry for 'codex'.
10. The entry titled 'Criticisms of Wikipedia' is longer than the entry for 'terrorism'.

Wikipedia is like a digital circus where the clowns are in charge of feeding the lions.[8] If we are to move, as Daniel Pink suggests, from the Information to Conceptual Age,[9] then the wikiworld must be recognized as the king of the former and the fool of the latter.

This wiki-probe chapter is not a *Daily Mail*-fuelled attack on popular culture, shrilly defending the value of national testing of all eight-year-olds on their knowledge of ancient civilizations. In fact, I am a huge *Star Trek* fan, maintaining a slightly obsessional relationship with Captain Kathryn Janeway from *Voyager*. But even with this love of the programme, there is no way to justify why the entry for Klingon should be longer than the entry for Latin. This is not a question of fact but emphasis. As discussed in the first chapter, what I call 'the Google Effect' constructs a culture of equivalence, where all Klingons and Romans are equal but only Wikipedian Lord Jimmy Wales is more equal than others.

I teach popular culture. I research popular culture. But it is not helping this study to allow fandom to be confused with academic expertise, or populism to overwrite an intricate discussion of popular cultural studies. Fan knowledge is distinct from academic knowledge. Wikipedia blurs these categories, so that Elvis is granted a greater prominence than Karl Marx. Seemingly, the King rules over all modes of production. But even within popular culture, there is a skewed emphasis on the present, rather than the past. Dolly Parton is a good country singer, but she will never be as influential as a songwriter, guitarist or vocalist as Leadbelly.

The Wikipedia discourse is also inward and self-referential. Yes, the entry for 'Wikipedia' (that started in 2001) is longer than the entry for 'library', an institution that can be conservatively dated from the Library of Alexandria in 300 BC. Yes, 'user-generated content' offers a longer entry than for 'codex', and perhaps most disturbingly, the page for 'Criticisms of Wikipedia' is longer than the entry for 'terrorism'.

This final paradox captures the deep flaw in the diamond potential of collaborative media. By example, Wikipedia – and even criticisms of it – are simply not as important as understanding the world outside of the 'edit this page' culture. We overvalue the movement of data and editing of words at the same time that we undervalue the movement of migrants[10] and the editing of history.

It's only food, dude

Is it just me, or is anyone else cheesed off at the Slow Food people? As I have moved around British and Australian towns and cities, I increasingly bump into a bunch of middle class tossers with too much money and time, getting their hands pseudo-dirty in 'authentic' produce, organic tomatoes and navy blue vein cheese. They are following a well-sodden path plotted by cooking programmes. You know the narrative. An overweight baby boomer bloke travels to deepest darkest Sicily – or New Jersey, Maidstone or Glebe – to talk to 'a local' (insert working class man) to discuss how we can not only exploit his labour but his stories, giving our mobile phone culture some depth and meaning. We have the phone. Now we need something to say on it.

It's only food, dude. These pompous cooks are practising appropriation of the worst kind. Celebrating olive oil tasting and homemade pasta will not redistribute wealth or power. Carole Cadwalladr let rip at the pretensions of the haves and have mores.

> Oh, it's so exhausting being middle class. What with the moral superiority. And the self-improving television programmes. And the quasi-religious food laws. Even going shopping is not the simple supermarket run of old: it's more like sitting A Levels that consist of memorizing an unwritten coda of increasingly complex rules pertaining to which stuff you're supposed to buy, which stuff you're not supposed to buy, and which you're simply meant to sneer at – existing only to be purchased by the witless chumps who are insufficiently bourgeois to know any better.[1]

This food obsession reinforces the division between those who produce and those who consume, those who work with their hands and those who work with their brain. Having an interesting foodie story to tell at the next dinner party adds sparkle to the conversation, but nothing to the understanding of work in our postfordist, deunionized and short-term contract society. The official *Slow Food Manifesto* reports their goal as 'a firm defense of quiet material pleasure'.[2] How this aim contributes to quelling religious fundamentalism, bringing peace to the Middle East or mediating colonial injustices that still resonate in the present is unclear.

When academics and foodie intellectuals talk about everyday life and slow cultures, they fetishize 'ordinary' people, while remaining comfortable in their squishy liberal politics of being inclusive, nurturing and open. The slow food movement had its origins in Italian left-wing politics. Yet as Petrini and Padovani confirmed, while some of these men and women who lived through the incomplete revolution of 1968 moved to the environmental movement, others welcomed a shift to conviviality.[3]

> Taste buds are neither conservative nor liberal, and, though it may be impossible to change the world, one should at least be able to change a menu.[4]

This is a political retreat. It can be dressed up with the language of sustainability, reclaiming diverse and historic seeds and varieties, more equitable payment for farmers or considered treatment of animals. Each of these goals is important and valuable. However, the core of slow food is the intrinsic value of taste. When wide ranging social justice imperatives have been lost, it is an unfortunate replacement to welcome a change in a menu. It is also a decontextualized response to postfordism and changes to the workplace.

It is strange to meet slow foodies. They live in one world. Then I telephone my mother. She spends (too) many hours each week buying specials at supermarkets all over Mandurah, a regional city near Perth in Australia. This city is also known as God's Waiting Room. While the grim reaper hovers, buying bargains becomes a competitive sport for the over-seventies. My mother loves specials so much that she had to buy another fridge to hold her quarry. When the nuclear winter comes, Doris Brabazon will be the pantry for the Western world. She is encyclopedic in her pricing knowledge of dish washing liquid, cheddar cheese and long life milk. This milk will probably outlive all of us, including the cockroaches. But my point is an important one. Whatever she gathers in these shopping expeditions is built into a meal. This is a true cook. No lavishly illustrated cookbook. No careful list of ingredients. No 'I like it really hot' advice from Nigella Lawson. Anyone can create taste sensations from rump steak and salmon. Try doing it with a shank or chuck-out cod.

Following Disraeli, there are still two nations,[5] and they are increasingly distant from each other. Reality television is meant to link them. One nation votes housemates off *Big Brother*. The other group studies why they do it. Text messaging substitutes for democracy. Such divisive times summon difficult questions. Why – after September 11 – have there been so many shows on home renovation? Why do we need to 'change rooms'? What happened to changing the world? Why are we filling our minds with paint colours, paving designs and the newest variety of fuchsia? Terrorism has transformed citizens into home decorators. These changes are not caused by television. We are not duped masses, eyes wired open in some revisited *Clockwork Orange* nightmare, grateful for the semiotic scat thrown at us.

The gritty truth is that there is little to watch except these bizarre, banal shows, featuring proto or post-celebrities, singing, dancing and ice skating through screen culture. Celebrating their worth does not mask the fact that they are poor quality programming and cheap to produce. This is not an elitist statement. The best of popular culture buzzes with dynamism, excitement, energy and a gritty critique of the powerful. As *Dancing with the Stars* winds down and *American Idol* winds up in a spiral of stupidity, we need an active and intelligent discussion about how class differences are lived in and through our lives.

Working class culture is not a pick 'n' mix of lifestyle options. The middle class cannot appropriate yokel food stories and then complain about the woman who cleans their house. Raj Patel realized this distinction.

> Beyond this, the most pressing problem for most of us as consumers is, of course, that to be able to go on a culinary odyssey in the first place and, even more, to be truly at liberty to savour food, to have the time to quaff and roll, the majority of people need that passport to all other freedoms – money.[6]

University academics may think they are studying 'everyday' life, but we are researching a moderated, mediated working class reality. Dinner parties are not a metaphor for living authentically. Life presents far greater challenges than an unfashionable plate design and washing a mountain of dishes.

And – really – how happy do you want your chickens? Obviously, no one wants animals to suffer unnecessarily, but there is a guarantee that chickens will die in an attempt to create chicken drumsticks, breasts and stir fries. If the eater is that offended by the life and death of chickens, then do not eat poultry. As Cadwalladr confirmed, 'who likes being lectured on ethics by a celebrity chef who trousered £2m a year from a supermarket chain? It's foodie fundamentalism is what it is.'[7] Then there is the issue of eggs.

> A properly cooked poached egg has to be really, really fresh and free-range. Barn eggs are also acceptable or, if you're really choosy, barn conversion eggs, which are eggs laid in barns with original exposed beams. Free-range is a relative concept: you'll know chickens are really free-range when you find one in the lift at work.[8]

A serious decision must be made for those of us who eat and think, and it involves confronting the ruthlessness of professional food production. Supermarkets require a guaranteed supply of produce, requiring animals to embark on a pre-programmed life for a pre-scheduled death. I am not a vegetarian or vegan. I have respect for those who make these life choices. For the rest of us, we have to recognize that how we manage food in our lives has a consequence on other animals in the world. It is the disconnection of food production from food consumption that is the problem. Foodie stories fill this gap, configuring a pseudo authenticity and pretence that blanching vegetables is equivalent to growing them, or matching a Chablis with peppercorned scallops is similar to pruning grape vines. Dinner parties are the crucible for this performance.

I have always hated dinner parties. There are two reasons for my disgust. Firstly, during much of my adult life, I have been single. As every single man and woman reading my words knows, married couples dislike those without the weighted ball and chain of mundane monogamy. Maybe dislike is not the word: confusion and ambivalence are better. With the whole culture paired up in wedded despair, single people ruin the symmetry of a well laid-out table. Crockery and cutlery sets are only available in even numbers. Without children's schooling, home decorating or extra virgin olive oil to talk about, the conversation stutters around the difficulty of single women finding good men. Or I think that is what happens. My only experience of these dining disasters is from Bridget Jones. I am so unpopular with paired-off heterosexuals that I have never been invited to one of these dinner parties. Maybe I remind them of what they could have been doing for the last two decades if they could just close that home decorating magazine or stop proselytizing about expensive wine.

My second reason for the pathological fear of dinner parties – not surprisingly – involves my mother. I attended a convent school, as did three generations of women in my mother's family. But my mother intervened in the taken-for-granted education of nice Catholic girls. She staunchly removed me from sewing and cooking classes. The teachers believed I was ill-prepared for looking after a husband. Bugger, I didn't think of that. I was wasting my life trying to get into university. I should have put down that compass and picked up a spatula. Then my future would be secure.

To this day I sew badly and cook unsteadily, but made it into university and stayed there. And I have not cooked for a dinner party in my entire life. The world as we know it has not ended. It's only food, dude. Have a piece of fruit. Make a sandwich. This is the problem with the slow foodies. It is profoundly ungenerous to the generations who came before us to now decide that spending our lives cooking for others is the best way for a woman to use her time. Our mothers and grandmothers fought for our right to make a toasted cheese sandwich for ourselves and feel good about not making a beef stroganoff for the family. Love is not found in salad dressing. Success is not switched on with the refrigerator light. Intimacy is not stirred through a Belgian chocolate mousse.

Those who believe in progressive politics need a way out of this lifestyle Prozac. While we slumber with satiation, there is a war going on. We need a method to connect the lifestyle of some with the life and death struggles of others. I am not sure when it happened, but at some point it became acceptable for supposedly left-leaning academics to celebrate consumerism, drink fine red wine and eat the best organically grown vegetables, while placing children in private schools. Academics are not alone in replacing good politics with good food. It is incredibly difficult – post-Clinton, post-Blair and the Coalition of the Willing – to ascertain what the left actually represents. Both New Labour and Republican governments went to war and justified their decision in starkly similar language.

Looking around the world, those of us who think, write, create and build must do so with responsibility. Whenever I hear people talk about slow food, I hear implicit and condescending laughter at the poor, and ridicule of those who are not self-aware (or self-absorbed). Two nations are splaying once more. One is successful, content, complacent and able to plan for the future. The other struggles, fights and tries to get through the day. To go slow – to make a sea change – is a choice beyond the reach of most. This is a fast, frightening time. Retracting back to the kitchen will not bring us peace in the Middle East. Instead, make yourself a cheese sandwich and think about the House of Saud.

Crazy Frog capitalism

My father has reached – in cricketing parlance – 80 not out. Now retired and surrounded by digitized screens, sounds and searches, I never have to worry that he is silently suffering from Alzheimer's disease. He manages a box of remote controls so complex that landing the space shuttle is less taxing. While now bouncing around the digital bubble, he has lived the conventional analogue working life for a man of his age. A skilled tradesman, he finished a railway coach-building apprenticeship at the end of the Second World War. In remembering this period, he recently told me how his days were regulated.

Kev Brab not only clocked on and off for an eight-hour day, but also had toilet breaks timed. It was one man's job to monitor these ablutions. His name was Wal. My father remembers Wal had a small desk and chair assembled at the entrance to the toilet block. As each apprentice or tradesman arrived, Wal would write down his worker number and time of arrival. Only eight minutes were permitted to occupy the toilet. When this interval was up, Wal would knock on the toilet door and end 'the break'. The worker would then be logged out of the facilities.

This was how work was managed in the late 1940s and 1950s – controlled, patrolled and ordered by time. Kevin's story has been a trigger for my recent quizzical gaze at the contemporary working environment. Work has changed, but our identities are increasingly defined through leisure and lifestyle. The spillage of leisure technologies into the white collar workforce is piquant to watch.

I am being polite.

I am seething with rage at the incompetence and rudeness of self-important fools with small mobiles and big voices who seem to think that I am remotely interested in their wife, children, office romance, drinking habits, hangover, lunch appointment, lack of a mobile phone charger, newly pregnant receptionist, newly appointed receptionist who is not yet pregnant, new trainers, new phone because they have lost the charger, new tie, new lounge suite, new plasma screen television and – much to their horror – new credit card bill that they are unable to pay. My cochlea is bursting with microtraumas in microtime. I am not going to be polite any more. Let me explain.

I have spent the last 20 years in universities, which means long meetings with short agendas are the spectator sport of choice. Men in shiny polyester charcoal-grey suits, with sensible socks and ties and sharp haircuts, try to make us believe that we work in the hedge fund department of a bank rather than in the enterprise of education. I have been fascinated to watch the mobile phone behaviour of these charcoal-clad corporate commandos. Our students are easily disciplined. My promise to answer any phone that rings in my lecture theatre and chat to the person at the other end in front of 140 people, or send a pseudo-intimate text message to their mother, scares students enough to switch off their social life for one hour.

No, students are not the problem. It is the adults that are behaving badly. I have noticed that as staff file in and sit down for meetings, their mobile phone is placed on the table, within easy reach and view. It is switched on. No pretence of privacy or politeness is enforced or enjoyed. I am old enough to remember when people used to apologize if their phone went off in a meeting. Now the ring etches another notch on their corporate belt. They are so important that they do not care if they irritate fellow workers. No one is as cutting edge, significant or important as them. Their time is valuable. Their business is urgent. The shrieking, disruptive ring confirms power over sound and space and therefore people.

There is a performativity to this rabid phone behaviour. Part of it is a *Kath and Kim*-inspired 'look at moiye – look at moiye' attitude. For teenagers, the endless beeping of arriving text messages signals popularity. When I was 15, I wanted spike heels and big hair for the same reason. For suited baby boomers, incoming calls in meetings confirm the scale and depth of their workload, and how incredibly fortunate we are that they have spared a few minutes to share with us. I once attended a meeting where the chair's phone not only rang, but he proceeded to answer it and have a conversation while the rest of us wondered where to look. At a meeting of local government representatives, a man's phone rang while a lecture was being delivered. He answered the call and spoke for five minutes *in the auditorium* while others were trying to concentrate on the presentation.

And we all know his ring tone. It is profoundly appropriate that in such crazy times that Crazy Frog continues to stutter and sing his way through capitalism. That a ring tone went on to become a number one single and continues to feature in endless iTunes remixes is digital convergence at its most camp and – let's be honest – weird. That such a silly song shrieks from serious business meetings – rather than The Stones '(I can't get no) Satisfaction' or The Kaiser Chiefs' 'Everything is average nowadays' – is a satisfyingly appropriate commentary on our time.

This is not only a blokey pseudo-phallus phenomenon. In fact, I think women are probably worse in this distraction factory. The endless chick checking of the screen, while mock apologizing that they are waiting for a call, is a desperate cry for attention. (Too) often, these women's phones do not ring, yet they continue to gaze at the screen, willing the tone to peel to confirm their supposed significance in the lives of others. That is the greatest trouble with mobile phone culture: the arrogance and egotism. Nobody is that important. Nobody needs to be contacted so urgently that an hour-long meeting must be interrupted by this digital garbage. Mobile phones are crucial for drug dealers, prostitutes and leaders of the free world. Everyone else – *everyone else* – can wait an hour to clear their messages.

In trying to understand the sociology of text messaging and ASPOs (Attention Seeking Phone Opportunities), I have been drawn again to Andrew Goodwin's brilliant *Dancing in the Distraction Factory*.[1] Although taking popular music as his focus, the title has been bouncing around my head for years. The consequences of not concentrating on daily tasks – of dancing in distraction – will only be revealed in the long term. As someone who teaches for a living, one of the major skills I have to develop in first year students is their capacity to focus, concentrate and silence the clutter and clatter of their lives. The ever-shrieking mobile phone punctuates the silence of contemplation and thought, making us too busy – or appearing too busy – to actually think about and complete important tasks in a considered and effective way.

Fordism, with its assembly lines, mass production and mass consumption, granted the factory system efficiency. The difficulty in this mode of production was how to convince and motivate workers to operate in such a pressurized environment. That is why consumerism and leisure became the sweetener for running our days by a bell, clock and timesheet imposed by others. In a postfordist environment, we (only) work to gain access to goods and services through consumption. Work is brought into the leisure context, and leisure is brought into work. The mobile phone is often the conduit. Unlike pre-industrialization, where most of the day was spent gaining food and surviving, now shopping and gathering items has become an act of leisure, embedded in virtual consumerism and lifestyle through e-commerce.

Concurrent with these radical changes to work, 'lifestyle' has replaced leisure. Too often we use the word 'lifestyle' without recognizing what happens when our life has a style rather than an experiential reality.[2] Through such a transformation, the workaholic has morphed from a pathologized, hard-drinking insomniac in a crumpled suit on a train into normal corporate behaviour.[3] The phone is a marker of those men and women in the workplace who wish to prove that they are invaluable to the corporate enterprise, endlessly – and literally – on call for their management masters.

What happened to thinking about a life, rather than a lifestyle? The focus on lifestyle makes us believe that we as individuals choose our destiny. Such an assumption lets governments off the hook in making structural changes to work, health, food and safe exercising and sporting environments. The pleasures of lifestyle have replaced the opportunities of living a balanced life. We have traded text messaging for free time. Pinpointing the alienation of workers is not new: Marx's 1844 *Manuscripts* took this topic as its primary focus.[4] The biggest change since Marx's interpretation has been the shift from a predominant blue collar to a predominately white collar workforce. A new language of management creates an artificial consensus that hides the volatility and antagonism of workplace relations. This disconnection between the white collar worker and management is mediated by new vocabularies such as corporate objectives, professional development, multiskilling, generic competencies, occupational health and safety, mission statements and strategic plans. Through such phrases, there is little mechanism through which to express resentment without fear of redundancy.

With our mobile phones, shopping malls and civilized workplaces, we may seem to be a long way from my father's timed toilet breaks. Certainly, we have traded a life for a lifestyle. Now we have the freedom of ablutions and can determine the colour of our bathroom. But we do not have the time to think that there may be alternatives to a lifestyle of artichokes in extra virgin olive oil, pay television and mobile phones. We work to consume. We do not work to think. Maybe we should think a bit more.

What are the young people wearing?

As a Generation Xer, I have spent most of my adult life working for and with baby boomer men. Mostly these generational and professional situations have been based on an affable truce, with disagreements surfacing over skirt length, shoe selection and musical tastes. But there have been the occasional shockers of bosses and some crazy characters. One bloke seemingly gained pleasure from causing fights between young female staff only to stand back to tit-tit-titter at the state of feminism. Another boomer bloke intentionally created vulnerable situations for women – personally and professionally – so that they would have to rely on his 'good nature' to get them out of it. There would be a bill presented for these favours.

In my deck of boomer horrors, the joker of the pack always trumps the rest. He wandered around menswear stores asking only one question of shop assistants: 'What are the young people wearing?' In the 1970s, this man would be mocked as the oldest swinger in town, with gold chains and chest wig accoutrements. In the early 1990s, our swinger was clothed in see-through mesh tops, cargo pants, boat shoes, platinum hair vertically gelled into a state of continual electric shock and a stud through his left eyebrow. The shop assistants saw him coming and used his question to sell all the hyped up, marked up excesses of the season's fashion before massively discounting similar items the following week. He thought he looked great. He didn't. He looked like he thought the young people looked. He didn't.

I recently met the new breed of cargo-panted chest wiggers. Not surprisingly, they no longer use clothes to prove that they are down with the kids. Skaters have physical dexterity to go with their dress. Goths get beaten up. Instead, Web 2.0 has provided the metaphoric hooded anorak to cover the bulge with bling. This new boomer species has emerged in the safest – but strangest – of settings: library conferences. Librarians are the Jedi Knights of the modern age, committed to reading, interpretation and thinking in a world of chaos, ignorance and fear. Like the Jedi, librarians have also been under threat by the evil empire of capitalism, as schools and universities reduce the budgets for books and staff. The justification of this downsizing is that Google is as good as a catalogue and the internet is almost a library. This statement is wrong, and about as dangerous as connecting Saddam Hussein to September 11.

In the case of libraries, the result of this intellectual hallucination will not be war, but ignorance. Google is a search engine. The internet is a random, corporatized electronic shopping mall filled with ghost sites, pornography and bloggers who demonstrate the confidence of Jeremy Clarkson at a car show. The most basic realization – that librarians do not provide information, but a path through information – seems lost in the 'I'm feeling lucky' cursor click age. There has never been a time when librarians have been more important. Yet there has never been a time when they have had to justify so strongly their expertise, professionalism and role.

The library profession has suffered profound challenges to its credibility. It is a predictable irony that this attack has emerged against one of the few professions dominated by women. It has been a study in power relations to attend library conferences during the last decade. I have seen auditoriums filled with intelligent, well-read and educated women being harangued, ridiculed and attacked by male baby boomer 'consultants' who prophesize doom, decay and medieval-style upheaval.

These men have discovered a new mantra through which to batter and frighten the women of the library profession: Web 2.0. We are all meant to be impressed at the moment a boomer summons this phrase. He is trendy. He knows what the young people are wearing. Web 2.0 aligns Flickr, MySpace, Facebook, YouTube, blogs, wiki-enabled media and Google as (supposedly) part of an end-user democracy where the readers of websites become the writers of websites. Our digi-swingers use Web 2.0 to ridicule librarians, rendering redundant expertise in catalogues and information literacy skills because – you've guessed it – 'the young people' are doing it. If libraries and librarians want to get down with the kids, then they need a blog. Urgently. And be prepared to wiki-enable those catalogues.[1]

Governments, employers and parents are placing demands on formal education to 'get with' the young people and/or the digital age.[2] A complete lack of understanding of curriculum, how it is written, evaluated by peers, assessed by quality assurance organizations, and improved over years rather than days is never featured in the pieces that berate how librarians and teachers are failing the digital revolution. For example, Bill Thompson became cross at his son's school because it did not teach students about the Trojan Horse code that spreads through online video sites.

> Despite the growing importance of computers and the internet in school I don't expect that this real threat to home computer users will make it into the school newsletter or be announced in assembly as part of the general school concern for pupil safety. And this highlights a real failing in the education system, one that betrays a lack of the sort of joined-up thinking that the government is trying to

achieve elsewhere … It would be nice to think that my son would come home from school to tell me that there was nasty Mac Trojan in the wild because his teachers realized that it might be important to him. It would be just as nice if he was encouraged to use social network sites to share his insights into the underlying causes of the First World War or MySpace to post his pop art inspired paintings.[3]

There are endless news loops reporting that seven, ten and twelve-year-olds are lacking 'the three Rs'.[4] Thompson does not mention this mode of literacy. Numeracy, reading and writing are not in his vista as he argues for the importance of his son being taught about computer viruses. Clearly, it is time for a reality check. The school and university timetable is a finite entity. New and fashionable ideas that may or may not be a necessity for the information age will replace other subjects and literacies if they are to be taught. Is it really necessary that students learn about computer viruses at school? Is Thompson satisfied that less geometry and algebra, less reading and comprehension will be taught to fulfil his request?

Technology has warped priorities. Like digitized sun stroke, pseudo-evangelistic commitments to computers have meant that more basic questions, goals and imperatives are not being addressed. For example, One Laptop Per Child's programme to supply children in the developing world with computers has found that orders have not been forthcoming from the planned market. Nigeria's education minister, Dr Igwe Aja-Nwachuku, explained why Nicholas Negroponte's scheme has not been successful.

> What is the sense of introducing One Laptop Per Child when they don't have seats to sit down and learn; when they don't have uniforms to go to school in; where they don't have facilities?[5]

Analogue injustice has been masked by the imperative for the newly digital. 'Needs' and 'wants' are not ahistorical, but meshed in inequalities of colonialism, sexism and homophobia.

But what are the 'young people' really thinking when YouTube and MySpace becomes part of their formal learning? Just because 'the young people' are using a platform in leisure does not mean that they want it to move into other institutions and discourses like work, libraries or education. Instead, this fetishization of the new has been used to scare librarians so that they feel that their expertise and experience is redundant in the Web 2.0 age. Such a fear is groundless, but is encouraged by these men who preach – and are paid to preach – a crisis, which lathers everyone into a fearful frenzy of discomfort and self-doubt. When suitably terrified and under-confident, the digi-swingers present themselves as the saviour for librarians, the rescuer from redundancy. Meanwhile, the real 'young people' are amused when taught Web 2.0 platforms in schools and universities.

From: luke

Sent: Sat 10/14/2006 11:36 PM

To: Brabazon Tara

Subject: RE: pom didlly um pom

that be great creative industrys sound good, i came home for the weekend to have a double think on everything, and the top up year on year 3 sounds like a good idea.

The first lesson i had was on "myspace" and "youtube" and i thought that was a joke as i already use them two, but the video production looks really good.

New zealand ah i wanted to go there and figi but backpacking i ran out of money i love oz and plan to go back there after uni. well let me know what room you are in and i will come see you.

Luke

Two crucial steps in logic are missed by digi-swingers. Simply because more people are involved in the construction of a set of facts or a document – the premise of Wikipedia – does not make it true. The reason that scholarly monographs and articles are trusted is because they have been refereed and checked by experts in the field. But Google has created confusion between finding information and possessing the literacy to actually understand, evaluate and judge information. We have spent so much of the last ten years focused on words like 'access' and 'content management' that we have neglected other ideas like 'motivation' and 'context management'. There is plenty of information available on the Web. What is lacking is the appropriate information in the correct time and place. Content is not the problem. Situating data in the correct context is the greatest challenge.

Secondly, there has been the assumption that information created by end users equates with the development of democracy. Supposedly, bloggers, through their daily diatribes, build citizenship through their posts. In other words, there has been a damaging confluence between affirmations of democracy and the promotion of right-wing populism. We must remember to ask who is *not* online, and what are the costs and consequences of this absence. With most of the world's population lacking a stable system of telephony – let alone the provision of broadband – we start to see how the democracy affirmed through Web 2.0 replicates many colonial structures of the nineteenth century. The empowered speak on behalf of the disempowered – the old, the disabled, the black and the poor. Instead of recognizing this ventriloquism, the loud affirmations of digital democracy drown out not only any critique, but any space to hear the silences in this pseudo-utopic discourse.

When scratching the taut cyber-skin of wiki swingers, the inconsistencies and inequalities emerge. Wiki is a software device that allows collaborative writing and editing. 'Anyone' can create a page. What this has meant is that global businesses and universities have used Wikipedia as another site of branding and marketing. This phenomenon is not too serious. What is ironic and important in this wikiworld is that the open source movement has its limits. In Wikipedia, there are increasing numbers of protected and semi-protected pages that can only be changed by administrators or 'experienced' editors. These include – no shock here – the entries for George W. Bush and Dick Cheney. Brilliantly, Uma Thurman is also a closed page. *Kill Bill* makes the wiki-heads delusional in their edits. There are more serious charges against these wiki profiles. In a famous case, Brian Chase created a page for John Seigenthaler in May 2005.[6] A former assistant to Robert Kennedy, the wiki-biography included complete lies in the listing, suggesting that Seigenthaler was implicated in the Kennedy assassination and had lived in the Soviet Union. He had done neither. Expertise did not matter in this case. It was popularity that determined truth.

In August 2006, a Wikimania conference was held at the Harvard Law School. Gary Younge reported that three quarters of the delegates were male, and 90 per cent were white. While the swingers are talking (at conferences) about what the young people are wearing, they are still only celebrating themselves. In a time where such digitized social dysfunction is masked by the label of democracy, there has never been a more opportune time to value the expertise of librarians. The e-library – if and when it does appear – will not be created through dumping the books, sacking the librarians and creating row upon row of keyboards. Content will not be created by wiki-literate white men telling us what the young people are wearing, thinking and doing. The electronic library will be built through information literacy classes and courses, document delivery, effective and accessible databases and a thoughtful transition between – not through – the analogue and digital collections.

Significantly, all these purposes, objectives and functions are dismissed by Jimmy Wales. At the London-hosted Online Information Conference at Olympia, he attacked teachers who doubted the value of Wikipedia. In fact, he described them as 'a bad educator'.[7] Once more, the fact that 'young people' are using it justified its deployment in formal education. He stated, 'you can ban kids from listening to rock 'n' roll music, but they're going to anyway … It's the same with information, and it's a bad educator that bans their students from reading Wikipedia.'[8] Significantly, he has blurred the divisions between leisure and education. It is not 1956. No one is banning rock 'n' roll or rap or metal or grime. No one is banning Wikipedia, Facebook, YouTube or MySpace. Instead, a legitimate judgment and statement about intellectual value is being made. No encyclopedia – not Wikipedia or Britannica – is operating at a sufficient scholarly level to be of use at university. Wikipedia, along with other Web 2.0 applications, is an object of study. It is not a method of study. Jimmy Wales has no qualifications or expertise in teaching or librarianship.[9] His inability to understand the value of expertise is what has caused the flattening of information and scholarly value in the first place. While the size and popularity of Wikipedia is impressive since its founding in 2001, with over two million articles in English, perhaps we should not be so impressed by this number. After all, Wikipedia also features 62 articles in Klingon.[10]

My fear is not of Flickr, Wikipedia or Google. They are simple platforms to use that require complex literacies to use well. My concern is that, in the confusion between finding information and building knowledge, we lose not only analogue objects and artefacts, but analogue ways of thinking. Our minds have been marinated by digitization. We think that every item and moment in our lives is infinitely reproducible, forwardable, compressible and transferable. The gift of this knowledge is that we can store text messages from our loved ones to be reviewed during times of sadness. What we have lost is the capacity to value the particular, the unique and the transitory.

Through digitization, we are reducing our ability to acknowledge and relish a moment in time, knowing that once it has passed it cannot be repeated. If we miss a class at school or university, then the PowerPoint slides will be available. If we miss a call, then a message will beep its presence. If we do not go online on Monday, then the emails will still be in the pop server on Tuesday waiting for us. This digital way of thinking has a cost. We become guest stars in our own lives, looking down at our phone's message bank, rather than up to be fully living in a moment. Analogue living has risks. The moments of intense happiness or tragedy quickly vanish. The gothic scale of emotions cannot be relived or renewed. Through digital mediation, we have been sucked into emotional and intellectual neutrality, medicated against excess, loss and pain. We do not have to fight for anything or feel anything deeply at the time, because we know the file can be reopened at our convenience so that we can relive the micro-emotion at a safe distance.

The best of learning – the best of life – is transitory, irreplaceable and analogue. How many hours and days are we living in instant replay, photographing analogue reality, creating a barrier around our bodies so that we can deny specificity, deny the loss of time for a later playback on digital delay? Losing analogue objects is a tragedy. Losing analogue ways of thinking will crush civilization more than a Tsunami or war.

You've been Jaded

And then suddenly – finally – it was all over. All the pseudo-celebrity nonsense. All the anti-intellectualism. All the attention to pedicures, makeovers, hair extensions, waxing, Manolos, ugg boots, thong bikinis, colonic irrigations, pilates, flat screen televisions, stainless steel ovens, gazebos, water features, designer clothes, designer jewellery, designer bags, 4 x 4s, miniature dogs and massive barbeques. All these micro-choices of no importance created a culture where how we looked was more important than what we thought.

But it has all gone now. One degrading and degraded woman in the midst of a reality television programme destroyed the façade of democracy buildt through 'celebrating' Wikipedia, text messaging and blogging audiences. The acidic ugliness of racism exploded over our faces. This is not television as usual, as Peter Bazalgette – chairman of Endemol – tried to suggest.

> It has been a fairly typical series of Big Brother, which has uncovered surprising and controversial aspects of our life … It goes to the root of who we are, questions about our identity. That's what happens when you put 12 people together. We have obeyed the rules of broadcasting. It's not a mistake, it has been successful.[1]

We have valued, laughed at and validated the stupid, inane, dense, dumb and thick. Now we see the consequences of a life where bread and circus television has replaced bread and butter decisions about social policy and military strategy.

There was karma to the crisis. Jade Goody, a single mother with little education and less career prospects, did not win *Big Brother 3*. She came fourth. On the basis of this 'fame' she made public appearances, went on the revolving door of chat shows, lost weight, did not tell anyone that it was through liposuction, released a workout DVD, put her name to a perfume and then – two years later – completed the cycle. At the start of 2007, Goody returned as a 'celebrity' to *Celebrity Big Brother*. It was the high water mark of reality television. A woman who was an 'ordinary person' before the programme had now become a celebrity in her own right. It seemed the conventional trash to treasure, zero to hero tale where a screened life was a successful life.

The problem was that the programme that made her also broke her.[2] When paired in the House with Shilpa Shetty, a Bollywood actress, all the nodes of tension and decay in popular culture and public life were revealed. Jade Goody was part of a gang of three, including Danielle Lloyd, the (former) girlfriend of a footballer, and Jo O'Meara, a (former) member of the pop group S Club 7. Like the worst bullies from high school, the three Queen Bees oozed their ugly opinions without the restraints of evidence, knowledge or reasoned discourse. They were beyond bitchy. They were an embarrassment to their gender, their country and television. Effigies of Endemol executives, the producers of the programme, were burnt in India. The Carphone Warehouse withdrew its three million-pound sponsorship. The Perfume Shop removed Shh…, Goody's best-selling scent, from its shelves. Lloyd lost her modeling contract and her opportunity to be the face of a motorcycle insurance business. Her relationship with Teddy Sheringham was in shreds.[3] *Celebrity Big Brother* – punctuated by racism – became the most complained about programme in television history. It was mentioned in the House of Commons. It summoned international protest and press coverage.

What did these women say and do to initiate such hostility? The following transcript provides some of their lowlights.

Date	Event	Comments
12 January 2007	Shetty bleaches her facial hair	Lloyd: 'Do you get stubble?' Goody: 'She wants to be white … She makes me feel sick. She makes my skin crawl.' Lloyd: 'She's a dog.'
14 January 2007	Shetty cooks food in the House	Lloyd: 'They eat with their hands in India. Or is that China? … You don't know where those hands have been.' Lloyd: 'Me and Jo and Jade are really good friends – you're just the cook.' Lloyd: 'Shilpa is a dog.'
16 January 2007	Ordering Oxo cubes	Goody: 'It's not the only fucking thing you ordered, you liar … You're not some princess in fucking Neverland … Go back to the slums and find out what real life is about, lady … You fucking fake. You're so far up your own arse you can smell your own shit.' Shetty: 'Oh please learn some manners. You need elocution lessons, Jade.' Lloyd: 'I think she should fuck off home.'

17 January 2007	Conversation between Lloyd, O'Meara, Goody	Goody: 'Shilpa Poppadom.' Goody: 'I look at her and I wanna headbutt her. I wanna wipe that smug look off her face.' Lloyd: 'She can't even speak English properly.'
18 January 2007	Goody talking with Shetty	Goody: 'A lot of stuff got said ... I didn't say it in a racial way ... I do not judge people by the colour of their skin.'
20 January 2007	After eviction, watching a clip of herself	Goody: 'I look like an utter nasty small person – the sort of person I don't like. I am not a racist.'[4]
21 January 2007	In an interview with the *News of the World*	Goody: 'It was racist. I am a bully.'[5]

It was political theatre at its most bombastic. But it was the response to these three women that captures – with jagged clarity – the xenophobic clashes after 9/11. They were racist. There is no doubt or questioning of this label. Goody, O'Meara and Lloyd saw a skin colour different from their own and made judgments about cleanliness, linguistic capacity and the value of a person. Yet it is the reaction to this racism from the encircling journalistic vultures that is the core concern of *Thinking Popular Culture*. The women's comments were used to confirm that working class values are intrinsically racist. In other words, this public racism was justified and explained through public class-based prejudice. Attacking racism through class is not the way to build social or political justice. Prejudice on the basis of race or class cannot be ranked or balanced, with one being worse than the other.

To attack three women for being working class – and therefore racist – is as offensive as these same three women abusing an actress for being Indian. Discrimination emerges when making assumptions about a person, group or community on the basis of a particular social variable and then constructing a narrative of difference, incompetence and ineptitude based on this bias. Matching intolerance with intolerance is not the way to enact social transformation or a consciousness that prejudice is unacceptable in public and popular cultural discourse. Finding another way to mediate and understand cultural differences is the key. In response to this challenge, the final chapter in the first section returns the thinking to the pop and asks how we regenerate and exfoliate the skin of civility and respect that will be necessary to build a post-terrorist and post-terrorized world.

Honesty, hypocrisy, racism

> Is racism really any worse than any other kind of prejudice? If someone
> mispronounces – even persistently – a name, or suggests that people of the Indian
> subcontinent eat with their fingers, or confuses them with the Chinese, does it
> automatically suggest that they would willingly man the gas chambers – or even
> read the *Daily Mail?*[6]
>
> Tim Lott

The Age of Terrorism has meant that 'we' need to be very clear on who is one
of 'us' and who must be excluded as a threat to 'us'. 'Fundamentalists' are the
easy targets of terrorist campaigners. 'They' hate 'the West', which is supposedly
synonymous with freedom, democracy, progress and modernity. In this fantasy
land of good and evil, any racism and prejudice instigated by 'the West' on 'the
East' can hold no place. Any label, libel or law can be justified if it is part of
winning the war against terrorism. That is why racism from the white working
class fits the narrative of middle class politicians and educators. 'They' can be
blamed for all the 'unfortunate' statements about 'moderate Islam', while a war
is fought against 'fundamentalists' without purpose or end.

The Chief Executive of Channel 4, Andy Duncan, hid behind the mantra
that 'discussion' about volatile topics on television is always valuable: 'The
debate has been heated, the viewing has at times been uncomfortable but, in
my view, it is unquestionably a good thing the programme has raised these
issues and provoked such a debate.'[7] Such a statement is like the manager of a
losing team braying to the waiting journalist pack that 'rugby was the winner
today'. A debate 'led' by narrow-minded, self-absorbed English women is not
'a good thing'. It was cheap television presenting inflammatory ideas without a
context or framework. Such a genre and platform is not the way to understand
the relationship between Britain and India, the colonizer and the colonized.
Instead, we require a careful grappling with history, geography and postcolonial
theory. It is no coincidence that some of the most complex research in the
media and cultural studies palette from scholars such as Gayatri Spivak,[8]
Etienne Balibar[9] and Homi Bhabha[10] was written in an attempt to grasp the
tissues of connectiveness between past and present, domination and resistance,
commerce and culture, empire and nation. In comparison, the theorization of
class has been neglected since the high water mark in the 1970s from scholars
like Paul Willis, Stuart Hall and John Clarke. This gulf in understanding leaves
space for three working class women to represent all the ugliness, narrowness
and banality of a little England that has traded its Empire to complain about
being part of Europe. We deserve better than Endemol framing and feeding a
debate on race.

Post class ↔ under class

> This repression and violent passion is analogous to the way Jade Goody became hysterical with rage when brought face to face – by an exasperated Shilpa Shetty – with the obvious fact that the only reason she was famous was because she had the luck to have been chosen to appear on a reality show. This manifest and incontrovertible truth penetrated to the heart of Jade's self image, and punctured it, leaving her fizzing around the room as pointless and angry as an over-inflated balloon pricked by the sharpest of points.[11]
>
> Tim Lott

This controversy over race is really a controversy about class. Michael Collins' *The Likes of Us*[12] is an important book that deserves not only a wide audience but constant re-reading. He shows how the white working class has become the one group that can be abused without fear of legal or social retribution. These attacks are not only built on middle class snobbery but supply the hyper-consumerism and credit cards that blur the line between the haves and the have-nots. The battle is now between the haves and the have-mores or – more precisely – the wants and the want-mores. Therefore new markers of class are invented and fresh strategies to undermine working class consciousness and collectivity are constructed. Alexander Chancellor presented this problem at its most evocative: 'Is the Big Brother row really about race – or is it more to do with old-fashioned class hatred?'[13] One answer to his question is to provide a context around the controversy, and recognize the consequences of placing fame on the shoulders of the freakishly inarticulate, inexperienced and ill-educated. Goody justified her reference to Shetty as 'poppadom' by explaining that she wanted to use an Indian word, and this was the only one she knew.[14] In other words, the fount of racism was a lack of reading and an attendant simplification of thinking.

Goody, O'Meara and Lloyd are all located outside of a clear class structure. Their affiliation with working class life, identity, agency and consciousness is ambivalent at best. They are a long way from the organized labour movements of the nineteenth century. Raised in Bermondsey, London, Goody's father had a lengthy criminal record. From such a family, gaining social mobility would always be difficult, but her route to fame and fortune was through reality television, therefore circumventing any challenges to her excessive emotions, malapropisms or intellectual flabbiness. Her aberrant behaviour created evocative sound bites and humour. For Endemol, there was no reason to circumscribe her anger or limit the exposure of her errors and inadequacies. Jo O'Meara grew up in Romford, became a singer in S Club 7 and then failed to develop a solo career. *Big Brother* was a chance for her to reclaim some connection with the word 'celebrity'. Danielle Lloyd was born in Liverpool and after leaving school studied as a beautician. She went on to become Miss Great Britain but lost the title for supposedly having been involved with one of the judges. The similarity in these women's stories is that they all used whatever media resources they had to 'be famous'. Their trajectory to this goal included reality television, popular music and a beauty contest. In class terms, they aimed for mobility without the struggles of formal education or the daily grind of conventional employment. They were grappling for fame. They were not aiming for integrity, credibility or sustainability. Their current difficulties could have been predicted. Fame is a fickle mistress. Early in his career, the writer and comic actor Ricky Gervais was probed about his attitudes toward popular cultural success.

> I was asked what advice I would give to anyone who wanted to become famous, and I said 'Go out and kill a prostitute'.[15]

Goody, O'Meara and Lloyd have not followed Gervais' advice. Instead, they have gone out and killed liberalism and civility. They were prepared to say the unsayable because they had a belief that all that matters is celebrity and opinion, not consideration and analysis. Since her earlier *Big Brother* appearance, Goody was supported in the press. The Cinderella story is an appealing distraction during a time of war and environmental destruction. For example, just hours before the racism became overt, *The Observer* columnist Kathryn Flett expressed support for Goody.

> I can only suppose that the desperately unhappy child-woman Jade's mum Jackiey, was voted out by the public on Wednesday to spare Jade any more misery because, you know, We Love Jade ... Jade isn't a moron any more – probably never was.[16]

This statement was published on the day Goody stated that Shetty made her skin crawl and just prior to the publicity cyclone encircling her behaviour. The 'we' who love Jade turned on her quickly. She did not have to kill a prostitute. She simply had to open her mouth.

The life narratives of these three women demonstrate that the relationship between class and race is intricate and intertwined. As Nigel Morris and Andy McSmith reported:

> For all the progress ... ethnic minority Britons often find themselves at a disadvantage compared with their white neighbors in their everyday lives. Many more [are] likely to be expelled from school, jailed, unemployed, poorly paid, living in sub-standard housing and victims of crime ... Home Office data published last autumn showed that black people were still six times more likely than whites to be stopped and searched, and Asians are twice as likely. Research has also suggested that black and

Asian people are more likely to be imprisoned than white defendants – and, if found guilty, receive longer sentences than whites.[17]

Structural inequality creates institutional racism. Colonialism continues through consciousness. Our eyes are ideological organs. We do not see the truth, but view the world in a way that reinforces our social position. That is why the statements by Goody, O'Meara and Lloyd were so offensive. Their grasp on 'fame' was tenuous and fleeting. To cling to their ambiguous social position, it was necessary to not only see difference, but to mark and judge it as inferior. As Justin Huggler and Saeed Shah realized, 'what Goody et al. are saying to these Indians is that no matter how rich and successful they become, they can still be called a "dog" by a white person'.[18] This prejudice perpetuates the injustice of colonial history but also the fear of losing a house of fame built on a deck of cards.

Shilpa Shetty slices through all of Goody, O'Meara and Lloyd's assumptions about Britain, race and class. She was born in a wealthy family. Her father is a businessman. She was well educated at St. Anthony's Girls' High School in Chembur and Podar College. Like Lloyd, she commenced her career as a model but went on to gain extraordinary success in the Indian film industry. The diasporic Indian community ensures an intricate network of audiences for such performers, reaching through the United Kingdom, Singapore, Malaysia, Fiji, Australia and Aotearoa/New Zealand. For Shetty, *Celebrity Big Brother* was a mechanism to build new audiences for her films and create new opportunities for her career. Her decision was without desperation. Shetty was naïve, as she perhaps expected civility and some awareness of her filmic portfolio. With Ken Russell and Leo Sayer leaving the House early during the programme's run, the inmates who could have moderated the racism and informed Lloyd, Goody and O'Meara about the size of both the Indian film industry and Shetty's profile were outside the discussions. The assumptions about India, which Shetty discredited, did not align with a simple imperial narrative of white supremacy.

The problem is that – post-Thatcher, Major and Blair – there is no space to think about the relationship between the economy and identity. Fame and celebrity have become circuit breakers to a rational analysis of social structure and social mobility. To rewrite Marx for the *Big Brother* discourse, life does not determine consciousness any more than consciousness determines a life. Jade Goody, by making millions from selling an identity based on reality television 'celebrity', was granted a public profile and role that she could not manage. Goody possesses the unfortunate combination of a slow brain and a quick mouth. She has spent the money earned through celebrity, not on an education, but on her body. When the time came for her to stand against racism and xenophobia, she merely recycled two centuries of assumptions about Britain and the colonies. In a violent re-emergence of Orwell's Big Brother rather than the Endemol translation, her celebrity self was killed through surveillance.

Thinking about education

> The current debate over Big Brother has highlighted the need to make sure our schools focus on the core British values of justice and tolerance. We want the world to be talking about the respect and understanding we give all cultures, not the ignorance and bigotry shown on our TV screens … We must teach children about our shared British heritage while fostering an understanding of our cultural diversity and the uniqueness of our individual identity.[19]
>
> Alan Johnson

Alan Johnson was the Secretary of State for Education under the leadership of Tony Blair. He was 'replaced' in the post when Gordon Brown became Prime Minister. Such a decision was fortunate as he was so mistaken in his curricula advice to teachers, parents and students. Actually, the last lesson that is needed at the moment is a celebration of 'British values'. The forgetfulness of British colonization and the active ignorance in recognizing the consequences of imposing law, language, religion and military power on the Middle East, Africa and the Asian and Pacific region through the nineteenth and twentieth centuries has forged the current attitudes of superiority. Whereas once British military power ruled the colonies, now 'core values' rule the political landscape. Only a deep unawareness of how British colonization affected indigenous peoples could trigger such a statement from Johnson. Parents, students and citizens of Britain need to know more about other nations in the world, beyond tourist documentaries and news programmes about frightening foreigners and insurgent terrorists. Instead of abusing India and Indians, a clear-headed recognition of the changing nature of international capitalism is required. India is second only to the United States as the biggest investor in London.[20] The Empire is buying back.

We need much less talk about British values and much more discussion of human rights. We need much less celebration of 'British heritage' and more critical interpretation of British history. For those of us who teach for a living, the culture of blame, retribution, ignorance and fear built since September 11 has been visible in our classroom for some time. *Celebrity Big Brother* simply screened this vision of the future. Trevor Phillips, chair of the Commission for Equality and Human Rights, stated that, 'What we are seeing is a noxious brew of old-fashioned class conflict, straightforward bullying, ignorance and quite vicious racial bigotry. It is outrageous, and it is unpleasant.'[21] While the diagnosis of what we have seen is correct and necessary, it is even more important to find a positive path to the future. We need to let a woman who was born on

Big Brother die on *Big Brother*. For the rest of us, her fame must be a warning to demand more from our popular culture.

Alan Johnson abused television in an attempt to reconnect education and 'core values'. While popular culture has been implicated in the bigotry, narrowness and meanness, it is also part of the solution. Racism has spilled out of television screens in the past, but the circulation of the comments through 24-hour news channels, newspapers, magazines, web fora and YouTube clips fed the *Big Brother* fire. It does not have to be this way. One month before the *Big Brother* controversy, the Open University severed its relationship with the BBC, leaving a vacuum of educational broadcasting on free to air channels.[22] Instead of blaming television, the goal for politicians, educators and citizens must be to develop a literacy and movement to create better television. The main problem is not racism or class-based oppression. Instead, women and men with few ideas and less vocabulary to express them have been granted a televisual space to express their limitations through ephemeral fame.

So much money has been spent on war, home improvement and breast implants. So little has been spent on education. It was not the class of Goody, O'Meara and Lloyd that created the prejudice. The convergence of working class people with racist attitudes suits the needs of a middle class who must endlessly displace discussions of their own wealth, waste and assumptions of superiority. As a recent migrant to Britain, and possessing all the advantages that a white face, a good job and speaking English provides, I have witnessed an inability to manage cultural difference, or even a slight variation in accent, when confronted by it. When walking on English streets, young men have responded aggressively when hearing my 'foreign' accent. I have been spat on three times in two years. When (trying to) exercise in a campus gym, a fitness manager kept interrupting my workout for no other reason except to flex his power over a 30-something woman with an accent. When I finally stopped answering his questions so that I could finish my remaining time on the stationary cycle in peace, he shouted in my face, 'Don't they speak English where you're from?'

In the context of a classroom, students have expressed pride in themselves that 'I can understand your accent'. When I laughingly replied in response that I understood their accent as well, their faces filled with confusion. A young man, in the midst of a discussion of obesity, alcohol and social exclusion, responded to my queries with the statement that, 'English people have to binge drink so that we can forget about all the foreigners who live here'. All of these statements express inexperience in managing differences in accent and origin, but all emerged from within a university, the supposed hub of social mobility for the middle classes. Remember, I am a white Australian. I am not a penguin from Antarctica. If I provoked these supposedly good-humoured responses, then it is understandable why other modes of diversity would be managed with even less respect and empathy.

To pretend that racism, xenophobia and discrimination on the basis of accent, origin or skin colour only exists in working class Britain is to deny a much more complex and wide ranging pattern of social exclusion. With great honesty, Brian Reade realized within the pages of the *Daily Mirror* that:

> We've always cracked gags about foreigners – I did on Tuesday about the French – but something far more sinister is creeping into our psyche. This is a country where ministers play the Muslim card to look strong and patriotic. Where elected parties demand repatriation and twist facts to prove how we need to shut our borders. Where Europeans are portrayed as out to destroy the British identity, multi-culturalism is a 'failed social experiment' and standing up to perceived prejudice is viewed contemptuously as political correctness gone mad. This drip-drip-drip of bigotry has turned us into a nasty nation, and these bullies have simply been caught on camera mouthing our fear and loathing. They repel us with their prejudices. But they also show us a glimpse of the future and what our tolerant country is in danger of becoming.[23]

One person – even three people – can never represent a nation. There is absolutely no indication that Britain is more racist and less tolerant than France, Malaysia, Australia, Japan or the United States of America. Yet this popular cultural display is a reminder of a necessity for vigilance. Racism and bullying are not entertainment. But television is not the problem, cause or origin for this crisis in managing difference. The problem is not the screen, but what has been presented on the screen.

Goody, O'Meara and Lloyd are ignorant. Even *The Sun* termed Goody 'the dim reaper' and a 'halfwit'.[24] Their inability to understand the life experience of others resulted in petty jealousies, unsubstantiated rage, tacky conversations about sex and endless fascinations with nail polish and bodily functions. Being working class did not cause these problems. Not being given the opportunity to read and think about a world beyond their small lives is the fount of discrimination. *Celebrity Big Brother* is a destructive fracture – but also an important opportunity – to transform popular culture and to reassess our cultural assumptions, biases and prejudices since September 11. This anti-intellectualism – where scholars are replaced by 'experts' with military rather than academic credentials – has presented a bill. Emma Cox, from the nest of *The Sun*, realized that even she had mis-read the cultural landscape. She stated, 'All those years I defended Jade to pseudo-intellectuals – saying, I admired her honesty and realness. I regret every second after last night's performance.'[25] This historical moment should be a lesson to journalists and the rest of us interested in promoting a thoughtful culture. Being 'honest' is a destructive force when it corrodes the matrix of modernity, civility and respect that is necessary to operate a working democracy.

The rest of *Thinking Popular Culture* takes this moment of clarity and consciousness on *Celebrity Big Brother* as the starting point to revisit the years following September 11, to rediscover the pop that mattered and was hidden below reality television, soap 'stars' and paparazzi shots of scrawny woman with cosmetic surgery scars or big women in bad tracksuits. We can build a buoyant popular cultural future by reclaiming the evocative, intelligent and important thinking pop of the past.

DESIGN

The last punk

Graphic design is the new rock 'n' roll. In the last 15 years, musicians, DJs, actors and journalists have been superseded in the fashion hierarchy. Graphic designers are the guerrilla fighters of capitalism, battling to align corporate objectives, stylistic innovation and interrogative creativity. Visual media have the potential for revealing, masking or solving social problems. White space is cut up, shredded and swamped with colour and punctuated with fine lines. Corporate types buy a design to sell goods, ensuring that visual creativity and freshness is tempered by a calm compliance with the capitalist order. As Peter Saville acknowledged, 'you realize why the men in suits say they're not interested in innovative creativity. It's because they can't afford to be.'[1] Neo-liberalism requires graphic designers to sell (out), not slice up, their politics.

Where a pencil meets paper, and art meets commerce, graphic design is enacted. As the service industry for screen and sound, clothing and corporates, designers create the look of capitalism. How they shape beauty, through lines and shading, determines the relationship between art and advertising. Peter Saville has fought 'the system' throughout his career. At his moments of greatest success and opportunity, he simply vacated the organization. Attempting to work in the United States, he left after a year. Saville justified these failures by asserting that, 'I have a real problem with going to work for the sake of going to work'.[2] He has moved from job to job, fight to fight, since he left the Manchester Polytechnic with first class honours in 1978.[3] Through this defiance and diffidence to a working day, he has managed to hold jobs – at least temporarily – for Dior, Yohji Yamamoto and Givenchy.

The goal of graphic design is to reframe the familiar, to make it new, fresh, distinct and disturbing. One of the most influential images on Saville's life and work was Kraftwerk's *Autobahn*.[4] A motorway transformed into a visual and musical collision of the industrial and the agrarian. But Saville has a gift that arches beyond the steel and chrome of Kraftwerk's aloof and modernist Dusseldorf. He was born in the right place and time. Manchester, at the moment of a music revolution, provided the soundtrack for his vision. Saville's austerity and crisp lettering was stark and severe in an era of excess, flamboyance and confusion. If he is known for two images, then it is his first album cover for Joy Division's *Unknown Pleasures*, and *Closer*, the last cover for the group, released after Ian Curtis' suicide. He realized that 'I was spoilt in my first five years working and only wanted to do things that I enjoyed doing and that would require incredible freedom'.[5] Manchester music was pivotal to him: it gave him an edge and a connection to popular culture.[6]

Saville was the ideal visualizer for Factory Records, a job without a client, contract or clearly definable brief. It was a label inspired by punk, but fuelled by Da Da irony. Punk morphed clothes and hair, music and symbolism. Punk cut up popular graphics through appropriation and pastiche. War-time imagery, Stalinist iconography and situationist scrawls were inscribed over the proto-Thatcherite wasteland. Most importantly, punk created space for change. Saville realized that, 'when you lose comfort in your own time, you seek comfort in another time'.[7] Perhaps that is why popular cultural historians and fans in our present so frequently return to Factory, Joy Division and Saville. While punk did not provide a fresh cultural language, it did create disturbing combinations. The border shifted between popular and unpopular culture, the compliant and the dangerous.

Punk offered more opportunities for musicians and fashion designers than for graphic designers. For Saville, it was Jan Tschichold's *Die Neue Typographie*, when traced over David Bowie and Roxy Music, which created new layers of design. Innovation was summoned through appropriation and synthesis of earlier iconography in a punked-up present. Besides Tschichold, Saville was also influenced by his former schoolmate Malcolm Garrett who started designing for The Buzzcocks in 1976. Inspired by this alliance, by 1978 Saville was commissioned by Tony Wilson to design the first Factory poster. What makes Saville's work significant to the history of independent labels is that he destabilized the link between the sonic and visual,[8] and the acceptable role of the single, album and 12" cover in relation to the music. He realized that 'the visual experience of New Order was Peter Saville',[9] being able to entwine design and popular music history, creating an edgy and unsettling dance. His work with Peter Gabriel, Suede and Pulp confirms his cold, Kraftwerk-inspired interpretations of sound and vision.

Christopher Wilson: Doesn't a record cover constitute a 'thing?'

Peter Saville: No, it's a record cover first, and a thing second. I like the idea of it being a thing first and only secondarily a cover.[10]

The almost competitive nature of vision shadow boxing sound for semiotic ascendancy made cultural artefacts out of New Order and Joy Division albums, ensuring they would live longer than transitory chart success. Peter Saville's designs for Factory capture the value of a prized relic.[11] Each of his designs was numerically itemized and given a FAC prefix. The goal was to attach equal importance to the musical releases, posters and buildings. FAC1 was a poster for the first gig at the Russell Club. FAC51 was the Hacienda Nightclub. A chronicle was established as a collection of aesthetic objects to narrate the Factory story.

Peter Saville remains the first and last design punk. He does not fit in. He does not produce goods on time and on budget. Working in the excessive egoism of the music and fashion industry, his shrill – but accurate – commentary was that 'I'm more interesting than any of my clients'.[12] His confidence (in himself) is contagious. He has confronted and publicized the hypocrisy of both the creative arts and the creative industries.

> It seems Pentagram now values the work I did there, which in retrospect I find upsetting and ironic. David Hillman, in particular, takes a distinctly hypocritical position towards me. I was put forward to be a Royal Designer for Industry this year, and David had it stopped. He lodged a personal objection, which didn't surprise me. What did surprise me was when I then heard that Pentagram now includes my work in presentations. The value of those fashion projects with Nick Knight for Jil Sander and Yohji Yamamoto, and Nick's own book were questioned when I was there. The work was resented because it wasn't profitable. They doubted the value of it then, but it would seem they don't now.[13]

There has never been a greater need for Peter Saville to reveal the contradictions, hypocrisies and inconsistencies of work, capitalism, culture and life. His great gift was to put design – passionate, punchy and difficult design – onto record sleeves during a time when music mattered. For a generation of young people, Peter Saville made design not only important, but a necessary part of popular culture.[14] He made music look important and gave music fandom credibility, unsettling clear determinations of cultural value.

When reminded that his designs must make money for his corporate clients, he replies – with edge – 'Well, actually that's not why I'm here. I'm here to make things better.'[15] In the duel between creativity and commerce, he has defiantly chosen to live outside of the capitalist order. Yet 25 years after he left the place of his greatest fame, Manchester City Council made him the creative director of the city.[16] A retrospective book, *Designed by Peter Saville*, was published in 2003. Between January and April 2004, his Peter Saville Show ran at Manchester's Urbis, the museum of the city. His value and credibility, built through decades of outsider status, is being recognized. But he is clear that his work is grounded in darkness, death and post-industrial decay.

> One great investment happened in Factory, and this is what made Factory happen. The investment was someone's life. Literally, the life of Ian Curtis was the investment that made Factory happen. That's what made Factory happen. Without it, it couldn't

have happened. Ian's life created the platform from which Factory was able to survive and New Order were able to continue for the next decade. That was the investment in Factory Records. And actually in modern Manchester. I mean, the last three years I've been creative director to the city of Manchester, and I see it very, very clearly and plainly. Ian's life was the sacrifice that made it all work.[17]

His coldness of style masks the jaggedness of grief and has constructed what he terms an 'original modern'. In an era of content – user-generated or corporate-delivered – he has affirmed the value of form.[18] His visual vocabulary has rewritten the industrial past, but also transformed himself into a brand.

The irony is that now he is famous, one of the most famous graphic designers in the world,[19] he is (re)drawing himself and his history as sharply as shiny black lettering on brittle white card. His war against capitalism – through lateness, endless talking and procrastination about details and alternatives – has been successful. He has punctured popular culture, slowed accelerated modernity, in a relentless search for visual solutions to social problems. He had to be difficult and defiant to do it. Saville infused punk with cool elegance and roughed up corporate sleekness. Although he actually produces few designs, he has transformed his body – let alone his body of work – into an early twenty-first-century art experiment.

Mad about the Boy (London)

I've been sitting on the nostalgia couch for a while now. It is well over a decade since I left Australia for Aotearoa/New Zealand, to take up my first academic job at the Victoria University in Wellington. I was young, green and tragically try-hard. My fashion was a bit Drag Queen 101 and I applied the polyfillar principle to makeup. Like an ageing Baby Jane, I assumed that more was better. A colleague at the time told me that – when I arrived – she had assumed I was a post-operative transsexual. Every now and again – after an aerobics class and under fluorescent lighting – I still approach my complexion like a DIY project requiring heavy duty sanding and a lacquer resurfacing.

There remains a lot of that style-lifing girl in me. I still believe that stronghold hair products offer a pathway to spirituality that televisual preachers will never understand. Big hair is closer to God. But design, as shown by Peter Saville's fame, rather than hairdressing, is the new deity for creative types. That's fine. Besides big hair, I have always had a fascination for big watches. Nearly fifteen years ago, when arriving in Wellington, I was wearing the most beautiful watch I had ever seen. It was black and chrome, chunky and had two dials. I loved it so much that I bought a bag to match. The label was fashionable and obscure, and the perfect accoutrement for a wannabe Generation Xer cultural studies academic. This was the label – and world – of Boy London. The company was formed by Stephane Raynor in 1976. Like colostomy bag belts, multicoloured Mohawks and garbage bag dresses, it was a product of punk's blading of the body politic. The shock imagery of the punks seems a distant memory in our era where Ikea has taken out a patent over the planet. In 1977, The Sex Pistols released their single 'God Save the Queen' to coincide with the Silver Jubilee. It was a far cry from the 'safe' rock celebrations of Paul McCartney and Cliff Richard for Elizabeth's Golden Jubilee Concert in 2002. Bad language was replaced by Botox.

Punk emerged from the glam rock years of Marc Bolan and David Bowie. Bands like The Damned and Siouxsie and the Banshees collapsed the distance separating performer and audience, Ziggy and fan. The anger of The Pistols' lyrics and the violence of their stage performances offered a strident critique of the 'United' Kingdom. The success of their 'anthem', which reached number two on the British charts in June 1977, typified the way that style, consumption and resistance came together through a solid link between youth culture and popular music.

Punk – as an iconography and ideology – was unsettling. The swastikas, syringes, safety pins and garbage bags cut up history and dispatched the 'Greatness' of Britain with performative panache. With truth shredded, the symbols of Nazism – just like the Union Jack – were available for rewriting and reinscription. All culture was usable. It was uncomfortable and profoundly disturbing to stitch the symbols of the Final Solution into fashion. But that was the point.

Founded on London's Kings Road, Boy London combined star style with street style, grittier than Vivien Westwood and more wearable than Jean-Paul Gaultier. Aesthetic objects were produced that were beautifully designed and able to be worn. Like so much of the punk appropriation and reinscription, Nazi eagles were recoded and rebranded as the logo of the company. This was the punk dream: pop cultural quarrying of disturbing iconography that moved transgression onto the streets. For the Boy, watches, bags, sunglasses and clothing were the basis of this mobile politics. The packaging was also uncommon for these uncommon objects. Shut up in chrome canisters, like a sarcophagus in a tomb, opening these goods became a design adventure. There was nothing like Boy London.

The energy, adrenalin and aggression of punk were short lived. A truth of popular culture – as much as people – is that the brightest of lights flicker and extinguish. Crushing conformity and consensus suffocate innovative imag(in)ings. Through the mediocrity and melodrama of Thatcher's Britain, Boy London survived. The label rode through the post-punk cultural wasteland of Spandau Ballet's fluffy shirts, Rick Astley's dancing and the legendary quiffs of Haircut 100. The label gained new energy, direction and popularity through acid house and rave culture. A disturbing ultraviole(n)t palette was added to the staunch chrome and matt black, to build a tougher style partner for the loved-up Joe Bloggs. The staunch Smiley of Boy London moved from the streets of punk to the clubs of house.

Part of the Boy's attraction was – and is – that its designs and products are difficult to find. There is only one shop in London, appropriately located on Carnaby Street. Painted light blue and with enormous 'Boy' lettering on the front, the shop is a single, long room filled with their wares. From this base, Boy London has pushed into the world. English culture always means more beyond Dover than in Polegate or Slough. Boy London is big in Holland, Sweden, Japan and the United States. In fact, there is no English-housed website for the company. A little shop in Camden has built colonies of style. Boy creates a London for foreigners.

Years passed. Somewhere in the movement between jobs and lives, the watch and bag were lost. I now own a briefcase that – while functional – is about as sexy as a washing machine in the midst of a spin cycle. From the nostalgia couch, the sensual memory and desire for the matt black and gleaming chrome watch of my past life returned. This is where my story becomes embarrassing. In remembering Boy London, I was not in a trendy designer shop fingering consumer items from the latest style guru. I was not google-shopping for virtual couture. Instead, I was in Target, buying an enormous knock-off watch that looked every inch Boy London. With some embarrassment, I can report that I received change from 20 dollars for this aforementioned item. A knock-off design that was inspired by the Nazis, pogoed through punk, jacked through house and kicked back through the 1990s was bought in a suburban shopping mall at the edge of the Antipodes.

Wearing it to work on Monday, my students loved the wide cuff watch. While (trying to) discuss cultural politics, creative industries initiatives and tourism, my students' eyes would glaze over and shift their focus, only to smilingly admit later that 'I really like your watch'. At lunch with a group of my postgraduates, I told the Wellington story and wondered aloud – whatever happened to Boy London?

Stories punted from the table. One of my students, only a few years younger than me, told us about the first time he saw a Boy London watch in his youth. He said that 'in Tasmania, Boy London was the closest thing I'd ever seen to sadomasochism'. Silence greeted this odd – but strangely appropriate – revelation. His story makes sense: the leather, the size, the pseudo-machismo of Boy London teeters on the edge of excessive masculinity. It was a coldly distant and asexual design, a dominatrix of a dial. From the streets of punked-up London to a suburban shopping mall in Perth, the Boy has intervened in iconography through crisp design and a knowing, nostalgic consistency. Long after Sid's death, the chrome, the black and the staunch eagle have survived. This is style with an agenda.

Handbag nation

I have done something really stupid. I have seriously bought in – rather than sensibly avoided – the 'new fashion colours of summer'. I now own four dresses and suits in an impossibly light baby pink. The palette is glorious. The dry-cleaning bill that results from such shimmering fabrics and hues is horrendous. What the hell have I done?

As we all know, fashion disasters are the gifts that keep on giving. These purchases necessitate follow-up acquisitions of similarly dysfunctional accessories. Dark garnishing on light dresses is beyond the pale (pink). Therefore, two pairs of gorgeous pink shoes have been bought: the ever-present ballet pumps and fascinatingly complex high heels that look extraordinary but feel like a millennial mode of foot binding. In the shop, I rationalized that as long as I park close enough to a restaurant or club, then I will not have to actually walk in these shoes. Mobility is an over-rated skill anyway. Fashion has never been functional, but these stilettos extend this principle beyond the uncomfortable and into the downright dangerous. Luckily I have been increasing the frequency of yoga classes to ease the cramp in my upper calves caused by wearing these shoes. Balance is no longer a problem. I can now teeter my entire weight on a big toe and a crumbling thumb nail. Any questions about why I would want to enact this torture on my body are meditatively returned to the third eye.

The fashion saga continues around feet. Monitoring the dire state of the toenails peeping out from their new pink enclosure, I rushed to a suburban shopping centre for foot care. From step aerobics, stationary cycling classes and the aforementioned yoga sessions, my feet look like clumps of tenderized meat rather than the delicate, dainty morsels necessary to pull off these airy frocks. Much to my horror, the local Body Shop has closed since my last visit, and in its place is the gaudily titled Accessorize, a shop of bags, hats, scarves and shiny objects. Earth mother capitalism of the 1980s has been replaced by the bling bling excesses of the 2000s. Lavender aromatherapy oil has been superseded by dangly earrings. This seems a fair swap. Never one to miss an opportunity to contemplate the changing nature of consumerism, I entered the premises. As a temple to tack, it was a gaudy testament to bling rituals.

Dangling earrings and colourful handbags are an unexpected fashion trend. Culturally, these are odd developments. Handbags and enormous jewellery loudly proclaim femininity in a cultural environment where clothes no longer crisply demarcate between the genders. Women use handbags to absorb, construct and perform the contradictions of contemporary life. Handbags, and accessories more generally, do not cover the body, but carry around knowledge about women, class and identity.

Accessorizing transforms the human body into a DIY project. We create ourselves through the objects placed on, around or through our corporeal surfaces. We renovate our skin and senses through colour, texture and style. Handbags stretch the scale and limit of women's bodies. One profoundly sensual memory of the early 1980s remains my mother's glomesh handbag. At the time, glomesh defined glamour. Even Laura Brannigan wore a top made from the metallic beads in the video for 'Gloria'. Although returned to the stylistic attic, at the time glomesh was the epitome of style. As a young teenager, I remember the evocative tactility of grazing my fingers over the cold shards.

Louis Vuitton is glomesh for the 2000s. It was a designer label established in 1854, and is best known for the signature on luxury suitcases that punctuate VIP departure lounges. From this elite luggage line, Vuitton extended the designs into ready to wear clothes in 1996, including jewellery, belts, scarves, shoes, watches, pens, ties, notebooks, towels, rugs, wallets and handbags. Vuitton and its knock-offs have been the designer success story of the last few years. The LV insignia has accompanied Jessica Simpson in *The Newly Weds* – and through the divorce – and Paris Hilton through celebrity scrag fights. Obviously, looking to Paris Hilton for fashion advice is about as appropriate as passing Inspector Gadget through a metal detector. Still, the elegance of Vuitton summons the social possibilities of fashion, expressing both social identification and the ability to slot into an aspirational crowd. That the bags are both ugly and ubiquitous is proof that the purchaser has more money than sense.

These frock stars and scrag bags provide a rationale and context for the purchase of accessories. Louis Vuitton loans young woman a history and knowledge of design. It is a truth universally acknowledged that designer labels were invented for those who have no idea how to dress. Too often, the bling industry stitches pseudo-label coolness to ill-fitting and inappropriate choices. Designer jeans become so tight that women must put them on with a shoe horn.

Bling revels in these rituals of consumerism. Named after the sound of clanging metal, bling has an aesthetic that violates middle class notions of taste, decency, social and self-control. The conversations around bling – the dialogues between hyper-marketing, appropriation and creative transgression – allow the body to speak knowledge about race, capitalism, modernity, class, work and leisure. The more excessive the cut, fabric, colour and style, the less likely the wearer has had to work to pay for these altars to overkill. Bling accessorizing presents seductive challenges and choices for women. A September 2003 *Cosmopolitan* asked its young readers, 'Would you sleep with a guy for an expensive handbag?'[1] This is more than a tabloidized translation of *Sex in the City* for the suburbs. To exchange bodily fluids (let alone intimacy) for a shiny satchel of fake dead animal hide does not signal an entry into the post-feminist age. It is prostitution for a purse.

A game you play with your brain: Philosophy Football

I attend one of those 'lifestyle' gyms that matches the conventional aerobics class with chrome decor and bitter espresso. Indoor pools, outdoor pools, spas, saunas, squash courts and a sprung corked floor all transform sweaty exercise into a fashionable consumption of fitness. It is a place where thin, pastel-clad women, accompanied by their Nike swooshes, work on their bodies to displace thinking about the world. They talk about dieting, husbands and children. It is a small life punctuated by self-absorption and a coma of consumption. I watch these women with the horrific fixation of a car accident in slow motion. They are fighting a losing battle against ageing: 40-year-old women who, through botox, exhausting weight training and downward facing dogs, attempt to look like 40-year-old women trying to be 20. That is supposedly a mark of successful femininity.

Ageing is not an illness. The game of life is not won by those with the tightest skin and the perkiest bum, who lie to themselves and others about the value of a woman. Sport, leisure and fitness, let alone leisurewear, should encourage physical movement in all shapes and sizes of people, rather than demanding bodies be poured into tight tops and short shorts. Even better, exercise should encourage thought about our place in the world and how we build relationships between others, rather than inward fixations on the self.

Sportswear is part of this self-absorption. It encourages men and women to look in enormous mirrors and see overhanging flesh and a protruding abdomen. Corporations manufacture clothing that encourages dissatisfaction and desire: we see our weaknesses and desire new clothes to make us *look* better which supposedly will make us *feel* better.[1] Clearly, we require a rupture to this corporatized sporting sameness.

I made a decision to switch from the swoosh in my affluent gym and wear clothing to provoke thought rather than disgust. I choose to wear Philosophy Football shirts in bright colours of red, orange and blue, which feature slogans from philosophers, footballers and managers. Catchphrases range from Roy Keane's 'Happiness is not being afraid' to Bertolt Brecht's 'Art is not a mirror to reflect reality but a hammer with which to shape it'. I receive odd looks from gym members in these shirts. On one occasion while walking out after a Saturday morning class, a large man accosted me, aggressively demanding why I was wearing a 'Marxist' shirt. He had seen the word 'socialist' in one of the quotations, and the red colour of the shirt matched his mood. The slogan read, 'The socialism I believe in is everyone working for each other, everyone having a share of the rewards. It is the way I see football, the way I see life.' I tried to explain to him that this statement was derived from Bill Shankly. He blankly looked at me. I asked why he thought the shirt was red. He replied, 'because you're a socialist'. I suggested that he needed to read a bit more about football. Shankly was (obviously) the most famous manager of Liverpool Football Club. They play in red, the same as the shirt. My conservative accuser went the same colour as the team strip, but – with finger pointing in my face – stated that my clothing was inappropriate for the club. When I noted that I thought the same about his Nike swoosh shirt, considering the payments received by workers in Indonesia, the gym's personal trainers had to physically intervene and escort me to the car park. Clearly though, this moment confirmed the politics of the club, performed through women's clothing. Revealing and tight clothes with corporate logos are acceptable and naturalized. Anything political – or even 'clever' – becomes a problem.

For too long, football – the real football with a round ball – has been linked with an array of other nouns, like hooligans and violence. Instead, it is a metaphor for life, the pain, the injustice, the triumph and the lost opportunity. A clothing company with a political programme, Philosophy Football, tries to de-hooliganize soccer. The company was cofounded by Mark Perryman and Hugh Tisdale in 1994. Their slogan, 'sporting outfitters of intellectual distinction', transformed bodies into mobile billboards for the footballing thoughts of Cruyff, Clough and Camus alongside Naomi Klein, Pierre Bourdieu and Jean-Paul Sartre. The bright orange shirt featuring Cruyff's most famous slogan – 'Football is a game you play with your brain' – confirms that sport and clothing can be more than part of prosaic consumerism, but triggering thought, critique and reassessment.[2]

Clearly, this is not the time for such strange thoughts, for putting the oxy back in front of the moronic. The company has had its critics. Duleep Allirajah described Perryman as 'the man responsible for those geeky philosophy football t-shirts favoured by *Guardian*-reading nouveau fans everywhere'.[3] It is very easy to attack and undermine *Guardian* readers, rather than tabloid's tit-whisperers. It is also unproductive to attack those who encourage others to think. The existentialist/footballer Albert Camus provided the archetypal slogan for the Philosophy Football project: 'All that I know most surely about morality and obligations, I owe to football.' At its best, the company affirms the globalized nature of the game, featuring slogans from players, thinkers and dissenters from around the world.

Yet a new project – a parallel project – has been developing during the last decade that undercuts this internationalist goal. Philosophy Football wanted to create an English patriotism without prejudice, like a rock against racism for the boot. Mark Perryman wished to critique:

> the broader network of largely uncontested negative values associated with following England away [and] help to explain the significance of a violence relatively few are involved in. But the small numbers do not equate with the third fact, the huge impact of what is perceived virtually as a national trait, 'football hooligan'.[4]

He wants to create a positive English identity, disconnected from racism and violence. Perryman became disenchanted by the St George's flag at British National Party marches. Yet the colonial past of the United Kingdom cannot be so easily erased, marginalized or denied. Paul Gilroy, in *Postcolonial Melancholia*, has argued that September 11 has not only displaced multiculturalism but is 'transmitting an additional negative energy into this delicate postcolonial process'.[5] He believes that the threats to social justice and the welcoming – not only the tolerance – of difference are best understood through acknowledging the colonial structures perpetuated in contemporary institutions. Yet Perryman does not revise or reassess this colonial history.

> We represent England in the stands and the streets while the team represents the nation on the pitch. All of this could be read as a manifesto for a future fan culture full to the brim with the ugly inside of Englishness. But it can be read in another way. Fans as ambassadors not invaders. Enjoying rather than enduring. Pride without prejudice. War is over.[6]

Perryman's words raise the potent question: can a positive Englishness be summoned in the 2000s, having dumped the colonial baggage of the nineteenth century? With the scars of colonization marking most of the former landscapes of empire, it does seem (too) convenient that Perryman wants to create 'a practical project to construct an alternative, positive Ingerland'. No reparations. No sense of how English power was based on colonial oppression. No recognition that institutional racism has empowered white faces as the embodiment of truth and wisdom. Billy Bragg deserves credit in recognizing how the colonizing Great Britain still shapes and defines (post)colonial little England.

> The way we felt about our country as a child, the pride and prejudices we learnt at school, stay deep within us and, like the players who first inspired us to support our team, these feelings take on a legendary status – we yearn for a simpler world, an

innocence lost. If only we could get back to those days when we felt secure, before everything got complicated, before all these others came in and changed the rules and spoiled things for us. The way that we teach our imperial history leaves an indelible stain on our modern society. Having been brought up to believe that we should rule the world, some of our citizens have great difficulty coming to terms with the reality of Britain's post-war status.[7]

Perryman embodies Bragg's realization. While critiquing racism in football, the Englishness he backs is – by default – white. New shirts were added to their range in response to this project, including Blake's Jerusalem and Rupert Brooke's 'There's some corner of a foreign field that is forever England'. While the joke about Brooke's 'corner' suits Philosophy Football, the colonizing assumption of this statement goes unacknowledged.

Jean-Paul Sartre's contribution to the Philosophy Football project – 'In football everything is complicated by the presence of the opposite team' – captures the uncomfortable nature of colonialism and the difficulties confronting this new English project. It suits former colonizers to forget the past, evade the often genocidal injustices, and marginalize the institutional racism that survives in the present. English power is based on British colonial injustices. Those coming from the (former) colonies and often seeing Union Jacks remaining in 'national' flags, recognizing the Queen as head of state and speaking English, live with and through the consequences of British colonization every day. So while cherishing the intelligence of Philosophy Football and the worth of Perryman's project, the lightening, revisioning and refashioning of English style is undercut by the ugliness, injustice and denial of (a) black history.

Punking yoga

In the midst of postfordism and cold modernity, it is unworkable to differentiate between centre and margin, sameness and difference, us and them, threat and compliance. The speed at which semiotic incorporation transforms radicalism into advertising has increased. In an environment washed by the marketing of opposition, not only is resistance difficult to define, but it is harder to find. In response to this political and intellectual challenge and political disquiet, Michael Erben welcomed the value of this ambivalence, confirming that 'it is not a problem that the lives we study and examine should remain ambiguous, mysterious, discordant and confused'.[1] This chapter in *Thinking Popular Culture* builds upon my pensive questioning of Philosophy Football. Acknowledging Erben's realization, I probe the application of resistance through consumerism. The goal is to track an object of culture that is *intentionally* 'ambiguous, mysterious, discordant and confused'. Yogurt Activewear is a company attacking corporatized yoga wear by creating an anti-brand brand. They advertise their products as a combination of yoga and punk. The calm corporeality of asanas has now been clothed with threat and confrontation. The cost of this resistance and defiance – the price of building an anti-brand – is a loss in the complexity of yoga's pre/postcolonial origins.

To make this story of Yogurt Activewear even more complex and fascinating, Morgwn Rimel, one of the cofounders of the business, is a media and cultural studies graduate.[2] She has used semiotic and sociological expertise gained from this qualification to restitch the fabric of sports fashion. The origin of the business in Australia makes the post/neocolonial punking of yoga part of an odd dialogue with the London-based Philosophy Football. The brand, concept and logo were designed by Australian women. But from this Antipodean, postcolonial space, the clothing was sold to the world in a complex rebranding and reconstitution of tradition, history and nostalgia.

Resist this

When branded clothes are worn through sporting and fitness activities such as yoga, there is a cultural confirmation that any movement, practice or behaviour which may appear transgressive, radical or resistive is also implicated in neo/colonial corporations and casualized workforces that are a characteristic of sports clothing manufacture. While Becky Beal was able to locate concrete examples of 'social resistance'[3] and 'active consent'[4] in the 'subcultural' sport of skateboarding, yoga as a practice and Yogurt Activewear as a company does not offer a clean separation of dominance and subordination. To construct a workable definition of resistance for Yogurt Activewear that also contextualizes their 'punk meets yoga' slogan, it is best to return to one of the most recognized books in cultural studies history, Dick Hebdige's *Subculture: The Meaning of Style*.[5]

Subcultural theory, as associated with Hebdige and the Birmingham Centre for Contemporary Cultural Studies in which he was enrolled as a student and worked, has two formative parts. Firstly, resistance to dominant codes and ideas must be present. Secondly, through time, there is an incorporation of this resistance into the dominant discourse.[6] The term 'subculture' must be used with care as it is both historically specific and socially dynamic. A subculture in one year may become part of the dominant cultural framework and market economy the next. Such a model also carries forward many blind spots, particularly with regard to colonization and gender.

The benefits of bringing forward Hebdige's use of *sub*culture into terrorized times of insiders and outsiders, us and them, is that the concept provides a constant theoretical reminder that resistance is always possible, no matter how conservative and repressive the environment.[7] Yet with class politics and class consciousness being sidelined through the 1980s and 1990s[8] and rarely discussed in public discourse through the 2000s, there is an intricate conversation to be had – again – about the relationship between subcultural/symbolic politics, and real/parliamentary politics.[9] Subcultural theory was effective in showing that politically bland periods, like the 1950s and early 1960s, encased the fount of political challenge. The teds, rockers and mods shredded interpretations of the 1950s and early 1960s as being 'quiet times' or 'grey decades'. Political challenge – through subcultures – was always present through the disruptive rituals of clothing and music. The analytical difficulty emerges when these groups and modes of challenge through clothes, hair and music are overloaded with too much significance and importance. Groups like the punks, mods and rockers 'represented' far more than they ever actually achieved socially or politically.

Besides inspiring Peter Saville and Boy London, punk was also a pivotal movement and moment for cultural and media studies researchers. It seemed to perform cultural studies' arguments through the late 1970s and early 1980s. But through this dance between resistance, youth and punk, specific biases have survived in the subject. Harriot Beazley confirmed that the Birmingham Centre for Contemporary Cultural Studies approach 'has also been accused of being too focused on white, male, working-class youth'.[10] Gender and racial divisions were marginalized and then re-emerged through such books as *Women Take Issue*[11] and *There Ain't No Black in the Union Jack*.[12]

Punk was a specific subculture. Yet this word has a currency that moved far beyond Thatcher's Britain and the Birmingham Centre for Contemporary Cultural Studies. Punk has arched beyond The Sex Pistols, Nirvana and Green Day. Morgwn Rimel, founder of Yogurt Activewear, stated that 'it may seem like they are at odds, but if you think about it, punk rock is more than just music and style. It's an aptitude – a way of life and being, just like yoga.'[13] Punk – like yoga – has followed the historical trajectory of subcultural theory, occupying a space of transgression and then being emptied of resistive content to become part of dominant cultural frameworks. Both these trajectories of subculture – resistance and incorporation – are revisited and redesigned by Yogurt Activewear.

Don't be active – be proactive

Yogurt Activewear is an Australian-based company formed in January 2006 by Morgwn Rimel and Gaylee Butler that described its project as a fusion of punk and yoga.[14] Manufacturing men and women's clothing along with yoga props, the company offers resistance – through clothing – to both the neo/colonial spirituality of the practice and the increasing commodification and branding of the shirts, pants, mats and bags. They consciously deploy punk resistance. Morgwn Rimel's expertise in media and cultural studies means that Hebdige's arguments are applied to popular culture and fashion. Deploying an e-commerce portal – http://www.yogurtactiveculture.com[15] – the company uses humour to prick the (mock) seriousness and pseudo spirituality of yoga. One of their shirts features the slogan 'Poser'.

> Practicing yoga postures (asanas)
> is to calm the mind
> dissolve tensions of the ego
> and put an end to the duality you perceive
> between who you are and who you want to be.
> STOP POSING. START PRACTICING.[16]

Such a statement notes that while popular cultural renderings of yoga focus on the asanas – the poses – actually it is the practice, the fluid movement between static postures without investment in the result, which is the primary goal.

While celebrating the different relationship between mind and body, the ideology of rock cuts through this discussion via a black shirt featuring the slogan 'Rock hard core'.

> Build rock hard core strength.
> In yoga, you can do this by pulling your chin, abdomen and
> pelvic floor upwards and inwards while you practice.
> Jalandarabandha (chin lock)
> Uddlyanabandha (abdominal lock)
> Mulabandha (pelvic floor lock)
> Lock your core.[17]

The alignment of the words 'rock hard core' masks the construction of women's body shape. While making their products available in small, medium and large – without any sense of how that sizing standard is constructed – all the photographs feature thin and gently muscled women. While there may be

resistance to the 'hippy' components of yoga, there is little sign of change, critique or transformation of normative body shape for women.[18]

Clothes punctuate our identity. Through our fashion choices, sexual differences are assumed, hidden or overlaid with social meanings. Examining a clothing company like Yogurt Activewear, clothing is placed into the context of both reinforcing and threatening normative social values and exchanges. A.C. Sparkes realized that 'certainly, much recent theorizing about the body has tended to be cerebral, esoteric, and ultimately a disembodied activity that has operated to distance us from the everyday embodied experiences of ordinary people'.[19] Clothes are part of this distancing and disconnecting function, but also reveal the visual literacies operating in our lives. We learn expectations about women's bodies and how they are shaped and covered. Even when positioned in unconventional poses, as is common through the cycles of yoga poses where breathing patterns and normalized bodily movements are questioned, viewers learn about 'natural' shapes and conventional definitions of beauty.

In acknowledging how yoga can be inserted into conventional narratives of feminine slimness, beauty and vanity, Yogurt Activewear deploys bricolage to rip through some of these expectations of normality, as was a characteristic of punk resistance.

> Don't be active – be proactive
> Our clothes are comfy to practice and cool to live in.
> Our designs communicate ideas we hope more people will think about.[20]

Particularly of significance, in terms of activating a punk threat, is the construction of a gritty urbanity around yoga. The portal into their e-commerce site features a wall with the graffiti-like inscription of their company name. Instead of yoga's alignment with nature, city-based graffiti transforms the meanings of the practice. Shirts feature slogans including 'Cobra' and 'Enlighten Me', showing a skull and crossbones. Such slogans are part of the punk challenge, to deploy bricolage so that familiar – and often disturbing – images can be repositioned

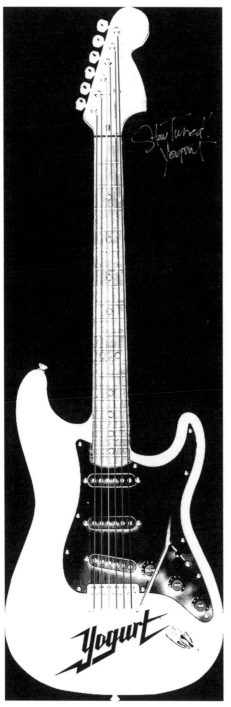

into a new context to confront assumptions about the peacefulness of yoga.

The aggression of the clothing – the directive to the instructor and other participants to 'Enlighten Me' – is a perpetuation of punk's visual intimidation. The punk challenge amidst yoga practice also spills into the advertising of the 'six-string mat'.

Certain lights or sounds can stimulate emotional, mental, physical or spiritual responses in our bodies. Each of the 6 spinal chakra centers corresponds to a particular color and musical note. Regular adjustments of the chakra centers helps keep our organs functioning properly. When they are balanced, your energy or life force flows freely. STAY TUNED.[21]

The guitar featured on the mat displaces the colours, images and fabrics that align yoga with nature. Instead, electric instruments and Western systems of musical notation are overlaid with discussions of life force and energy.

Clothes allow body surfaces to be read, signalling belonging or difference. Yoga signifies 'the east'. Commodified branded yoga clothing signifies 'the west'. Yogurt Activewear – through its punk allegiance – moves between these categories and offers uncomfortable but productive alignments of neo/colonialism and anti/orientalism. Rimel states that she is 'using western language to talk about an eastern philosophy within the context of their own pop cultural experience … Yoga is thousands of years old and was punk before punk rock even existed.'[22] This mixed (up) history cannot stop resistance or uninhibited incorporation. The company works through the ambiguity, aligning threat and humour. Through the confrontational comedic slogans – 'Enlighten Me' and 'Poser' – there is a recognition that challenge and change is part of yoga. It is not an ahistorical, depolitical and 'natural' practice untempered by politics, the market economy or colonization.

To capture this incorporation (with attitude), the clothes and products have been promoted in women's magazines and websites. Marilyn Perez, in Venuszine.com, stated:

> Some may cringe at the idea of 'Disco Yoga' or 'Punk Rock Yoga,' believing it defeats the purpose of relieving stress and finding peace within. With the popularity of Yoga in the West, along with yoga clothing lines such as Lululemon and Be Present taking off, it's become apparent that people want to look good while holding Vrksasana (Tree post). Sweatpants and a tee just won't do anymore. Its popularity is especially growing among younger people. Some practitioners are concerned that the true meaning of the practice will be dumbed down for the secular crowd. Thanks to yogis like Morgwn Rimel, founder of Yogurt Activeculture Wear, they are hoping their product will not only draw people to yoga, but also show that it is safe to spice up this ancient practice. Yogurt Activeculture is using western language to introduce an eastern philosophy.[23]

The trajectory and confusions of punking yoga with both subcultural and corporate infusions is revealed through this statement. In acknowledging that yoga is Sanskrit for 'union', (literally) embodying a fusion of mind, body and spirit, there are racial and colonial applications that reveal the costs and consequences of suturing semiotic systems through punk bricolage.

Active denial

Yoga is now part of popular culture. It has become the cure for a range of 'diseases' of consumption, whether it be an eating disorder[24] or stress management.[25] The 'East' once more rescues and cures the 'West'. This is an orientalist discourse, with the 'East' exoticized, romanticized and objectified. While yoga's 'Eastern' ideologies have been appropriated and used in the 'West', Indian workers have been the cheap labourers that make the clothes in which 'their' asanas are performed.

In 1992, the Vice President of Reebok Technical Services for the Far East recommended that India be the base for their operations, as an alternative to

China.[26] This shift was made after the Indian parliament made a decision in July 1991 to deregulate their economy, encouraging 'free trade', privatization and the movement of international capital. This governmental deregulation was matched by a reduction in direct social welfare. India then became the base of operations for international subcontracting in sportswear.[27] So while 'India' is deployed in yoga discourse as a spiritual home and the origin of the asanas, the actual landmass of India is the basis of corporate power and profits, based on the manufacture of the clothes in which the postures take place. Bernard D'Mello realized the consequences of this gap between the 'real' and 'imagined' India.

> India has a vast pool of surplus labor living in abject poverty. The wage rate at which India's poor are obliged to offer their labor services is so low that India can possibly emerge cost and price competitive in a whole range of relatively labor intensive manufactured goods ... From a social perspective, the cost and price competitiveness may not reflect the strength of the Indian economy but rather the weakness, because it is predicated upon the relative poverty of the Indian people.[28]

This is the context in which any threatening bodies should be placed. While Yogurt Activewear stresses the 'punk' element in their designs, they provide no information about fair trade practices, or how their garments and products are made. They certainly resist the pastel-infused Nike/Puma/Reebok yoga wear. Yet capitalism remains the default position: punk has become a brand and a strategy to differentiate yoga clothing in the branded market. Yoga has been incorporated into sport: yoga wear is part of sportswear. Despite its long history in India, yoga has not been spared from corporatization. In 1999, Christy Turlington 'designed' a yoga range – titled Nuala – for Puma. In 2005, Stella McCartney released yoga clothes through Adidas. There are Gucci yoga mats and Hermes yoga bags. Yogurt Activewear is part of this story.

The branding of yoga may seem to both corrupt and corrode the 'authentic' history of the practice. But yoga is not a stable practice. Throughout its long history, it has changed and moved. As Sarah Strauss confirmed:

> To Indians, the type of yoga re-oriented by innovators like Vivekananda and Sivananda suggests empowerment, using an imagined shared history to create a progressive, self-possessed and unifying identity. In this light, yoga can be understood as part of a methodology for living a good life. Because of its basis in bodily practice, the yoga tradition is easily linked with physical health maintenance at the level of the person. The physical development of the person was seen by many as the first, necessary step to be taken in the service of improving a larger community, whether local, national, or global. Yoga re-oriented this new theory with old practice.[29]

Strauss offers the important argument that physical and cultural movements like yoga must be dynamic. To deny change is to deny the formerly colonized the right to move and change. The key recognition is what is lost and gained through the movement of yoga out of India. Significantly, the rights of textile workers in India are disconnected from the practice and ideology of summoning a spiritual India in the midst of a yoga class.

Quite impressively, this ownership, proliferation and popularity of yoga is being discussed by practitioners. In the magazine *Australian Yoga Life* for March to July 2006, a long article was published under the title 'Who owns yoga?'[30] Greg Wythes confirms that:

> Yoga is now a practice that straddles both its Indian birthplace and the broader Western world. However, there seems to be mounting evidence that there are growing tensions in this process of adoption and change from the traditional culture of yoga's beginnings to the contemporary culture of today's capitalist society.[31]

Wythes acknowledges that yoga is a business. He also notes that Indian-based practitioners are losing ownership of practices and sequences. By 2005, the United States patent office had granted 134 yoga-related patents on 'accessories', 150 yoga-based copyrights and 2,315 yoga trademarks.[32] To make the question of ownership of cultural ideas even more controversial, many of these copyrights, brands and patents were granted to expatriate Indians. Recognizing what is being lost to India through 'Western' creative industries management, the Indian government has assembled a taskforce with the goal of creating a database of yoga practices to protect Indian knowledge systems.

This postfordist, (post)colonial situation is a provocative case study to probe and question Charles Leadbeater's phrase and directive in *Living on Thin Air*.[33] In February 2003, Bikram Choudhury copyrighted a sequence of 26 poses, and the verbal directions used to teach the sequence. He also threatened to defend these rights through litigation. By 2004, Choudhury himself became enmeshed in litigation. Yoga practitioners and teachers – under the title of OSYU (Open Source Yoga Unity) – challenged his 'ownership' of the sequence. They argued that the poses were hundreds of years old and therefore in the public domain. Unfortunately this case was settled out of court, which meant that the legal status and copyright over yoga postures still remains debatable.[34] Wythes confirmed that this case captures the challenges – politically and economically – of yoga's immersion in popular culture.

> This case highlights the broader concerns about the way yoga is being commercialised in the West. OSYU initially challenged Bikram along ideological lines, espousing the view that their concern was for the rights of the yoga community at large. But

when they were able to come to an arrangement that suited their own purposes, i.e. to be free to teach and practice without legal threat from Bikram, they accepted a settlement.[35]

Once more, resistance is difficult to track and determine, as practitioners and teachers become implicated in intricate power struggles over ownership. Such moments of commercialization and vested interests are particularly troubling within yoga as affirmations of spirituality, higher powers and a divestment in the self are part of the practice. This issue was raised effectively by Kausthub Desikachar, son of T.K.V. Desikachar and grandson of T. Krishnamacharya.

> Yoga was created for the purpose of nourishing a spiritually oriented life. However, we are living in a capitalist oriented world, and therefore, I think we must use yoga to help us find balance. Yogis have to work and earn an income to pay for their own food, shelter, education, and clothing, as well as support a family. However a $100 yoga mat wrapped in a $200 yoga tote bag that is slung over a $300 yoga top is not the way to go either. I think finding a balance between the material and spiritual world is the key today. And it is definitely not easy.[36]

This interpretation is probably the clearest and most accurate way to assess yoga in the contemporary environment. Yogurt Activewear is resisting the corporate branding of clothing. Yet – with self-aware irony – they are enacting this process through appropriating the codes and signs of earlier modes of resistance, such as punk. So threatening 'punked' yoga wear has become a marketing strategy, not a political imperative.

When cultural practices move from formerly colonized nations, there must be attention to how the complexity of ideas are either maintained or lost. Suzanne Hasselle-Newcombe realized that:

> Given the mixed religious and philosophical background of yoga practice in the Indian context, one cannot make many assumptions about the beliefs of yoga practitioners in the modern British context. When the British practice yoga, is it simply for health benefits or is it a meaningful spiritual activity? … To what extent do yoga practitioners adopt Indian religious worldviews? Could yoga be a new form of religion for a pluralistic, secular culture.[37]

Iyengar yoga places attention on the sequence of postures. 'Religious' or 'spiritual' attributes or characteristics are less associated with this practice. The reason for this separation of body and mind emerged when B.K.S. Iyengar visited Britain in 1954 and worked with Peter Mackintosh, the Chief Inspector of Physical Education in the Inner London Education Authority, to design a yoga curriculum. It was a condition of those classes that the attention was on the 'physical' and not 'religious'.

Through such curricula strategies, yoga became equivalent to – and incorporated within – other fitness practices, erasing much of its history. This transformation has occurred in the era where 'creating a brand appears to mean more to sports marketing executives than any real connection the fans have to their teams'.[38] With yoga divested of history, origin and context, the postures and clothes can be filled with the corporate branding. This branding is now organizing social identity, removing the complex and contradictory history of India. Vincent Carducci confirmed the consequences of removing history, politics and struggle from sports media, to be replaced by a brand.

> Nike epitomizes the postmodern 'hollow' corporation. The company owns little by way of fixed assets, focusing instead on managing its cultural capital and maximizing its financial strategies ... From a postmodern perspective, it can be said that Nike owns the surface effects while leaving the risk of investment in fixed assets to others.[39]

This focus on surfaces is against the historical imperatives of yoga. Morgwn Rimel tries to reconcile these variables through her clothes and company, providing a rationale for her fashion/yoga project.

> We hope to develop an Activeculture that's NOT just about yoga, but that broadly promotes truth and beauty, encourages playfulness, cultivates individual style and wellbeing, and most importantly, inspires us to make positive changes in our lives and the lives of others.[40]

With this goal in mind, Rimel articulated her target market for the clothes.

> 25–40 age group where yoga is part of your life and you're not a hippy and not a mum ... Yoga's not always relaxing ... It can be quite confronting and intense and we wanted to express that mental and emotional side.[41]

There is no mention of yoga's history, or the goal of aligning mind, body and spirit. Instead, this new brand has created an anti-brand that excludes 'hippies' and 'mothers'. This difference becomes the basis of a resistance, but the target of the resistance is unclear. Even *Slimming & Health* magazine entered the yoga/ punk discourse by outlining the company's goal.

> Created as an alternative to the boring pastel and conservative range of clothing currently out there, this kooky range of T-shirts and pants will put a smile on the face of your fellow posers.[42]

Humour and difference render yoga clothes one more consumer project that creates pleasure through the purchase.

Threat, challenge and resistance are difficult to define and even more complex to find in an era of lifestyle, brands and logos. While Yogurt Activewear is not Nike, it still captures an investment in a brand. It is part of what Clive Hamilton and Richard Denniss described as *Affluenza*, where 'we are confused about what it takes to live a worthwhile life'.[43] The buying and selling of identity creates desiring selves that must constantly manage disappointment. Shopping is the stitching that aligns the ideal and actual selves. While consumerism creates an investment in surfaces, there is a parallel desire for authenticity. Richard Butsch argued that 'the future of leisure studies and cultural studies lies weaving together the threads of domination, resistance, and incorporation in order to understand leisure and popular culture in an era of hyper commodification and consumption'.[44] In this space between commodification and authenticity, Yogurt Activewear is positioned. It is a clothing of resistance within capitalism, and a fashion choice for threatening bodies posing through postcolonialism.

Kindle surprise

I came from a house with few books. Old Encyclopaedia Britannicas and a large white dictionary were well-worn tools of my school years. But public libraries were crucial to my education. The university library was a citadel, cathedral and lolly shop. Some of the most precious moments in my late teens and early twenties were spent wandering around the stacks, taking out books and thinking about how knowledge is structured through numbers, spaces and shelves. It was quiet. It was solitary. It was transforming.

Reading was not a pleasure, but a necessity. It was the way to become a person that I was not, to live a vicarious life of possibility and excitement. My first professor, the historian Richard Bosworth, proclaimed in my first university lecture that 'from this point forward, you will read six books a week, every week, for the rest of your life'. Stunned silence in the auditorium. There were only two options in response: comply or leave. Education was not pleasure. But it was important. There was never any doubt that we were privileged to be reading books, ideas and theories that had changed the world. In sharing this history, we had a chance to move forward in our own lives and as a community of scholars.

Our universities – and our students – have changed. This transformation offers opportunities for renewal, but also creates a gulf of expectation between academics and the scholars in our care. I once reported Richard Bosworth's comments to my first year students over a decade later. They were stunned. One young man said that he had not read six books in his entire life. A young woman asked if reading the *same book* – a Harry Potter book (it had to be, didn't it?) – six times counted in that total.

Changes in reading, thinking and teaching are not the problem: how we manage this movement is the key. I am a believer in books and committed to ideas on paper. Most of our students are not. That lack of shared passion does not mean that academics should stop conveying the passion of ideas, the gift of great words and the debt we owe to other writers. It does mean that we must establish an effective curriculum that moves students into an environment where they are safe and secure, but also challenged, questioned and probed about their lives, ideas and attitudes to the word and the world.

Reading on a page is different from scrolling on a screen. As long as we are conscious of these differences, high quality scholarship can be produced. But the publishing industry has also ridden this rupture between page and screen, print and text, turning and clicking, content and design. Publishing has been waiting for its 'iPod moment' – a crack in an industry that discredits and destroys past protocols and platforms and transforms the relationship between product and consumer. Ebooks had promise, but stalled. The Sony Reader failed. The reason for these disappointments is that books are analogue. They have been a stable and functional platform – and therefore the 'failure' of the digital age – for a reason. The book is matched well to its project: it is intimate, mobile, durable and effective.[1] Our eyes glide over the page. The paper, spine, cover and binding disappear.

Music and video have worked well off mobile digitized platforms. The difficulty in digitizing books is how to display words. With the improvements in electronic paper and electronic ink, comfortable reading is possible on a high resolution screen, with no backlighting. Once the design, navigation and display issues were resolved, Amazon's Kindle could be released. Amazon was the e-commerce firm that understood the relationship between analogue and digital, books and convergence. They may also change reading.

The advantages of the Kindle are clear. It is self-standing, not requiring a computer as a dock for updating, as is the case with the iPod. Actually, it resembles a telephone more than a computer. It uses EVDO, a high-speed data network, to create a Whispernet and is not reliant on wireless hotspots. A dictionary is also resident on the platform. As with eBooks, the interior text can be searched and bookmarked. For specific communities of readers, font size and type can be changed, and audio books are supported. It is mobile: long trips by train or aeroplane can be accompanied with books, just as the iPod provides a soundtrack. For publishers, the Kindle has enough features to make it financially viable: books are never out of print or stock and initial print runs never have to be approximated. Also, new authors can be discovered. First chapters of books are available to download for free, ensuring that digitized sampling can replicate a bookshop browse. These features were enough to ensure that the first release of the Kindle from Amazon sold out in less than six hours.[2]

For consumers – rather than readers – of books, there are great advantages in wireless delivery. We can watch a programme, listen to a podcast or read a review and buy the book immediately, with delivery in 60 seconds. Also, the Kindle is only ten ounces in weight. For those of us with semi-permanent lower back strain from years of carrying books, our ligaments may have a chance to recover. The disadvantages involve the digital rights management on content, the complexity of migrating from other formats including PDFs and the small charge waged for the delivery of freely available blogs. However, the enthusiasts are clear.

But the digerati don't get it and don't like it and that creates a compelling investment opportunity to buy Amazon shares now. The stock market doesn't appreciate this game changer. Kindle will be the iPod of books, you read it here first … There's one particularly misleading notion floating around in the blogosphere that the Kindle is closed to free content or that you can only read what you buy from Amazon. Totally wrong. You can load any file you want in a couple of formats including plain text and HTML. You can email those to your Kindle for a dime or load them free using a USB cable or SD memory card. Check out the gazillions of free offerings at Project Gutenberg, for example.[3]

For more ephemeral, leisure-based reading, the Kindle seems ideal. Newspapers and magazines, already transformed through the Web, now have a new paid digital delivery option. The *New York Times* can be fed to the Kindle overnight and read with the morning coffee. By working with the great strengths of digitization – searchability, compression, convergence, wireless connectivity and immediate gratification through downloadable consumerism – opportunities for new modes of reading are created.

There are losses when dropping the physicality of books. There is also no desire or strategy to link this individualized reading project into public libraries. The Kindle is a personal reader, ensuring that affluent consumers will increase their reading options, platforms and purchases. The commodification of (public and free) information into individualized downloads increases through the Kindle. Perhaps surprisingly, heavy readers have shown the most resistance to the project. Amazon boasts that 100,000 books are available for the Kindle and base their future business on ensuring that the *New York Times* Best Seller List is downloadable. When remembering Richard Bosworth's early interventions in students' lives, 100,000 books is not an impressive number. My personal library holds 10,000 texts and it grows at a rate that threatens the foundations of the house. Kindle is based on popularity and mass market publishing. I am not interested in the *New York Times* Best Seller List. It includes wireless access to Wikipedia. I do not need wireless access to Wikipedia. No one does. The digi-literate who have run out of friends to text message on the train do not need to enlarge the listing for Klingon while they are on the move.

The other problem for scholars is that the Kindle only holds 200 titles at one time. In the advertising campaign, this is a huge number, replicating the attitudes of my young students who cannot imagine reading six books in a lifetime, let alone a week.[4] But I would use many more titles to write a single article or book chapter, let alone a more sustained research project. Amazon promotes two solutions to this problem. An optional memory card is available. Also, every downloaded book is saved online in Amazon's Your Media Library. That is a great initiative. Anyone who has either lost an iPod or changed computers knows how finicky it is to move iTunes libraries between platforms. However, the necessity to transfer material off the Kindle and onto Your Media Library – and back – is a weakness of the project. The size of the Kindle hard drive is the most urgent improvement necessary for the project to succeed.

Academics are no corporation's target market. Our Kindle, a customized academic Kindle, could use some general features but in a different way. While it does not hold sufficient books for a research project, it is valuable as a holder – and delivery bay – for electronic journal articles. These smaller documents could saturate the Kindle for the duration of a task and then be saved on Amazon's storage facility. The other function – which has great academic benefit and is not mentioned in the promotional literature – is the possibility to email word documents with pictures to the Kindle so they can be viewed while travelling. Therefore, it has a strong editing and proofing function for those of us working on our own projects and reticent – because of security issues or weight – to lug our laptops around the world. Academics are not Kindle's target market. The obvious audience is readers of fiction, particularly Oprah's Book Club. But the mobility of a few scholarly documents, when combined with wireless access to the Kindle store, will be the value. It will be a personal travelling database of materials for research.

While reading may change through the Kindle, so may writing. The surprise of the iPod was that it rejuvenated the dying singles market, while destroying the CD-based album in the process. Remarkable creativity emerged from this change. Not only singles, but live releases, DJ sets, even premixed exercise music, all gained an audience. The Kindle may refire poetry,[5] short stories, investigative journalism, book reviews and serials, delivered wirelessly and like a podcast. It is an ideal way for writers at the margins of profitability – poets, freelance journalists and short story writers in particular – to gain a wage and an audience. Like the single, the Kindle may be a new platform for consuming shorter prose genres.

As with all digital revolutions, these transformations and opportunities are available to the affluent few and the geographically fortunate. Those who live beyond Kindle's electronic pages are excluded and invisible. At the moment, only citizens of the continental United States can use this device. The rest of the world can merely look through the virtual shop window at its potential. The Kindle will not replace books. It will transform particular modes of reading, researching and publishing. Portable media make different demands of readers, writers and listeners. It is not equivalent to analogue reading. It is not better or worse. It is different. Kindle's name confirms this distinction. Amazon's Tieresius – Jeff Bezos – reports that his product is meant to start a fire for reading. Once more, we may be disappointed at the gates of electronic books. But perhaps, in this digitized kindling, there is a spark for both change and preservation.

SONIC

Two bars

The 2005 Brit Awards were the usual combination of drunk, daft pop singers, pseudo-goth guitarists and drummers who spent much of the night in the toilet. But there were some piquant differences. Of the 17 awards given, 11 went to bands and performers for debut albums. Through all the talk of iPod insularity and retro redundancy, music is changing. It is renewing. We are – after a decade of disappointment – hearing new and challenging popular music.

While the brilliance of the new was being rewarded, the old was being respected, or so it appeared. BBC Radio 2 listeners voted for the best song of the last 25 years. The palette of performers from which to choose was odd enough: the *Pop Idol* winner Will Young, Queen, Kate Bush, Robbie Williams and Joy Division. The omissions were odd: where were The Smiths, New Order, The Stone Roses ('Waterfall' anyone?), The Happy Mondays or Oasis' 'Wonderwall'?

While aware of the gaps, let's unpick this list. Queen produced high quality stadium rock. Will Young who? Kate Bush's 'Wuthering Heights' was a better choice. It changed the structure of popular music, lifted the standards of lyric writing and produced one of the strangest dance sequences in a video. Ever.

And the winner was … Robbie Williams for 'Angels'. The decision caused controversy. The BBC website was filled with complaints.[1]

You've got to be kidding
Daz

I'm actually embarrassed to be British if that is the best song we have produced in the last 25 years!!
Thomas Crawford

A sad day for music
Chris Ward

Predictable and laughable
Andy Smith

'Angels' is a fine song, but it is a ballad used by ugly boys at discos to stick their tongue in the ear of an unwilling pubescent girl. For me, there was only one choice from the list, and the BBC complainants generally agreed.

While I am biased in that I thought Love Will Tear Us Apart should have won ...
Tom

It [Angels] certainly isn't anywhere near as good as Love Will Tear Us Apart by Joy Division or Wuthering Heights by Kate Bush
Laura

Have Radio 2 listeners even heard of Joy Division? A band who, through two albums, have had a bigger impact on music, and continue to do so, over the last 25 years than Robbie Williams ever will.
Lee

The punters' passionate certainty in their choices was fascinating to witness. Such enthusiasts of music – let alone life – require support and encouragement. Without this bubbling energy, we are left with Nick Hornby's *31 Songs*[2] which, just like *Fever Pitch*,[3] transformed blokey egomania into a slapped-up bestseller. We need music bloggers at the moment because there are far fewer great pop journalists than great pop songs. While Greil Marcus is the Emperor of rock, Paul Morley is the Yoda of pop. His *Words and Music*[4] spans from the second century BC to 2003. The image of a hot panted Kylie Minogue driving through a post-industrial city singing 'na na na – na na na na na – na na na – na na na na na' is the propulsive rhythm of his prose.

What has made Morley a stellar music writer is his obsession to convince the world that Joy Division is the best group to emerge from popular music.[5] His mania is convincing. Like Peter Saville, he was given a gift through birth, growing up in the right time and place, to be the chronicler of post-punk Manchester. His obsession with New Order and Joy Division has accompanied him throughout a writing career, producing a large and self-standing book.[6]

Not surprisingly, he believed 'Love Will Tear Us Apart' to be the greatest song ever written, not just the best British track of the last quarter of a century. While his reasons are personal, there is also a musicological basis for his decision. The trajectory of dance in the last 20 years was foreshadowed in the shift between the eighth and ninth bars of this song. In the space between these bars, *something* happens. The music transfers from a minor to a major key. On a dance floor, the repercussions of that movement is a feeling of euphoria, that anything is possible, we can dance all night and be young forever. There is also a shift from the guitar-based past of rock music towards the synthesized future of dance music. The change is significant, self-evident and pronounced.

To ignore these two bars and displace Joy Division is to forget about how dull rock music has been through much of its history. After disco's demise, rock was a soundtrack for growing old. Dance music is the endlessly inventive genre. Sampling translates and transforms aural and tactile memories into a bricolage of possibilities. Digitized divas warble with a re-energized beat and imported rhythms from Spain, Italy, Brazil, Jamaica, France and Germany. Techno, offering a break with Motown's past, fused with the intensely European sounds of Kraftwerk, Giorgio Moroder and Tangerine Dream.

While Kraftwerk is frequently praised by critics (who have never heard their music), what makes this German powerhouse so important is that they prised open the gaps between the notes. They knew the musical value of silence and disruptive noise. Their embrace of technology created new theories of metre, melody and mixing. These fusions continued through the 1980s with Cabaret Voltaire, Depeche Mode, Heaven 17 and Human League. Techno brought this merger of the corporeal and computer into clearer profile.

There is a trace of this rhythmic journey in the first nine bars of Joy Division's 'Love Will Tear Us Apart'. Certainly it is an evocative, powerful track, but its beginning is shocking in its innovation. While BBC 2 listeners did not vote it the best song of the last 25 years, I claim a smaller significance. 'Love Will Tear Us Apart' enclosed the two most important bars of music in the twentieth century.

Beyond the bars, beyond the song itself, the context of the track marinates the significance. There is tragedy evoked through the chorus. The single only entered the upper reaches of the British chart in the weeks after Ian Curtis killed himself. Joy Division produced frightening music and Curtis captured the fear. The jagged dancing, terror-filled eyes and melancholic intensity of the lyrics combined to cast a long shadow over Manchester music. Ian Curtis has become singular and potent in popular memory through a combination of words and vision: Kevin Cummins's photographs and Paul Morley's journalism. Ian Curtis has tragedy tethered to him and his music, encasing all the conventional baggage of heterosexual masculine angst.[7]

What makes Curtis significant, and adds even greater intensity to 'Love Will Tear Us Apart', is what happened after his death. The three remaining members added a woman, Gillian Gilbert, to their ranks and continued to produce music under the name New Order. Few bands survive the death of their lead singer. Ian Curtis and the first nine bars of 'Love Will Tear Us Apart' facilitated this survival by fading out the thrash of punk and fading in the synthesizer soar. New Order took that ninth bar and built a career around it.

Manchester is one of the birthplaces of the industrial revolution. The rip of change to time, work and identity scarred the landscape. Manchester, so integral to histories of commerce, culture and politics, offers a stark reminder of the uneven nature of globalization. Manchester, in moving from the 'old' industries to the new creative industries of music, screen, design and tourism, is now in the business of marketing differences, rather than homogeneity. After the death of Curtis, Manchester could export music as it had once exported textiles. Like wrinkles on a forehead, a city reveals its past. Manchester's derelict cotton mills were overwritten by the popular music that created a newer vision. These sounds and images – from Take That to 808 State, The Buzzcocks to Simply Red, The Smiths to M-People, and New Order to The Happy Mondays – intertwined the histories of music and Manchester. It would be impossible to write about contemporary electronica without a sizeable chapter based in the north of England. The industrial past punctuates present rhythms.

It is no surprise that the Pied Piper trajectory of Joy Division's ninth bar was followed by so many. New Order learnt to dance with black armbands, like most of us.[8] In remembering the greatest songs of the last 25 years, few can claim a moment of creative genius. Between the eighth and ninth bars, Ian Curtis arched beyond his own death. He sang a future that he would not share.

126

As cool as The Crickets

I have a secret love for Buddy Holly and The Crickets. At least once a month, generally after hearing 'It Doesn't Matter Any More' or 'True Love Ways', I become emotional like Oprah Winfrey's guests, sniffling vigorously to avoid the ugly streaking of leaky mascara. I wonder how the world would have been different if that plane had not crashed, or if he had decided to travel on the tour bus. With all the focus on Buddy, the fog and the flight, we forget and undermine the innovation to instrumentation, rhythm and harmony of his great band, The Crickets.

A three-piece is sparse and economical, beckoning instrumental innovation through a frugal melody or lilting syncopation. Joe B. Mauldin slapped a stand-up bass and J.I. Allison's drumming filled out the extremities of a track. Three-piece bands expand the sonic landscape in innovative ways. The Police built a reggae cadence with Andy Summers' Telecaster soaring above Sting's understated bass line. Johnny Cash developed the boom-chicka-boom-chicka rhythm through his early collaboration with the Tennessee Two, sans drummer. Cream and The Jimi Hendrix Experience could allow two of the greatest lead guitarists in rock music to showcase their virtuosity rather than being muddied in the mix. The Thompson Twins were dominated by percussion instruments, weaving melody around the intricate rhythms of 'Hold Me Now'. The Jam sutured thrash, mod style and political rage through Paul Weller's staccato flagellation of his strings.

The innovations of the three-piece band have been underwritten through musical history. With all the attention on 1960s rock and the default lineup of two guitarists, a bass guitarist and a drummer, the subtle distinctions of a three-piece have been marginalized from influence. We have become so accustomed to the configurations of The Beatles that more frugal ways of managing sound have been under-represented. Too often the risks of the three-piece band are misunderstood in the fleshed-out sound of rock's default instrumentation.

There has not been an equivalent to The Crickets. But in 2007, I attended what I hoped would be one of the greatest gigs of my life: seeing the Scissor Sisters in Brighton. Their legendary show at the Brighton Dome was saved for posterity on DVD.[1] Performing live again in the gay capital of the United Kingdom, much was promised. Perhaps predictably in response to the hype, the Scissor Sisters were mediocre on that night, held back by their fans. Now that they are part of stadium rock, the radical edge of 'Take Your Mama' has become a sing-along, affirming the importance of spending quality time with our parents. It was good performance. It was not great.

Even though the Scissorhood was a drag rather than in drag, it was the opening act that changed my life. I had heard rumbles about a three-piece from the United States called Gossip. They happened to be booked for the Sisters' support slot. Out walked a five-foot, 15-stone lesbian in a seriously stretchy green dress. She wore enormous stilettos and enough eyeliner to satisfy the most hardcore Cure fans. In a queer reinscription of The Crickets, Beth Ditto is a lesbian feminist Buddy Holly. This is quite an image, but unerringly accurate.

Emerging from this startling green frock was a transcendental voice, summoning 50 years of soul divas, the best of Motown and the anguish of the blues. She was Aretha Franklin, Janis Joplin, Sandy Denny, Patti Smith and Yoko Ono in one body. She had Aretha's range, Janis' rage and Yoko's scream. She was terrific. Even better, she 'played' her stilettos. In a sparse and percussive three-piece, she slammed her stilts hard into the floorboards in time to the music. The thump resonated through the auditorium. While Buddy Holly played (off) his glasses, Beth Ditto played her shoes. Within days, *The Guardian* newspaper was calling her 'The Next Big Thing' and putting her on the cover of their magazine. The NME named her the 'coolest rock star on the planet'. Both these headlines are understatements. She is changing how we think about women, bodies and voices. Beth Ditto is the new normal.

Gossip is punk-pop and pop-punk. They howl and shout. Most importantly they ask questions about what it means to be in love, to be lost or to change. While the Scissor Sisters helped us party through the Iraq War, Gossip will be the soundtrack for the retribution and rehabilitation that follows. Significantly, and like The Crickets, Gossip works the spaces between the notes and through the instruments. Like Holly, Ditto stands out in a crowd and dominates the band. If there is a diametrically opposite point to Victoria Beckham in popular culture, then Ditto lives there. All of us should move there, to save us from weird lips, weirder breasts and a wardrobe that is one part dominatrix, one part WAG and two parts spray-on tan.

Against the odds in an era where thin women are only matched by thinner ideas, Ditto is fashionable. Resisting the leggings and jumper combination that is meant to block big bodies from the offending gaze of skinny sensibilities, she wears tight dresses, swimsuits and enormous shoes. But this parallel to The Crickets does not stop with a riveting lead singer. Gossip's guitarist Brace Paine has the Holly capacity to move smoothly from an innovative riff to a lead break. Hannah Blilie continues the pounding tradition of female drummers and J.I. Allison's capacity to puff out a track with rhythm.

The single that led to their popular cultural breakthrough was 'Standing in the Way of Control'. Written in opposition to the Bush government's decision to deny gay men and women the right to marriage, it has become a wider anthem against indifference. The importance of resistance, amidst banal television and YouTube executions, has never been more important. Ditto's voice is so clear and Gossip's sound so crisp and punchy that they are the Pied Pipers to our political future. Howling the rage and hammering for change, Gossip stand in the way of stupidity.

It's not easy being Johnny Cash[1]

There were some shocking years in the last two centuries. For completely different reasons, 1939 and 1945 duel for ascendancy in gothic violence and suffering. A young president died in 1963. Al Gore was not elected in 2000. The global community stood back from the genocide in Darfur through 2006, coating Europe and North America in shame. But 2005 was a distinctive and damaging popular cultural year. It was like an old dog that needed to be put out of its misery. It was a time of confusion, denial and loss, when the crisply pressed linen line between good guys and bad guys – the white hats and the black hats – was frayed and crumpled. George W. Bush's pronouncement to the Congress that 'either you are with us or you are with the terrorists'[2] suddenly became a refrain of resistance. No matter what the cost or consequences, those crazy hawks with their claws exposed could no longer be supported as they ripped the civility and tolerance from our daily lives. Blood-soaked news continues to ooze from a supposedly post-war Iraq. It is now accepted that the country was invaded, not to depose a dictator who would suffer a YouTube execution, but to salve domestic American concerns. During this time of loss, horror, confusion and alterity, we needed leaders, people who were prepared to ask difficult questions and listen to those who resist, critique and do not acquiesce to the directives of the market economy. Being an outsider is not an act of sedition, but of necessity. In this time of war, torture, injustice and a flattening of debate and expertise, there is popular culture that is hot and fiery. Bad times produce attacking, probing and angry culture. Outsiders make us think and feel more, giving us courage to live with both respect and responsibility.

Outsider status is difficult to sustain in popular culture. Being popular often means compliance, smiling on the red carpet, answering inane questions from ill-prepared journalists, knowing the best designers and being on the most fashionable diets. Johnny Cash never fitted into such a narrative. He sang at the White House. He sang in prisons. He sang to soldiers in Vietnam. He sang for their return. He sang for indigenous Americans, recording 'The Ballad of Ira Hayes' before postcolonialism was chic. He sang 'What is truth?' to Richard Nixon. George W. Bush presented him with an award, but it was Al Gore who spoke at his memorial service. A follower of Billy Graham, he was also the supporter of an AIDS charity.[3] He described himself as an independent voter, who was interested in issues, not political parties. He was also a courageous drinker and excessive drug-taker. When he sang 'Cocaine Blues', there was powder in his throat. Even when Cash selected Joaquin Phoenix to play him in the filmic biopic, the twinned black and white hats of life and identity justified his selection. Phoenix remembers:

> he was incredibly down-to-earth and it was really nice, just dinner with his family … At dinner, they were praying, he and June would sing a song, Banks of the River Jordan, and look into each other's eyes – their love for each other was palpable and amazing. He finished the song and I said I had to go … and he said, 'I loved that Gladiator movie you did. My favourite part is when you said, "Your son squealed like a girl when I nailed him to the cross and your wife moaned like a whore when they ravaged her again and again." … It was so odd that this beautiful soulful man who'd been looking into his wife's eyes as he sang a beautiful song liked the part of a movie I did where the wife moaned like a whore. That is Johnny Cash for you.[4]

This tussle between the secular and the sacred was not resolved through Cash's performance of either gospel or rock 'n' roll. Cash was special: one of only two performers who are members of the Rock and Roll Hall of Fame, the Country Music Hall of Fame and the Songwriters' Hall of Fame. Johnny Cash sang of an America that the rest of the world could live with, work with and respect. The uber-masculinity was undercut by the grinding relentlessness of work, exploitation and death. Every violent act held a consequence. The America of Woody Guthrie and Johnny Cash can be respected in a way that Bush the Elder and Younger could never grasp. Stephen Miller, a Cash biographer, described him as 'the thinking man's John Wayne'.[5] Like Wayne, Cash was an icon, but he was much more complex than a Hollywood career could script.

By the time Johnny Cash started to make records, he already sounded old, like his larynx had been a percussive punching bag for life's disappointments. His brother Jack died by evisceration: a spinning circular blade chewed up his young body. Johnny was 11. There is both a cause and consequence for his rough cut music. Before signing to Sun Records, along with Presley, Lewis and Perkins, he had worked as a door-to-door appliance salesman, an automobile assembly-line worker and managed a three-year stint in the US Air Force. Cash was a country singer. But he could be – and became – so much more. Appropriately, he was at Sun, a label that fused rhythm and blues with pop. It was an ideal context for Luther Perkins to create 'the Cash sound', best associated with the boom-chicka-boom guitar picking.[6] 'Folsom Prison Blues' and 'I Walk the Line' were both released in 1956, staying in the American charts for most of that year.[7] While the Perkins rhythm is present on both, they are unique. 'I Walk the Line' commences – not with a lyric – but a husky single note. The chord progressions are odd and the bass C in the vocal line transforms the modulation of the entire melody.

This was new music that suited a tough context. Cash never did hard jail time. He only sounded like it. He was arrested for smuggling 1,163 pills across the Mexican border. He also spent a few nights in jail for disorderly conduct. His damage was not to other people, but to himself. His amphetamine use in the late 1950s and early 1960s was of such a scale that even the Road Runner would have baulked at the speed. Considering this history, it is not surprising that Cash had played prisons since 1957 and wanted to record one of these concerts. This event would only emerge deep in the 1960s.

Cash's concert in Folsom Prison on 13 January 1968 was extraordinary. Nearly 40 years later, it inspired Michael Streissguth to write the book *Johnny Cash at Folsom Prison: The Making of a Masterpiece.*[8] An evocative work of historical reclamation, Streissguth demonstrates how one event – one concert – can summon a dervish of social resonance.

> Among everything else and perhaps above everything else, Folsom was also a social statement on behalf of disenfranchised peoples, as potent as any such statement in the rolling 1960s, for by appearing in front of America's modern-day lepers and recording and releasing what came of it, he unapologetically told his listeners that these locked away men deserved the compassion, if not the liberation, that the 1960s offered.[9]

This concert transcended 1960s protest music to become a trace of how the disempowered can be granted a voice and agency through popular culture. The resultant album spent 30 months on the American chart. This success led to a renewal in his career. The following year, the queer anthem that is not one – 'A Boy Named Sue' – emerged. This comedy/country/performance art record commenced a rediscovery of his back catalogue. By 1969, nine of his albums were in the pop charts. In that one year, he was responsible for 5 per cent of all record sales in the United States.[10]

It is the humour that makes Cash – even at his most staunchly Christian – endearing. In comparing the songs of Cash with recent tracks from Madonna, we see our current political and popular traumas at their most overt. The former material girl, even when using an Abba sample and Eurotrash rhythms, does not see the comedy of a 50-year-old woman wearing a pink leotard, beige fishnets and discoball shoes. We want to laugh with her, not at her. Really we do. But Madonna has seemingly lost the ability to see her own life and music at an ironic distance. Madonna, in the latter stages of her career, had a great opportunity to offer commentary about the complex nature of femininity and sexuality, and how the expectations of being a woman have changed through her life.

Instead, she wrote children's books and returned to Abba and the lycra. Cash was different. He continually put the guilt, blame and retributions of masculinity into his music. 'I Walk the Line' – a lyric written by Cash in 15 minutes[11] – sang of monogamy, fidelity and faithfulness. But his grain of voice suggested that he slipped from this standard, and often.

Johnny Cash was a man of style who transcended fashion. Rebelling against the rhinestones of country music, he wore black with a purpose. Typically, he commented on his own image and gave his clothes a context. In his song 'Man in Black', the jacket had meaning: carrying 'a little darkness on my back'. It was the grinding struggle of daily life that marinated Cash's voice. These were adult struggles encircling sobriety, fidelity and citizenship. He was a patriot who attacked the dense injustices of America. His level of recognition and visibility over 60 years – a popularity created through confronting unpopular issues – makes him a rarity: a singer that not only minstrelled to the sick, dispossessed and disenfranchised, but actually shifted the trajectory of pop in the twentieth century.

It is appropriate that 2005 – that dark year of self-loathing and squelching guilt – saw the release of *Cash: The Legend*, a four-CD retrospective of 107 tracks from Sony. The 'deluxe' version of this package included a lithograph and limited edition coffee table book. The timing was important: it was 50 years since he first recorded music at Sun Studios. Beautifully packaged, the discs themselves are black. All the hit singles are included, along with duets, Cash's personal favourites and the surprisingly noteworthy compilation, 'The Great American Songbook'. His renditions of 'Rock Island Line', 'Goodnight Irene' and 'Born to Lose' are chilling and addictive. Previously unreleased material is plaited with the hit singles. The significant Sun and Columbia recordings are included, but not the material from his American series. Not only are the discs dippable, but as an entire listening experience it commands profound respect for his voice, his songwriting, humour and range. For long-term fans, or those discovering Cash after the publicity of the filmic biopic *Walk the Line*, it is satisfying and revelatory. This man is a great, complex[12] and contradictory American. Near the end of his life, he confirmed that 'our government scares the daylights out of me'.[13] He was flawed. His bass baritone voice was cracked and shredded. But he not only asked 'What is truth?' but offered more answers than most.

Even this great collection of four discs does not capture the whole story. In effect, there are three different versions of Johnny Cash. The first started with 'Hey! Porter' in 1955. Then an older and harder Cash emerged through the 'comeback concert' at Folsom Prison in 1968. The final stage was the greatest phase and the ultimate surprise. Johnny Cash may have faded away through the 1980s, but something remarkable happened. In February 1993, he was approached by Rich Rubin, the producer of the Beastie Boys and Red Hot Chili Peppers and cofounder of Def Jam Records. Like a postmodern Sam Phillips, he invited Cash to his house in California, and asked him to play some music. Rubin justified his commitment and belief by affirming that 'It just didn't seem like he was cherished. He's a great man.'[14] Cash's voice, guitar and Rubin's tape recorder produced 13 songs and the *American Recordings* album. The music was so raw and authentic that he did not even use a pick on the strings. It was a movement away from Nashville and towards the Doc Marten-ed, leather jacketed post-grunge, post-acid house audience. He showed how the supposed differences between country and rap could be erased through Cash's status as an outsider. Through Rubin's influence, the link between rap, heavy metal and country was fused through a desire to capture the life of the crushed, the angry and the beaten. The album went on to win the 1995 Grammy for the best contemporary folk record. This project was a Generation X marketing dream. The tough image of the old man of American music – dressed in black – was accompanied by a shredded voice of a life punctuated by drink and pills. His iconic status was confirmed. He even played Johnny Depp's Viper Room. Bono described him as 'a saint who preferred the company of sinners'.[15] He became the great American outsider.

The four albums Cash recorded with Rubin are stunning. He was fighting pneumonia and diabetes, but his re-recording of 'Hurt', a Nine Inch Nails classic, was fresh, potent and horrifying. The video for the song captured the indignities of illness and ageing.[16] It also won a Grammy for 'Best Short Form Video' at the 46th Grammy Awards and was named the top music video of the past three decades by the BBC.[17]

Johnny Cash was concurrently authentic, serious and laughing at his mock gothic grandeur. The distinctive terrain of his music demanded rapid twists in emotion and perspective. In 'Folsom Prison Blues', one of the most disturbing lyrics involved shooting a man in Reno. To view Cash singing this line to prisoners is extraordinary. It is hypermasculine, violent and frightening, but also very funny. As shown by The Village People, when masculinity is pushed to excess, it becomes camp, a farce.[18] Prison songs have always been part of country music, but they are filled with regret at a loss of love. Cash's version of the genre was different: the killer knew he deserved the punishment. Retribution was required.

Johnny Cash had originality, honesty and respect from peers.[19] He was handsome, imposing and edgy. He was a musical innovator – who else would have added Mariachi horns to 'Ring of Fire'? – and protective of those who shared his rebel status. He defended Bob Dylan from irate folkies who did not forgive him for 'going electric'. He was also humble and modest. Famously, he introduced himself before he started a concert: 'Hello – I'm Johnny Cash.' There are very few people, faces or voices who less required an introduction.

It was only a matter of time after Cash's death – and with Hollywood rejuvenating the biopic genre – that the man in black's story would be filmed. It was also inevitable that his second marriage would be the frame for the music. While Cash often credited God for his redemption,[20] it came – in an ironic inversion of Genesis – in the form of a woman, June Carter. This couple had five marriages between them and seven children, with John Cash Carter the only product of their union. The evocative and complex performances of Joaquin Phoenix and Reese Witherspoon in *Walk the Line* 'made country music sexy'.[21] The celebrity magazine *Who* listed them as one of their 'Beautiful Screen Duos'.[22]

Although now anchored in memory through the success of the film *Walk the Line*, the man in black finally faded to black in September 2003. It was proper that he saw the start of a new century, because he had been the minstrel of the twentieth. He gave us songs of mayhem, darkness, consequences and redemption. MTV termed him the 'original gangsta'.[23] But he was more than any genre or label could encase. He was bigger than country music, and he was unbounded by a single nation. He sang for the broken people, the desolate and the lost. He was hurt, but he sang for healing.

Play 'Great Leap Forward', you bastard

Play 'Great Leap Forward', you bastard.

Fan/heckler, Billy Bragg concert encore, 2003.

The final concert of Billy Bragg's Australian tour was held at Perth's Concert Hall on 24 September 2003. It was the archetypal cold, wet and windy night that the city produces before the stark, scorched summer that stretches out for half the year. Entering the auditorium from the September chill was an audience composed of (way too) many greying buzz cuts and sensible shoes. A near-sell out crowd of 40 and 50-somethings came together once more to celebrate the revolution that never was, and commemorate a social democracy that is further away now than during Bragg's mid-1980s peak. His band, composed of The Blokes and The Small Faces' keyboardist Ian 'Mac' McLagan, produced such smooth renditions of well-known songs that they almost made Billy Bragg appear cool – at least until he danced. He still moves with the subtlety of a post-it note on a tiled floor. Thankfully, he is one of the great post-punk rhythm guitarists, which gives him something to do with his hands.

I was among the youngest in the crowd. For me, Bragg's *Worker's Playtime* album is invested with mid-teen angst and hopes. The singer represented what a man should be: socially just, politically attuned, intelligent and funny. The first time I ever heard of Antonio Gramsci was on the back of a Billy Bragg album. His ability to combine emotion and politics, personal relationships and social change, probably led me into my current career in media and cultural studies. As an academic rather than a school girl, his concert performance was not only nostalgic, but intensely sad. Billy Bragg's music hot-wires melody to melancholy. Old Lefties believe in Billy. For example, the late broadcaster, John Peel, offered an appealing portrayal.

> A genuinely decent man in an often loathsome business. Unless he has deceived me – and many thousands of others – there's something about Billy that is immensely reassuring. As a pretty much unreconstructed old Labour type myself … I admire Billy's politics too. Politics that are prone to ridicule these days although they rest essentially on the proviso that you do as you would be done by.[1]

It had been ten years since I had seen Billy Bragg live. In that decade, he became a better singer and guitarist, and the all-star band provided a luminous backdrop. Hearing those songs, I realized how much we have lost during the 2000s. Two decades ago, Billy Bragg fought a political battle that – even in 1983 – was already lost. Thatcher's victory in the Falkland Islands, which was compounded by 'victory' over the miners and the destruction of the coal industry on which Britain was built, signalled an end to a particular form of political challenge and social organization. Bragg's songs and mid-set monologues offered alternatives in a time of no alternatives. Even now, when the battles of the 1980s have been lost in ways we could not imagine at the time, his words remind us of asylum seekers, gripping poverty and an environmental disaster that dare not speak its name.

While the skeletons of songs remain, Bragg's dreams of collective responses to collective troubles are vanquished. Tony Blair's governments provided few effective answers to dense social questions that – put bluntly – require redistribution of resources rather than tinkering with words like 'new', 'creative', 'collaboration' and 'facilitate'. Consumerism has bought us individuality. Now that the credit card is full, the price we have paid for satiating our acquisitiveness is a wardrobe of clothes we never wear, and refrigerated food we should not eat. The children of the revolution have been fooled. Again.

A pop musician has left a legacy to the planet when they produce one song that captures the energy of a time. Billy Bragg has a catalogue of such tracks. 'Levi Stubbs Tears' has a lyric which still creates an absorbed, pained silence from a live audience. It is too painful, too real, and depicts a damaged femininity better than any disco diva or celebrity chanteuse. Similarly, in a post-feminist environment, 'Sexuality' is an important song. Emerging from a collaboration with Johnny Marr, it was a crucial anthem to post-AIDS intimacy. The fear triggered by this seemingly unpreventable disease was eased in Bragg's probing but joyful lyric. Although still included in the live Perth performance, the band and Bragg could not recapture the energy of 'Sexuality' on stage without its post-house rhythm track. This song was a product of dance culture fuelled by Johnny Marr's guitar. The reinterpretation from his band into a pseudo-reggae rhythm did not work. This was the only song of the evening to suffer in live performance.

Bragg's truly influential song – his musical manifesto – is 'Waiting for the Great Leap Forward'. This much-loved track – and the subject of Perth heckler commentary throughout the evening at the Concert Hall – never moved above 52 on the British charts, but offered one of the finest linkages of pop and politics: 'the revolution is just a t-shirt away'. Billy Bragg made pop political before Clinton's use of Fleetwood Mac or Blair's appropriation of D:ream's anthem. Bragg welded the join, made the audience uncomfortable, but created a thinking space for activism and social change through popular culture.

Bad times produce creativity. Consensus facilitates banality and compliance. Thatcher produced Billy Bragg. Tony Blair summoned Oasis. This contradiction is a significant one. Bragg – even ironically – sang about a 'New England'. Oasis summoned an Old England of The Beatles, football and beer-soaked masculinity. They produced three-minute pop songs to whistle to, but little more. The Gallagher brothers are not alone. Popular culture is frequently inarticulate. The first rule of journalism is never – ever – interview models. The second rule of journalism is never – ever – interview footballers. Pop stars come in third for their level of inarticulate posturing. That is why Morrissey and Shaun Ryder were so extraordinary, because of their intelligence, humour and wit. But Bragg was always more than a sound bite. During dark times, he revealed a (seemingly) fully developed political plan.

In Andrew Collins' biography of Bragg, *Still Suitable for Miners*, the musician made a comment that still resonates: 'If someone says to me, what did you do during Thatcherism? My conscience is clear.'[2] Perhaps this is the lesson from Billy Bragg. We – his fans – must stop wanting him to stay the same, to maintain the rage, to be vacuum sealed with his guitar. His example of doing all he could when times were hard is the greatest message to emerge from popular music. If we stand by and watch injustices in our daily lives – knowing that we could have done more – then we are complicit in making a melody not of our choosing.

Singing a city

I was born in Perth. That is always a conversation stopper. Living on the cusp of a continent and the periphery of power creates a community of resident-tourists clinging to the edge of a coastline. Inhabitants of Sydney, Melbourne, Canberra and Brisbane are accustomed to seeing their cities as cinematic and televisual backdrops. Perth rarely pops up as an outer suburb of Middle Earth or an Antipodean Paris in *Moulin Rouge*. Being peripheral is a fashionable address in postcolonial theory, but it is difficult to live there. When Perth does feature, it is – in soap opera speak – like going to Coventry. Characters from *Neighbours* or *Home and Away* are either killed in mysterious circumstances, or they are sent to Perth. This is supposedly death of a different kind. If there is a chance that a character may return from a Maidstone pantomime season, then Brisbane is always a safer option.

When migrating to the United Kingdom, these local differences did not matter. Being foreign is enough. I remember being introduced to another professor soon after my arrival in the country. The stuttered, stunned response from a colleague was worth bottling: 'I've never met an Australian who doesn't work in a bar.' Stuart Hall could have predicted this response. In 'Minimal Selves', he reports that migrants are asked two questions: 'Why are you here?' and 'When are you going back home?'[1] In thinking about 'home' while 'away', it is the popular cultural imaginings that haunt me: of chalk white beaches, turquoise waters and dry heat that both warms and burns.

One special cinematic moment does use Perth as a vista of discovery rather than a soap opera Alcatraz. *Thunderstruck*[2] is the tale of post-mullet clad heavy metal boys who – in their thirties – decide to place the ashes of their mate near the departed remains of Bon Scott. Bon was a great rock tragedy. The lead singer of AC/DC with the paint-stripping voice, he died too young – as the best rockers do.

Secretly, we know that rock stars never die too young. There are only three options for the high rolling (ex) rocker. The first choice is a big bang early death and lifelong fame. Janis Joplin, Keith Moon and the two Jims – Hendrix and Morrison – mobilized this path to posterity. The second option is looking like Mick Jagger, who is only attractive to models so starved of carbohydrates that their brain has ceased functioning. In a calorie-starved hallucination, Mick looks sexy. Pass me the cheesecake. The final option is to become Keith Richards, wearing a face like the worn tread of a Doc Marten boot and a mouth that works ten seconds out of phase with his brain. Keith is living in two time zones most of the time. Bon, having taken the first option, permanently resides in a Fremantle cemetery where fans make a pilgrimage to the site. They keep going back in black.

Thunderstruck used Bon's resting place as the basis of an Australian road movie where disillusioned Generation X men drive across the Nullabor, the bitumen smile of a road that slices the continent. While fulfilling their friend's final wishes, they use the driving time to determine when their life hit the gravel. Filled with Xer angst and a nostalgic head-banging soundtrack, it is a great film. Now separated from this landscape that has been the near-constant companion through my life, this celluloid city has made me see the intense sunlight, stretched urbanity and laconic strangeness of Perth in a new way.

Such cinematic expeditions are rare. It has always been music that captures the spaces and emotional landscapes of Perth. The Triffids are our greatest sonic ambassadors. The scale and grandeur of 'Bury Me Deep in Love' and the silent desperation of 'Wide Open Road' offer more than a tale of gutted relationships. They are a soundtrack for ambling along a disturbing and desolate beach or cruising enormous freeways that carve through the suburbs.

Music has always been made differently in Perth. The city has – for two decades – been a dance music capital, with the two tribes of house and drum 'n' bass claiming their share of the drugs, DJs and door bitches. But the success of Eskimo Joe, The Waifs, John Butler Trio and Little Birdy is extraordinary. The music is so diverse – so good – that it has been one of the great pleasures of my Generation Xer life to see a city bloom with sound. Seattle had the grunge revolution. Manchester raised its hands in the air to acid house. Bristol pulsed with dub. I watched these musical revelations through a metaphorically grated dirty window, excluded from the great clubs by an accident of geography and history. I was a spectator to the excitement, not a participant. Then suddenly The Panics emerged, a band that grasped this stretched space and dark displacement of Perth, mashed The Stone Roses with The Triffids, and created a pop opera for this isolated, solitary, difficult, staunch and robust city locked between the sea and the desert.

The Panics had a guide to move them through this sonic journey. Pete Carroll – broadcaster, producer and manager who is also the brother of Matt and Pat Carroll from Central Station Designs, and the cousin of Shaun and Paul Ryder – signed The Panics to the littleBIGMAN label. He is still their manager now that they have moved to Universal. The relationship between Perth and Manchester was built into the music and design, with Central Station responsible for the iconography and visual style of the band. Framed by a wider history of migration and movement, art and music, The Panics pluck around the last 50 years of guitar-based history, gliding effortlessly from the 1960s to the 1980s, and on to the 2000s.

The Panics' first album used Carroll's connections in Manchester to record songs between the two cities. Through such a process, it is no surprise that *A House on a Street in a Town I'm From* sounds like the 'great' second album that The Stone Roses never recorded.[3] It is important to remember that the two Stone Roses albums were separated by five years. When released, *The Second Coming* was seen as 'a noticeable jump forward; it was, as some pundits promptly pointed out on its eventual release, like listening to the third album and missing out on the second one'.[4] The Rosetta Stone linking the two records has been produced – some ten years later and in an Antipodean city. The Panics' effect on an audience is similar to the Roses. As John Robb realized:

> The truth is The Stone Roses became massive without anyone's permission; they became massive because this was a great album, an album that friends played to friends and raved about in a breathless whisper.[5]

Similar responses emerge from The Panics. When I saw them live soon after the release of their first album, the audience was both hushed and in awe. Watching The Panics perform was the only time in my life when I knew – implicitly and definitively – that I was watching musical greatness. They seem aware of their moment. As Jae Laffer of The Panics realized, 'it's a great time to be a Perth band … and it's a great time to be a pop band. So take it now or else.'[6] The Panics are trans-local, trans-genre sonic historians. It would take a band from Perth, signed by the cousin of Shaun Ryder and brother to the great Factory Records designers, to provide a fitting conclusion to The Stone Roses story, a denouement that Ian Brown never managed or imagined.

Their second album, *Sleeps Like a Curse*, was also demoed in Manchester, while the band were listening to Johnny Cash. It sounds like a combination of The Byrds, Buffalo Springfield, Motown and Led Zeppelin. Following from this sonic tapestry, they have created their most unified, brooding release: the award-winning third album *Cruel Guards*.[7] They complete the cycle, continuing the legacy of The Triffids, by wrapping personal tragedies into a burnt landscape of isolation and despair. Jae Laffer, their lead singer and lyricist, confirmed their intent.

> I tried to keep the language and descriptions distinctly Australian; songs like Sundowner, Something in the Garden, and Get Us Home are all set in Australian landscapes and backstreets, mostly drawn from growing up in the outskirts of

Perth and road trips when I was younger. Scenes I remember vividly that have always stayed with me. They sum up my feelings of the country. The unused bridge, weatherboard shacks of the orchards, a disused train's cabin door swinging, fly wire, the distance that plays tricks on the eyes.[8]

As a writer, I have always admired musicians. The capacity to write a song that splinters a listener's life is a profound cultural gift. To produce one great track in a lifetime is remarkable. To be able to sustain success in an iPod age is extraordinary. Those of us who write words on a screen, rather than chords for a guitar, are on a different journey. A writer's goals are smaller in scale. Shorten the sentence, blade the adjectives, cut the clause. To write music that talks to a time and a place is a startling contribution to a city and its people. Writers only grasp at the coat-tails of such influence.

Once more, it is Stuart Hall who, besides being the great scholar of difference, offers a guide for those of us who are a long way from home in an age of terrorism and too close to the suffocations of a terrifying xenophobia. He confirmed that in 'thinking about my own sense of identity, I realize that it has always depended on the fact of being a migrant, on the difference from the rest of you'.[9] By moving our feet and seeing streets in new ways, we can challenge ourselves to not only hear difference, but meet it and – just occasionally – understand it.

Downloading democracy

Although my day job is as an academic, at night (and early morning) I am a closet bibliophile and pop cultural collector. During my 6.30am cycling class, I invent lists of pop trivia:

- Best use of hair straightening products on a news broadcast
- Best use of running mascara in a soap opera
- Best use of Ikea furniture in a talk show
- Best use of a Wham song in a retro police drama

No one else is needed to play this game. This obsession with the best locks, mascara runs and flat packs is matched by an even more piquant 'worst' list.

- Worst tie in a news broadcast
- Worst boots in popular music
- Worst celebrity use of hair extensions
- Worst attempt by baby boomer rock critic to appear 'down' with the kids

These lists categorize and judge the culture around us. It is ruthless, but with *X Factor* judges becoming the arbiters of quality and innovation, it is a defensive action from the desperate to remind those satisfied with the mediocre and banal that great singers use a songbook beyond the greatest hits of Mariah Carey and Celine Dion. There are other genres beyond the tongue-in-the-ear ballad, which has always been more of a sonic contraception than soundtrack for seduction. The lyric 'eyeiiiee wil alwaaaaas laaaaav youuuuuuuooouuu' made me want to call divorce lawyers. And I wasn't married at the time.

While television is close to unwatchable at the moment – if I see another diet story masquerading as investigative journalism, then I will spoon a tub of (low fat) yoghurt into the ear of a breakfast presenter – we do live in a rich, changeable and fascinating time for music. MP3 files and the platforms built for their use have reconnected listeners with a rich musical past and the potential for innovative remixing opportunities in the future.[1]

In retrospect, the compact disc was a ridiculous way to access music. It held the digitizing potential of convergence and compression. But record companies continued to apply vinyl – analogue – standards of length, structure and genre to the new musical platform. The changes from vinyl to compact disc were so rapid during the mid 1980s that we rarely considered what happened to our musical database, taste and literacies through that accelerated sonic transformation. Record companies focused on album-based artists like Dire Straits, U2 and – the best haircut of the twentieth century – Michael Bolton. Through the poor sales of white elephant platforms like the CD single and cassingle (remember those?), it seemed that adults were buying safe and packaged music for its clean and crisp resonance, rather than its radical and disturbing reverberation. I have memories of men satiated in sonic bliss while ensconced in a beanbag, headphones and Dire Straits' *Alchemy*. That bass line from 'Private Investigations' shattered glass. But this fetish for the pure, perfect and loud severed the relationship between youth and music. Adults took over the charts. Men in bad shoes took over the business of music.

The dissociation of youth and music, hearing and danger, would last less than 20 years. The permeation of the World Wide Web through leisure and work was enhanced by the compression algorithm within the MP3 encoding format. New modes of music recording, remixing, listening, copying and retailing emerged. Through this remarkable and rapid transformation, the single returned but without its vinyl platter. If we review the last 50 years of popular music history, we see the survival of the single – through iTunes and ring tones – and the decline of the album, with a 20-year blip through the compact disc.

There is now a fascinating rejuvenation in the chart books that dominated my youth. Instead of the Billboard or NME listings, I now have *The Downloader's Music Source Book*. A physical delight, it is a brick of a book. Included is a list of most of the notable performers from the United States and the United Kingdom in the last 40 years. No chart places are listed. The only relevant data in the iTunes age is the performer, song title and date of initial release. No album of origin is required. The single is all that remains in digitized music history.

How the compiler Dave McAleer actually selected songs is a mystery. But that adds even more spice to the book. To view someone else's arbitrary selection of popular music is both bizarre and obsessive. He describes his aim as 'to act as a reminder to you of all those fantastic hits of the last 40 years that you may have temporarily forgotten about but would like to add to the growing collection of downloads on your digital music player or PC'.[2] The lists by both performer and song title have an addictive quality, and there are some profound oddities. Bob Dylan has 17 listed songs. Duran Duran has 29. Helen Shapiro has three hits listed, which for the hyperlisters like me *does not* include 'Walking Back to Happiness'. The Smiths have more listings than Smokie (thankfully), and Will Smith is kept to less than half a page.

My copy of this brick book is dog-eared and post-it noted. The spine is bent from multiple readings and flickings. Through all the oddities, entering McAleer's downloaded history of popular music has honesty to it. Although acknowledging the breadth of our musical past, there is an emphasis on the last 20 years, rather than the 1960s and 1970s. Orbital has a longer listing than Orbison. There is also an absolute domination of British and American music. The former British Empire does not exist musically. Even wider European music is under-represented. I was relieved to find Kraftwerk in the listing. Any music list book without 'Autobahn' included in the most important pop of all time must be physically removed from the house.

There is also a blithe – but oddly comforting – denial of intrinsic musical quality. For example, The Smurfs have five songs listed. Fats Domino has one. I know this because after seeing Spike Lee's documentary on Katrina, and remembering that the legendary Domino had been air-lifted out of the water-logged city, I wanted to check if 'Walking to New Orleans' was mentioned in my book. It wasn't. Only 'Red Sails in the Sunset' was included in the downloading party. What about 'Blueberry Hill'?

In truth, there is great joy in flicking through the sonic history of this downloading 'source'. The completely arbitrary nature of the selections only adds humour and fascination. But there are serious and fascinating consequences of books such as this. We learn how music moves through time and what will survive in this downloaded, digital age.

While the iPod and MP3 player engross the listener in the endless replaying of musical favourites, it is also clear that the longer history of the single, so integral to the history of youth and social movements in the 1950s and 1960s and the punk 'moment', has been returned to us. Music – once more – has become short, snappy and hyper-personal. The potential for a two-minute triumph of a track, like The Chiffon's 'He's So Fine', Johnny Cash's 'Five Feet High and Rising' and Buddy Holly's 'Rave On', is matched by The Wombats 'Tales of Girls, Boys and Marsupials', Kate Nash's 'Play' and Digitalism's 'Jupiter Approach'. Now that the judicial proceedings against illegal downloaders have subsided, it is clear that not only will the best parts of our musical collections survive in the new format – with filler tracks and prescriptive linear album presentations lost – but experimentation with unknown and unfamiliar music and formats is now possible through guides such as this *Source Book*. While album sales have declined, singles sales were up by 40 per cent in 2006, with 90 per cent of UK sales now digital. Significantly, over 200,000 different titles are sold each week.[3] This is the long tail in practice. It disoriented the music industry, but rejuvenated the singles market. The long 1970s progressive rock keyboard solo has finally ended.

The challenge for those of us who love music outside of the transatlantic song pool is to ensure that we support artists in this new environment. We must create a context where they can brand, digitize, market and sell their music through online shops like MP3.com, wippit.com, Amplifier and Indiestore, along with the sites from major record companies and Apple. MySpace is great for 'exposure' but less useful in assisting new musicians in making a living. Instead of older creative arts funding models subsidizing the albums and tours of the few, we need to understand the new commercial future of the single and the remix beyond arbitrary notions of 'quality' that are frequently nostalgic for a 1960s that never happened. Creative industries initiatives, in city imaging, branding and copyright, may help new performers support themselves and their music in this unpredictable future.

These are exciting times for a new community of musicians, remixers, home recorders, software designers, samplers and engineers. Music is entering listeners' lives in a rapid, direct and intimate way. List books such as those by Dave McAleer are racing after these changes. This is a creative *and* corporate process. Our task is to ensure that democracy – for musicians, songwriters and producers – remains in the download.

I know I won't be leaving here with the Archduke

When all of us are nannas moving around city streets with walking frames and automated wheelchairs, young people will ask us why 'we' went to war with/in Iraq. Luckily I have about 50 years to develop an answer, because no clear justification comes to mind at the moment. Armed conflicts trigger tough questions. I had a student ask me about the causes of the First World War. As a proto-nanna in my thirties, I am clearly of the generation that must have been hip deep in the mud of French trenches for this fresh-faced seventeen-year-old. But as my first degree was in European History, obtained when dinosaurs still roamed the earth, I have had some time to think about this question. Replacing experience with scholarship, I mentioned the assassination of Archduke Franz Ferdinand in Sarajevo. Horror filled her face and a confused reply spluttered from her mouth: 'you mean the band caused a war?' Well, sort of.

The First World War is one of those great historical puzzles that endlessly fascinates scholars. There are so many possible causes. It was a context ripe for intrigue and subterfuge. There was an arms race between Britain and Germany – in the form of the Dreadnought brinkmanship rather than nuclear weaponry. There was the rise of the union movement, expressing the rage of a working class that had fuelled the industrial revolution but been engulfed by the *Modern Times* machines. There were the stylish suffragettes being force fed in prison while staunchly maintaining their right to vote. Art nouveau made flowers out of cast iron. Decadence made sex into farce. The 15 years before the First World War enfolds enough intrigue to keep historians debating for a lifetime. In our outcome-oriented education, this sort of subtlety and complexity is lost in high school essay questions asking students to list the causes and consequences of the First World War. In such an answer, our Archduke features strongly, but the band does not make the cut in most marking criteria. Amidst a culture of bullet points and textbook simplification, popular music since September 11 has revealed an intelligent, funny and strange re-cycling of the First World War. The Archduke is back in popular culture and fashion. The most difficult mix in music – and life – is wit with simplicity and humour with creativity. Creativity is not only the word of the new century, but it is difficult to define and even harder to find, like intelligence. We all maintain assumptions about creative people, generally involving a black turtleneck, bitter Turkish coffee and earnest conversations about the upcoming revolution. Frequent synonyms for creativity include innovation, newness, difference and challenge. These semiotic affiliations and relationships are derived from the fount of high culture, not pop. Without thinking, we summon the image of a poet sitting on a rock and 'being creative (dah-ling)'.

When popular culture is added to such an exclusive narrative, creativity becomes much more tightly bound to relevance. While J.R.R. Tolkien's *The Hobbit* and *Lord of the Rings* were written by an academic for a small audience, he wanted to create a new mythology for England through Literature (capital L). Tolkien invented an alternative world, language and geography around Middle Earth. Yet this book found new audiences and relevance through the 1960s and the birth of the counterculture. The hippies loved the hobbit, man. Drugs are like that. A tab of acid makes hairy feet far more plausible. Yet this extraordinary narrative of creativity did not end with the drugs. By the start of the twenty-first century, the films of Peter Jackson fully immersed the words and ideas – the creativity – of a don into popular culture. Middle Earth became relevant for the next generation seeking a battle between the forces of darkness and the light, mainly because the second – or was that the first? – *Star Wars* trilogy was such a disappointment.

Creativity in music is probably easier to track than in literature and film, by monitoring rhythm, instrumentation, song structure, melody, lyric or voice. When one or more of these generic, technological or musicological rules are breached, new soundscapes and aural literacies are summoned. I have always thought that we can predict a hit of popular music with reasonable certainty. If there are three transgressions – three innovations – on a track, then it will be successful. Take, for example, Johnny Cash's 'I Walk the Line'. The three innovations were, firstly, not starting his vocal with a lyric. The song commenced with a single (bara)tone – 'mmmmmmm'. Secondly, the rhythm from his guitarist, Luther Perkins – boom chicka boom chicka – was simple and effective, aligning boogie woogie with country. The final innovation that changed music was the transformation of melody. The overwhelming majority of popular music ascends the keyboard at the end of a verse and chorus. Johnny Cash's 'I Walk the Line' went down the scale. It sounded odd. It sounded strange. The success of this song – through innovations in rhythm and voice – meant that it continues to live as the title of the Cash biopic, again finding new audiences through the alignment of creativity and relevance.

Fifty years after Cash's 'I Walk the Line', the Archduke was back to transform pop as he had transformed the world through the First World War. In 2004,

Franz Ferdinand – the band rather than the assassinated royal – transgressed and agitated popular music. Their single 'Take Me Out' is amongst the most bizarre and extraordinary of songs in the suite of popular music. The track starts, not with a guitar introduction, but the crash of a cymbal. It moves into a fast and propulsively bouncy rock track. Then, at the moment when we think we have worked out this track's genre, the rhythm slows – painfully – and transposes into a completely different song. Instead of a rock track, it becomes body glitter disco through the syncopated cymbal and the stomping 4/4 dance beat. Then – at two minutes and 15 seconds into the song – the bridge of 'I know I won't be leaving here with you' transforms the rhythm again. In other words, 'Take Me Out' is three different songs – all of which are remarkable – but are jump cut into four minutes of energetic confusion. The innovations of genre, song structure, rhythm, melody, instrumentation and lyric are startling. If any song is able to freeze dry the brittle shambles that is life, politics and culture in the 2000s, then it is 'Take Me Out', where three separate songs fight for ascendancy in one track. If Franz Ferdinand had never recorded another song, then it would not have mattered. They changed music. They were creative. They came from Scotland. Go figure.

Scotland – indeed Glasgow – is important to this story. Not being from London or Manchester, being excluded from the main game, necessitates independence and confidence to make music from 'the outside' of the industry. The members of Franz Ferdinand are smart, snappy and self-aware. They are not four baggy-trousered mop tops exploited by a ruthless, cigar-smoking Las Vegas-type. They are educated and not frightened to show it. Alex Kapranos, the lead singer of the band, was a speaker at the 2005 Edinburgh Lectures, discussing Scotland's role in the twenty-first-century music industry. Other speakers included James McMillan, composer and conductor with the BBC Philharmonic, Nigel Osborne, Reid Professor of Music and Tia DeNora, Professor of Sociology at Exeter University.[1] This speech followed the band's Mercury Music Prize, the award for originality and creativity in the industry. They decided to use the £20,000 award to set up a centre in Glasgow to assist young people in music.[2] Such an awareness of place and space has a resonance in the early history of the band, where they 'appropriated' a disused art-deco warehouse in the city centre, which they named, with tongue firmly in architectural cheek, The Chateau. A police raid ensued, and Kapranos was arrested. The charges – of running an illegal bar, creating a fire hazard and contravening health and safety laws – were dropped. Appropriately, they then moved their musical and artistic 'happenings' to an abandoned Victorian courthouse and prison.

Their greatest talent was not only opening up an edgy and defiant Scottish space, but also grasping the semiotic nettles in our era where silliness, obesity and a clingingly desperate desire for fame at all costs has marinated the mind of everyone except the drunk, the sleeping and the dead. Paul Thomson was working at Glasgow Art School when he met Bob Hardy. Kapranos was studying English at university but socialized at the art college, and Nick McCarthy joined the band when he moved from Munich to Glasgow. Their intelligence, work ethic and group bond meant that when press and popular success exploded over their music in 2004, they were able to withstand it with clarity and perspective. Even *The Guardian* let them edit a G2 supplement.

As someone who teaches for a living and has to manage student complaints about 'boring' reading, 'difficult' assignments and 'hard' lectures, to find a group of people who make intelligence not only fashionable, but attractive and vital,[3] is the tonic I need at the end of a working day. The video for 'Take Me Out' is nearly as extraordinary as the song itself. While journalists call it postmodern – indeed journalists call anything that does not involve Paris Hilton postmodern – it is grasping the gritty entrails of modernity in its sparse coolness and antagonistic and agitated imagery. It was that effervescent and incongruous art movement – Dada – that was their iconographic database. No Baudrillards and Lyotards were harmed in the making of the music video.

For their album and single covers, they moved to the Russian avant garde for their canvas, with the cover for 'Take Me Out' revisioning Aleksandr Rodchenko's 'One-Sixth Part of the World' and their single 'Michael' sampling from 'A Proun' by Lissitzky. They continued their homage to Rodchenko on their second album, using the famous poster image of a headscarfed woman, hand cupped to mouth, shouting the word 'Books'. Instead, she now screams for the Archduke.

They take art and politics seriously, donating 'This Fire' as the background music for the advertising campaigns for the UK's Green parties for the 2005 British election. It was a busy year for them. They worked on the impossible second album. How was it possible to follow 'Take Me Out'? Offering a political commentary and a personal critique, they used the title *You Could Have It So Much Better* for their October 2005 release. They wanted to rewrite the old Harold Macmillan slogan to blast people out of complacency and comfort.

Through their serious deployment of history, they also claimed the energy and humour of the best popular music. One of the triggers for the band's odd and innovative song writing is the highly desirable goal of not sounding like Radiohead. Kapranos realized that the 'post-rock thing … seemed to be doing its damndest to avoid any bloody tune. We want people to go away from the gigs humming the tunes that we were singing. But at the same time bringing an edge to it.'[4] In playing music on and from the edge, they have become visible contributors and representatives of the Scottish music industry, building on the legacy of Orange Juice, Annie Lennox, Wet Wet Wet, Texas, Travis and Belle and Sebastian. Their success has meant that Scottish governments are finally recognizing the social and economic value of popular music beyond bagpipes and the Edinburgh Tattoo.[5]

When Matthew Arnold published *Culture and Anarchy* in 1869,[6] he constructed a model of high culture distanced from the gritty hands of exploitative capitalism. Pop – in such a model – became commercial trash, initiated not by creativity but the forces of money-making managers. Such an ideology survives in our time whenever a film, song or brand is successful with audiences in society beyond the chattering classes. If young women shriek and dance to something, then it must be garbage. Often the girly screamers understand the value of great pop before the rest of us.

The division between creativity and commerce is not as stark as this Arnoldian nineteenth-century ideology suggests. Still, issues of cultural value – even implicitly – operate in any discussion of creativity. To label the passions and interests of a particular oppressed group as 'mass culture' or 'commercial' is to degrade their experiences and naturalize 'high art' as embodying 'quality' without question, discussion or debate. Just as Peter Jackson took Tolkien's dream of a new English mythology and transplanted it into Aotearoa/New Zealand's postcolonial landscape, so have Franz Ferdinand reclaimed and repackaged a minor historical figure that had a major historical impact. In a case of scholarly revenge, Kapranos describes their greatest musical ambition as to make people think of 'four daft guys that met in Glasgow'[7] when they hear the name Franz Ferdinand. They are on their way. Wikipedia has a longer entry for the band than the man whose assassination triggered the First World War.

The Archduke is dead. Long live the daft Glaswegians.

I'm with stupid

I fell in love with the jacket first. It was long, black and nipped at the waist. It took several days to notice the man filling out the coat, and several weeks to realize that the song he was singing and the duo in which he was performing would become the sonic punctuation of my adult life.[1] The Pet Shop Boys are the museum curators of *Thinking Popular Culture*, offering an intelligent guide through the dusty cavities of media and identity. Even in my thirties, they remain the soundtrack of my life. No other popular cultural performer has been as influential and credible – for as long – as PSB. Unlike Madonna, they do not use Abba samples to out bling the kids. They are satisfied to grow up and age in public. Adult love, loss, triumph and decline is catalogued by PSB's words, rhythms, clothes and politics.

The Pet Shop Boys have staying power. Twenty years after Neil Tennant appeared in that flowing coat clumping through London's streets, they released their fifteenth album, the ninth of completely new music, in May 2006. It is already listed amongst their best. Titled *Fundamental*, it attacks weak political leaders holding strong views on war. Neil Tennant and Chris Lowe have always been political, in a stoic and coldly threatening fashion. Songs such as 'Rent' and 'It's a Sin', from the *Actually* album, poked the duplicity of an Iron Lady with a caustic will for social destruction. Although the bends and twists in sexual relationships and intimacy have been constantly attentive to their backbeat,[2] the excesses of greed, jealousy, envy and pride have been dominant textual fodder. During our era of limp gossip being reported in the news as news – Nicole Richie buying new sunglasses, Victoria Beckham attending another party, Lindsay Lohan choosing a new shade of lip gloss – The Pet Shop Boys draw us to the urgent and important. Using the relentless rhythms of disco, they create a disco(urse) of difference. They use pop to attack pap.

There is a font for their chic smartness. Tennant holds a history degree and his interest in Russia and the Soviet Union was to serve both the lyrics and iconography of the band well through their career. Songs like 'My October Symphony' and even the cover version of the Village People's 'Go West' became anthems for rethinking socialism after the fall of the Berlin Wall. Yet there is another member of The Pet Shop Boys who watches history and is stoic and reserved. Chris Lowe moved through the 1980s and the 1990s behind sunglasses, transforming the iconography, ideologies and clothing of masculinity. There is an origin for his subtle understanding of bodies, space and meaning. Chris Lowe studied architecture at the University of Liverpool. His consciousness of fashion and physical spaces bled into the sonic architecture and style that would provide the bedrock and façade of The Pet Shop Boys, making them much more than another electronic band, like Erasure or Depeche Mode. They are electronic(a) icons of the 1980s and 1990s.

They are intelligent and articulate, and they know it. PSB were not invited to Number 10 after Tony Blair was elected into office. The Prime Minister could counter the (verbal) punches of Noel Gallagher. He simply could not fathom the political or linguistic palette of The Pet Shop Boys. After such active avoidance of the duo, in his third term Blair had to manage urgent sexual barbs from Tennant and Lowe's new album, which suggested that he was also an inept lover. This album will remain amongst the most blistering attacks on Blair and his legacy. It is not unusual that such a staunch critique should come from popular music. Words matter to the duo, almost as much as rhythm. They have given their albums single-word titles – *Please*, *Actually*, *Introspective*, *Behaviour*, *Very*, *Bilingual*, *Release* and *Fundamental* – and often deploy full sentences for their song titles, like 'I Don't Know What You Want But I Can't Give It Any More' and 'You Only Tell Me You Love Me When You're Drunk'. For *Fundamental*, they adopted the full Kraftwerk effect, with sharp song titles as well. 'Psychological', 'Minimal', 'Numb' and 'Integral' duel with the disco excesses of 'The Sodom and Gomorrah Show' and 'I Made My Excuses and Left'.

This combination of words and images – history and architecture – creates a soundscape with a fully realized world view. They have maintained a singular function for the last 20 years: to translate underground dance rhythms into popular culture through smart lyrics, puffed up jackets, pointed hats and more pointed politics. Their persona has created an archetype. These quiet, understated, unmoving and laconic anti-pop stars move through dance music without dancing. Their videos show them watching other people at parties, watching other people having sex, watching other people living their lives. They are distanced – disconnected – aloof – from their context. They perfected their image in the videos for *Very*. Wearing dunce caps and egg-shell helmets, along with primary coloured jumpsuits, they wandered through post-Soviet Russia and a computerized matrix, looking more comfortable than in their 'real' context of Major's Britain.

The gift that the 1980s gave to popular culture was to bring edgy design into the loops of sound. While fashion cynics became fixated on the Joan Collins shoulder pads and the Molly Ringwald water-stained taffeta, it was the razor-edged lettering, the clean lines of design and the splash of colour that was the greatest stylistic revolution of the 1980s. The Pet Shop Boys, through their detached view of the world, created an intimate fusion of pop and design. Working with the extraordinary but under-recognized Mark Farrow, the details of their visual work was precise and conscious. Graphology, packaging and texture mattered from the start of their career and it has continued in the subsequent 20 years. The tightness of this alignment of sound and vision was only matched by the dense dialogue between Peter Saville and Factory Records in the late 1970s and early 1980s.

They also took chances by deploying operatic and theatrical techniques in 1991 through the staging and costuming of David Alden and David Fielding. They then produced their own musical, *Closer to Heaven*, in 2001 and a new soundtrack for the extraordinary film, *Battleship Potemkin*, in 2005. They have been prepared to make mistakes and take chances. It was no accident that their career anthology was titled *PopArt*.[4] It signalled either a double-barrelled noun to describe their work, or a linear trajectory from pop to art. More likely, the two words provide semiotic tennis rackets that allow their sounds and vision to bounce and resonate between these categories.

Fundamental has tracked this Pop↔Art reverberation, seeing a revival of their career and a reassessment of their influence.[5] Although their hardcore fans have stayed with them since *Very*'s release in 1993,[6] each subsequent album enacted a stark separation from the previous remix. *Bilingual* remade the English duo into the soundtrack for a European community. *Nightlife* brought rhythm and movement back to the night-time economy and *Release* – their great experimentation with rock structures and rhythms – was an album of regret and loss. But for the chart-based fans of music, they have been quiet since the brilliance of *Very* and the charting singles 'Go West', the stomping disco cover, and the fag hag anthem, 'Can You Forgive Her?'

Spurting from this recent history, *Fundamental* becomes even more extraordinary. It aligns their long journey of suits, sights and sounds. For those who have not followed their career in the last ten years, it seems like a comeback. For those who have commuted on their musical journey with faith and openness, the sheer quality and topicality of this release could have been predicted. The revelation is the breadth and freshness of their vision. It is an album glacial in its emotional intimacy.

The War on Terror has provided the hook on which to hang these tracks. The Pet Shop Boys are sharp and probing in their anger. These musicians have found their time. Again. The neo-conservative fear of foreigners bubbles into the lyric of 'Indefinite Leave to Remain'. An attack on identity cards and the disappointments of the Blairite third way pumps through 'Integral'. The pounding politics of 'I'm With Stupid' transformed the Blair and Bush 'special relationship' into a homoerotic encounter between the mediocre and obtuse. The video highlights the camp comedy of the track, with the *Little Britain* writers Matt Lucas and David Walliams re-staging The Pet Shop Boys' video history. This collaboration has overshadowed the more significant reunion between The Pet Shop Boys and the producer Trevor Horn. They first worked together on the 1988 single 'Left To My Own Devices'. Horn has thrived on bringing Barry White orchestration and the bumping excesses of disco into the 2000s. Alexis Petridis realized that 'The Sodom and Gomorrah Show' allowed Horn to 'pull … out what you might call the Full Frankie: timpani, thwacking hi-NRG bass, cascading synth lines, jagged guitar chords and, as was once mandatory on his productions, a booming voiceover that breaks into puny-earthlings-I'll-destroy-them-all cackling'.[7] For one album in this confusing time, romantic love and monogamous, heterosexual, suburban family life is placed in the backseat of the four wheel drive. During *Fundamental*, the outsiders to such heteronormativity can slam down a couple of Brandy Alexanders and unsteadily strut to a club with dull interiors, bright lights and sweaty rhythms. It feels good to be part of a community of listeners, dancers and thinkers who care more about ideas and politics than a tax rebate or a plasma screen television.

It is the random but trackable movements between the bright past and pallid present that make *Fundamental* a landmark in pop. Andy, a fan from London, described his response to the album for the BBC.

> Just when the dumper seemed to beckon, it's an astonishing return to form – right up there with the PSBs finest albums, Very and Behaviour. Minimal is a better New Order song than anything on the last New Order album, the Sodom and Gomorrah Show is a 21st century Welcome to the Pleasuredome, Integral is a furious disco stomper. Even Numb isn't bad. A great Trevor Horn album, a great Pet Shop Boys album… back! Back! BACK![8]

I understand Andy's enthusiasm. Popular culture generally, and popular music specifically, has let us down since September 11. Pallid ballads and try-hard rock has been the soundtrack to the Iraq War. We needed a sonic circuit breaker, a rupture in the conformity and consensus of war and hyperconsumerism. That is why this album is the pop musical equivalent of the film *Casablanca*. This metaphor drills down to the level of songs, with the hard, painful and frighteningly intense Bogart moment of 'Minimal' playing off the Bergman softness, silence and secrets in 'Numb'. The fragile confidence, performed to perfection by Peter Lorre, resonates with the final album track, 'Integral'. The wisdom and reflection of Claude Rains is captured in the lyrical masterpiece of the album, 'Twentieth Century', that remains second only to 'Being Boring' as The Pet Shop Boys' theme song. Just as *Casablanca* is more than a war movie, so is *Fundamental* more than a war album, offering a way to critique talk of terrorism and foreigners.

This survival is against all odds. With George Michael regularly being arrested and Britney Spears continually breaking up with new husbands, The Pet Shop Boys have settled into an important role: the undertakers of popular music. They gather the dark, damaged and decaying. Tennant's mournful tones confirm that there will not be a happy ending to romance, love or lust and are counterpoised with the hopeful swirling synthesizers of disco. Luke Turner understood that 'they've rightly realized that making an album chock-full of screaming camp bangers would merely make them look like a pair of decaying, bleach-blond queens spilling out of their sleeveless vests in some forsaken provincial nightspot'.[9] Instead, the evenness of Tennant's tone is tempered – lightly – with an ice cold slither of rage. There is none of Coldplay's blandness or Madonna's leotards. Right now, we do not need legwarmers. We require a bright, sharp spotlight hitting the paradoxes of this paranoid time. As Alexis Petridis confirmed in his review of *Fundamental*, 'you listen wondering who else in pop music would do something like this. And for the first time, the answer comes back, nobody.'[10] Being defiant rather than boring or compliant, it is The Pet Shop Boys who might be able to fuse popular culture with political change.

They have always been the pop stars that most captured the ambivalence of Generation X: inauthentically authentic, socially courageous, media-literate, intelligent, but also endlessly distracted by the cut of a good jacket. When opening the blackness of *Fundamental*'s packaging, a promotional card tumbles from the disc, advertising Pet Shop Boys ringtones. While the teen ringers are part of the pop audience, they are not the primary listeners for this work. Optimism and hope are for the young. Regret and disillusion come with experience. In the opening song, 'Psychological', Tennant asks 'Is it a cry for help or call to arms?' Life teaches us that despair – to survive this long dark night of hyper-capitalism – must be tempered by rage. The Pet Shop Boys' role in teaching Generation Xers how to age with an edge must not be underestimated. *Fundamental* exposes the next stage in understanding the changes in the mirror, and the changes to society. In April 2006, a month before *Fundamental* was released, Edward Said's posthumously published book *On Late Style* was released by Pantheon. Said remained interested in the creative abilities of artists in their final years. Beethoven, Genet, Mozart and Strauss are of particular focus. Said confirmed that the late works not only capped a lifetime of creativity, but an expression of 'artistic lateness not as harmony and resolution, but as intransigence, difficulty … unresolved contradiction'.[11] The tension between disenchantment and pleasure creates the impetus for innovation. The mastery of technique when matched with experience creates an aptitude for resistance and refusal. Instead of a late style showing clarity and confidence, self-assurance and peace, it is the darkness and denial that characterizes the quality of artists in the latter stages of their career.

Popular cultural time will always move at a greater pace than high cultural texts. For The Pet Shop Boys to have survived to produce charting music in the 2000s is an astounding example of pop longevity. They confirm Said's argument: *Fundamental* has captured their late style. Andy Gill, in *The Independent*, believed that 'the result may be the very best album of their career, a mature and considered work which satisfies head, heart and feet simultaneously'.[12] They are masters of form and technique, but need to express the paradoxes and contradictions that have emerged in their music and lives.

The label of 'dance music' has blocked The Pet Shop Boys from being recognized as powerful social commentators. Their critiques of Thatcher, through the songs 'Opportunities', 'Shopping', 'King's Cross' and 'Rent', were profound. Yet their attack on Blair is even more cutting and damaging. While *Fundamental* is their *Casablanca*, their Claude Rains track – 'Twentieth Century' – should be played on repeat for every political leader with aspirations for war: 'Sometimes the solution is worse than the problem.' Tennant's history degree has served him well. Concurrently, Chris Lowe has worn sunglasses through his pop life in the last 20 years. Through his shades, he sees the future more clearly than most. The Pet Shop Boys offer a lesson from pop, and a lesson from the last century, to be carried into the next 100 years. They not only sing the problems, but are the soundtrack for the solution.

VISION

What have you ever done on the telly?

The Office is set in Wernham Hogg, a paper mill in Slough, Berkshire. Before the programme was broadcast, the city's only claim to fame was a mocking poem by Sir John Betjeman. Swindon is sophisticated in comparison. Like fingernails down a blackboard, *The Office* is an observational comedy that is so close to the ruthless boredom of contemporary labour that it is almost unwatchable. While some critics have termed it 'a wry, dark comedy set in a dysfunctional workplace',[1] it has actually stitched together a mock-realist re-presentation of contemporary labour. Just as *The Royle Family* rewrites family life, revealing the comfortable silences and dinner-on-the-knees-before-the-television archetypes, so does *The Office* reinscribe the micro-traumas punctuating the open plan. The viewers hear echoes in the dialogue, setting and workplace relationships. The programme continues the British comedy tradition of appalling men directing the narrative: from Basil Fawlty in the 1970s through to Alan Partridge in the 1990s and David Brent in the 2000s. Brent and Fawlty have much in common: both are dreamers, aspirational men who use frustration, humiliation and sarcasm to understand a world where their lived experience does not match their hopes. Brent, unlike Fawlty, is unable to mask his embarrassment with anger. Ricky Gervais commented on his comedic creation:

> We don't despise him or hate him, we feel a bit sorry for him. He's not a monster or the bastard some people think he is, he's just a bit misguided, his only real crime is he's not as cool as he thinks he is.[2]

Brent's awkward smile and the pensive silences add to the discomfort. Gervais has recognized that not being cool is probably the greatest crime of a celebrity-fuelled best- and worst-dressed culture.

In creating David Brent, a great comedic archetype has emerged. His hubris is overt. As Stephen Moss realized:

> Most of his staff are, indeed, leading lives of quiet desperation and he wants to make them better, but his fatal lack of self-knowledge defeats him at every turn. All his attempts to be a caring boss – his self-proclaimed distaste for sexism and racism,

his championing of the rights of the disabled – end up undermining those he wants to defend. He is part of the problem, not part of the solution.[3]

The Office has translated the boredom and pettiness of office life into comedy. Ricky Gervais has experience in summoning these emotions, having had a varied career from pizza delivery man to university administrator, manager of the rock group Suede to performing in his own band, Seona Dancing.[4] His programme – at the start – appeared to have as little success as his band. The first episode of *The Office* was shown on BBC 2 on 30 August 2001.[5] Few watched it. It was a show without stars, without plot and lacking a laughter-infused backing track. Slough paper merchants were unable to capture an early, intrigued audience. Slowly it built a following. In early 2002, the first series was repeated,[6] and went on to win two BAFTA awards, for best comedy series and best comedy actor. By September 2002, an innovative DVD was released, which value-added context and detail to the programme. In that same month, the second series was broadcast – after great promotion.[7] By 26 January 2004, *The Office* had won two Golden Globes, for the best TV comedy and best comedy actor, the first time that a British comedy had received such acclaim. That the programme prevailed over *Sex in the City* is important. Slough won out over New York, intelligent critique triumphed over sexualized gossip, and dysfunctional masculinity was valued over empowered and self-assured femininity. Bad polyester suits gained a prize – even over Manolo stilettos. This success has been even more extraordinary considering that *The Office* was screened on BBC America, a small cable network, attracting viewers in the thousands, not millions.

This critical validation in the United States, leading to a successful remake with an American cast, masks the realization that *The Office* is actually a de-globalizing programme. It does not address 'universal' truths, but the specificity of a post-Blair, post-union, post-industrial, post-feminist, insular, open-plan office. Slough is not Christchurch or Perth, let alone New York or Madrid. The programme is built on the local, specific and particular. It is part of a radical restaging of Britain for America, beyond Reagan–Thatcher, Clinton–Blair and Bush–Blair. *The Office*, by focusing on Slough, creates an alternative Britain for the United States, after the death of Diana, the birth of Austin Powers and the recycling of Jane Austen. It is not heritage television but set in a (post) industrial business park. Such a construction is important in the current political environment. As Antoinette Burton has realized:

> there will be many for whom the events of September 11 signal a high-profile return of Britain to the world stage, with the old imperial power advising the new (though by no means unexperienced) American hegemony in which is the most dangerous moment in world history yet.[8]

Within such an interpretation, the spectre of Winston Churchill is looking over Blair's shoulder, guiding George W. Bush. *The Office* emerged through this period of increasing American power and the proliferation of new modes of imperialism. Unlike Alf Garnett's Tory working classness in *Till Death Us Do Part*, *The Office* cuts away public domain politics. Intriguingly, Tony Blair is not mentioned. Neither is September 11. Workplace drudgery saturates all other concerns. It is a small show, set in a bland, insignificant and grey place, with minor and irrelevant cities encircling it. The programme confirms that globalization is always uneven in its application. The global, cosmopolitan citizen, unrestrained by location, is not part of *The Office*'s world. The programme is strained and conflictual in the presentation of race, gender, sexuality and age, probing how these differences operate through labour.

The Office is a pointed portrayal of a 'new' management style in the workforce. The management language is vacuous and addictive. For example, when David Brent tries to mould a career trajectory for his staff by denying the value of returning to university, the Sales Manager Tim Canterbury ends up mouthing his mentor's vocabulary.

> No, I said 'moving up.' Yeah 'Moving up.' Moving up can mean within an internal ladder framework or sideways to external, then up. You know, you've got to look at the whole pie, vis a vis my current life situation, you know.[9]

This is the management culture created by David Brent, who believes he is the most charismatic boss in the country, with a great sense of humour. He is neither a great boss nor funny, but he is able to deploy manager-speak with vacuous skill. This language narrates not only the contemporary workplace reality, but reality television.

Dumbing down the plonkers

> Stitch up. It was a stitch up. They filmed hours of material most of it showing a good bloke doing a good days work and the one time I actually head butted an interviewee makes it to the programme, you're gonna look a prat. So you head butt a girl on the telly and you're labelled a prat. That's the game … We want a scapegoat. We wanna dumb down. We want to give them the biggest plonker of the year, you know. I'm not a plonker.[10]
>
> David Brent

Before the screening of two Christmas episodes of *The Office* in December 2003, there was much concern that there was no way to match the quality of the landmark 12 shows. Critics wanted it to be like *Fawlty Towers*: finishing on a high.[11] However, the best moments of the programme were saved until this 'new' ending. While the first series tracks the life and disasters of David Brent, creating more cringes per minute than any previous British comedy, the second series – brilliantly – shifts narrative focus, recognizing that Brent has become too appalling to watch. A focus on Tim Canterbury and Dawn Tinsley allows overt and poignant commentary on life, love, work and masculinity. The final two Christmas episodes summon a new imperative: working through the problems of reality television. David Brent – no longer in the office or the boss – is 'managing' the consequences of his (mock) reality television celebrity.[12] He is continually humiliated in nightclubs, or by grocers and women in a desire to stretch out micro-fame, while simultaneously being critical of the format that granted him minor notoriety. In a brilliant inversion, he passionately craves celebrity, but criticizes how he received it. Like countless (post) reality television 'stars', he is unable to understand how fame can be so quickly delivered, and even more rapidly removed. In rewriting Andy Warhol's maxim, Steve Redhead has realized that everybody will be 'famous for fifteen seconds'.[13] The mourning for a loss of pseudo-celebrity triggers brilliant black comedy. In a nightclub, and after a truly appalling simulacrum performance as Austin Powers (an already-existing simulacrum of Bond), he is labelled a 'beardy twat' by one of the punters. He can only reply, 'What have you ever done on telly?'[14] There is no way to dismiss such a rejoinder in an era where television *is* reality and the role of minor celebrity has become both a worthwhile aspiration and a full-time job.

It is no surprise that Ricky Gervais, after leaving the blistering success of *The Office*, took this desire for micro-celebrity as his new creative font. *Extras* is based around the 'professional' life of Andy Millman, played by Gervais, who works as an extra and suffers daily humiliations from his agent and other 'supporting artists'. Again, at the end of the programme, the male lead character cannot manage minor fame and leaves *Celebrity Big Brother* after a speech of flourish and attack. A deeper and more complex comedy than *The Office*, it continues the considered and horrifying commentary on race, gender, sexuality and disability, but adds fame and the media to the lists of targets. As Sam Wollaston has argued, '*Extras* is still just about the most original thing that's been on television since … well, *The Office*, I'm afraid.'[15] What was remarkable was that Gervais produced the 'difficult second album', which not only matched the first, but moved on from it.

The maturing of the situation comedy genre, which now involves laughing at reality television and pseudo-celebrity, revels in the confluence of documentary, mockumentary, representation and performance. Reality television offered a positive interpretation of CCTV and widespread video surveillance, changing the relationship between technology and privacy. While the 'original' reality programmes like *Cops* at least maintained some tether with an urban environment, the revitalized genre has removed people from familiar places, taking them to an island or 'the outback', or being situated in a house with strangers and filmed 24 hours a day.[16] This television is neither real nor live in any sense. The promise of spontaneity is tempered by intense editing. The aggression and ruthlessness of these programmes creates train-wreck television. *The Office* does not remove audiences to *Temptation Island*, but leaves them in Slough. As a meta-reality programme, *The Office* is able to laugh at the remaking of media. The desire to be famous is collapsed into the desire to be on television.

After September 11, news changed. Technology permitted 'hoover journalism'[17] without context or meaning.[18] Journalists become more crisis oriented, being dropped into 'trouble zones' to cover stories with little but the most provisional of notes. *The Office* hoovers up these news phrases, like dumbing down and scapegoat. Most importantly, though, programmes such as this track the changes to knowledge, expertise and value. Reality television has altered how we commit to and access information. As argued in the first chapter of this book, the plurality of voices, views and ideas supposedly 'represented' by interactive media has created a culture of equivalence. We are losing the ability to judge, interpret and rank expertise and importance. When ordinary people are placed in an extraordinary situation and granted value and celebrity, cultural and critical literacies are devalued. Mediocrity is celebrated. In moving away from the gleam of *American Idol* and back to Slough, the consequences of fêted ordinariness are revealed.

Sharing the carpet

> The people you work with are the people that you were just thrown together with. It was not your choice. But you spend more time with them than your own family. But probably all you've got in common is that you walk on the same bit of carpet.[19]
>
> Tim Canterbury

Work is defined contextually and historically, and in opposition to the home, family and leisure. By conventional and outdated dualisms: home is a site of consumption, while work is productive. Work is a set of practices and behaviours that are frequently determined through a specific space, but cannot be captured within a single definition. Greg Noble argued that 'cultural studies has often ignored the world of work'[20] because of an imperative to research media audiences, commodification and consumerism. Therefore *The Office* is a site on which to apply cultural studies theories of the media to the workplace. In *The Office*, workers do not have a private life. We never see their homes, families or children. Most of the programme is set in the open-plan office. Transitory excursions to clubs and pubs are made with co-workers. There is no commentary on the 'work and life' balance. The domestic sphere is irrelevant, with the ruthlessness of career jealousies and capitalism slicing away private lives. *The Office* demonstrates the consequences and fears of downsizing. The destruction of job security, when matched with the technological 'innovations' of pagers, mobile phones and email, means that work colonizes the rest of life. The cultural standards of a 'good day's work' are changing, with limits and boundaries more difficult to establish. Currently, hyper-consumerism has created a web of new needs and wants, and a lengthened work day to pay for it. In their 'Post-Work Manifesto', Stanley Aronowitz and others argued that 'the "workaholic" model, once regarded as an individual pathology, has become the enforced, ethically approved standard'.[21] Sharing office carpet has become sharing a life. There is no 'outside' to work.

Much of the discussion of work in *The Office* revolves around Tim Canterbury who, for much of the series, is the Sales Manager. Turning 30, he recurrently decides – and then changes his mind – to leave the paper mill and return to university to complete a psychology degree. Sitting adjacent to Gareth would be enough to encourage anyone to ponder and research delusional masculinity. In the last episode of the first series, Tim aligns popular culture and life narratives to validate the arbitrariness of Generation X career planning.

> It's like an alarm clock's gone off, and I've just got to get away. I think it was John Lennon who said: 'Life is what happens when you're making other plans,' and that's how I feel. Although he also said: 'I am the Walrus I am the eggman' so I don't know what to believe.[22]

Sources of alternative information about work – outside of neo-liberal ideologies – are difficult to find. Popular culture is as effective a fount for knowledge as any other. Such confluences between work and life are made even more unstable because postfordism has shifted the political vocabularies of capitalism. Postfordist labour is casualized, temporary, autonomous, responsible and 'flexible'. *The Office* workplace reveals none of those characteristics. Instead, it is a hybrid work environment, where white collar workers 'administer' a paper mill warehouse. There is intent and consciousness in the classed readings of these spaces.

> Tim: Okay, now guys we're about to enter a warehouse environment. Now, I must warn you that some of the people in here will be working class, so there may be arse cleavage. So, just find a partner, hold hands. Don't talk to anyone though, okay?[23]

Social changes with regard to gender and employment conditions first emerge in the working class. They are the first to confront downsizing, attacks on the union movement and a devolving of skill and expertise. In *The Office*, the warehouse workers do little except play cards, have lunch and discuss the distinctions between dwarfs, midgets and elves.

It is significant that Wernham Hogg trades in paper, not digital imaging or information technology. While paper is required for the information economy, it is not part of it. Creative industries initiatives often focus on the sexiness of design, not the banality of photocopying. The programme also offers a reminder of the big lie of the 1980s, the paperless office. Discussions of 'the global network'[24] do not seem relevant in Slough. The shift from manufacturing to an information-driven economy has required reskilling, but such educational imperatives are spliced from *The Office*.[25] For example, the 'training' episode deteriorates into David Brent playing his guitar and singing to staff.

As a study of workplace culture, *The Office* demonstrates the mismatching of the new corporate capitalism with the language of team building and flexible employment. Douglas Ezzy referred to this paradox as a 'managerial colonization of culture'.[26] It is a social engineering of the workplace, where the interesting ideas and debates are conducted by upper levels of management who take up life-long learning and creative knowledge initiatives. But there is also an incredible array of low-skilled repetitive labour, completed by workers who have few choices about how their timesheet is organized. 'Flexible' jobs are the most inflexible in terms of their content, career trajectory, function and rights.

Throughout the research and political talk about the new economy, creativity and the cultural sectors, there is a desire to provide an alternative to neo-liberal-styled globalization. The notion that individual creativity is required for productivity and competitiveness suggests that a clear demarcation can be made between the new and old economy. The shift from buying new machines to buying new concepts and ideas is matched by economic initiatives moving beyond the nation state. Kieran Healy described this movement as 'a focus on intellectual capital – and by extension, its container, the innovative worker'.[27] Yet so many of the old ways – insider trading, redundancy, underemployment and recession – are part of the current workplace. Obviously, since Daniel Bell's arguments – particularly his 1976 book *The Coming of Post-Industrial Society*[28] – there have been forecasts about the nature of a future working world. The predictions of growth in the knowledge class, particularly scientists and engineers, and a movement from manufacturing to services, is barely linked to the world of *The Office*. The staff use computers, but for few functions beyond emails and spreadsheets.

Brent: We're all online here. Hooked up to the World Wide Web. Internet.

Brent: [to female employee] No shopping! Everyone's got e-mail. Have you used e-mail before?

Donna: [slightly patronized] Yeah.

Brent: Yeah, it's easy, innit?[29]

This is not a creative use of the internet's potential for commerce. Older modes of sales, based on the telephone, predominate. Also, the gendered ideology – that women shop rather than work on the internet – is perpetuated.

The workers are in *The Office* from 9am to 5pm, with no flexibility in hours. It is a highly *uncreative* office, with basic and repetitive tasks conducted on a daily basis. In one episode, Keith, Dawn and Tim all express the place of work in their lives, and the mindless nature of employment.

> Keith: This job is just a stop-gap really … Job's not difficult. I mean, I don't take my work home with me, it's pretty brainless.[30]

> Dawn: I don't want to spend my life answering phones in some crappy sub-branch paper merchants.[31]

> Tim: I can't take any more of this nonsense. I can't take another boring call about Spa White Index Board at two thirty a tonne.[32]

This organizational culture is framed by mediocrity, low-level skills and boredom. It offers a sharp rejoinder to the aspirations of what the contemporary workforce should be. Alan Greenspan, the former Federal Reserve Board chairman, stated that 'today's workers must be prepared along many dimensions – not only technical know-how but also with the ability to create, analyze and transform information, and with the capacity to interact effectively with others'.[33] *The Office* reveals the brittle façade of this 'new' economy. Reskilling is not required. Slough's retail environment is not a creative place. In fact, it saps creativity.

> Dawn: For years I was an illustrator who did some reception work. And then Lee [Dawn's fiancée] thought it would be a good idea for us to both get full-time jobs. And you know, then you're knackered after work and it's hard to fit in time for the illustrating. So now, when people say, 'what do you do,' I say, 'I'm a receptionist.'[34]

One of the great changes in the workforce through the last few decades has been the increase in full-time female labour force participation. The instability early in women's careers[35] has consequences later in the building of labour market attachments, resulting in women revealing more complex employment histories and career scaffolds than men.[36] Dawn's lack of commitment to work, as a bright woman trapped behind a reception desk, and the loss of her passion and creative vocation, is one of the tragic plot arcs of the programme.

The Office has tapped into the dense anger towards the contradictions and hypocrisies of the workplace. In a time of labour surplus, where the great problem is not unemployment but underemployment, there is little mechanism through which to express resentment without fear of redundancy. In an online chat about *The Office* with the writers, one fan used the programme to express this rage.

> *The Office* has become a kind of outlet for all the frustration and pure hatred I felt towards my boss, and I think you've tapped into the bitterness and boredom of office workers the country over. Having exposed this, what next? Do we all continue to suffer in silence? Do you feel the very personal way in which people reacted to *The Office* puts pressure on you? (I personally was shouting at the TV in last night's episode, baying for Brent's blood, but I realize it's my own (ex)boss I want to see so humiliated!)[37]

In the same web forum, another contributor described it as 'the most subversive TV programme ever made. It completely undermines modern work culture.'[38] The stark truths of labour are revealed: clichés replace content, bullying surpasses expertise, and management speak is more important than questions of leadership.

Before the War on Terror, the 1990s was termed the decade of cultural crises, or at least the Oprahfied marketing of crisis. Kirby Farrell picked up this phrasing in *Post-Trauma Culture: Injury and Interpretation in the Nineties*.[39] After the traumatic movement from industrialism to post-industrialism, and a regrouping of political forces after the scarification of Thatcher, Reagan and Howard, many books were written to capture this post-traumatic millennialism and end-of-the-century hangover. *The Office* has addressed this trauma through laughter. The traditional managerial masculinity of the workplace is unpicked and restitched by David Brent. Through the 1990s, films such as *Falling Down* and *American Beauty* told the tale of the disempowered middle class white male as the drone of the late capitalist culture.[40] Personal development is a mask for this social dislocation. With femininity still dialoguing with consumerism, masculinity is being redefined through displacement in the workplace. Through white collar work, the tensions of modernity are actualized by men negotiating the challenges of contemporary economic and material conditions.

Wife, kids and endings

> I don't know what a happy ending is. Life isn't about endings is it? It's a series of moments and it's like if you turn the camera off, it's not an ending is it? I'm still here. My life's not over. Come back here in ten years and see how I'm doing then. I could be married with kids. You don't know. Life just goes on.[41]
>
> Tim Canterbury

Masculinity is determined by structures and institutions. When they weaken, so does masculinity. For much of the post-war period, competent masculinity has been determined through working hard, paying the bills and 'looking after' the wife and kids. Tim's awareness of this narrative is shadowed by the understanding of his own 'television' life. Men in each historical period, and within each society, approach and judge their lives through diverse criteria. Masculinity always has limits,[42] but is frequently taken for granted. While some men's studies theorists argue that the women's movement and feminism have unravelled traditional models of masculinity,[43] changes to the workforce need to be recognized as transforming the supposedly singular and naturalized ideology of masculinity into a plural, productive, ambivalent and dynamic formation. The managing of 'career transitions' and the rebranding of masculinity for new industries has caused stress and problems. Susan Faludi confirmed that homicide was the leading cause of workplace deaths in cities hit by downsizing. Termed 'going postal',[44] this destructive masculinity requires a new and careful theorizing of the relationship between men and work.

Elspeth Probyn – with tongue in scholarly cheek – stated that 'men are the new women'.[45] Moral panics about education, families and work are negotiated through the filter of masculinity. The social anxieties encircling men are built on globalizing capital, economic competition and the shift from a manufacturing to a service and information economy. Andrew Walzer argued that such movements had 'displaced white men culturally'.[46] These narratives of crisis have many 'solutions' and 'outcomes'. Some involve groups replaying traditional models of male bonding, teaching intimacy to men from other men, not women.[47] *Fight Club* and Susan Faludi in *Stiffed* asserted that men have been emasculated by consumerism.[48] Pop psychologists have sold millions of books based on the assumption that men and women do not understand each other, and speak different languages or are even from different planets. But masculinity is not a self-standing concept or a vacuum-sealed personal identity. It is part of a social landscape. Film and television in particular are ideal fora to track changing masculinity and femininity because of the fetishization of bodily surfaces.

Multiple masculinities vie for credibility, space and time in *The Office*. The most vindictive and ruthless masculinities utilize women's bodies to establish and perpetuate power. Chris Finch is the archetypal sexual predator in *The Office*. A misogynist, seething with repressed anger, he is a horrible man who displaces his personal inadequacies onto others. In the first series he states that 'give me half an hour with her and I'd be up to me nuts in guts'.[49] Bizarrely, competitive physical acts become the basis of ranking masculinities. Gareth attacks Tim with the rebuke: 'He's [Chris Finch] thrown a kettle over a pub, what have you done?'[50] We have all worked with Gareths: delusional men with the self-belief of Ronald Reagan at a press conference discussing the Soviet Union. Gareth is talentless, sleazy, inept and incompetent – but he is also a lieutenant in the Territorial Army. His negotiation of petty details in a working day is accurate and atrocious, spending much of the first series rewriting his job description from 'Assistant to the regional manager' to 'Assistant regional manager'. The workplace – like the military – has become a place where the mediocre hang on the words of the inept.

Heteronormative masculinity displaces conflict, struggle and contradiction onto other groups in the culture, surfacing through the archetypes of the potent black man, the effeminate gay man and the submissive woman. As men's bodies have been increasingly surveyed and judged, men and women with disabilities have also been enlisted in the project of maintaining the power and resilience of heterosexual masculinity. Throughout *The Office*, women, gay men, black communities and people with disabilities are continually ridiculed, categorized and implicated in the patriarchal project. As David Brent confirms:

> There are limits to my comedy. There are things that I'll never laugh at. The handicapped, because there's nothing funny about them. Or any deformity. It's like when you see someone look at the handicapped and go ooh, look at him, he's not able-bodied ... Yeah, well, at least the little handicapped fella is able-minded. Unless he's not, it's difficult to tell with the wheelchair ones.[51]

Continually, there is an overt demarcation of good and bad bodies. Gareth speaks the unspeakable, asking questions and humiliating those who are not like himself, a (supposedly) able-bodied white man.

> Brenda: What? Are you suggesting that people pretend to be disabled in order to claim money off the DSS?
>
> Gareth: I don't know. I'm just saying there should be tests, that's all.
>
> Tim: Oh God. What tests?
>
> Gareth: Well, stick pins in their legs – see if they react ...
>
> Brenda: That is not going to work. I have feelings in my legs, I just can't walk.

Gareth: Alright. I'm just saying there should be tests.

Tim: We're all ears, Gareth.

Gareth: Oh, I don't know. When they go down the DSS to make a claim, they should set off a fire alarm, a fake fire alarm. Everybody legs it out of the office, leaving them there. If they're a fake they'll be up and running with you; if they're real, they'll be left there screaming for help and then you just come back in and say 'It's alright, don't cry; it's just a test. You've passed – here's your money.'[52]

Instead of presenting a checklist of grievances from white, heterosexual men, *The Office* tracks the brutality of their daily failures and humiliation by displacing them onto the disempowered. The 'accommodation' of disability results in the oppression of difference. In *The Office*, Brenda is a female worker who is also – because she is confined to a wheelchair – pushed around the desks, discussed as if she is not present and assumed to be mentally limited. The overt presentation of this prejudice and inequality is important. Alex McClimens argued that 'the continual absence of genuine portrayals of disability or impairment reveals something about the cultural values that underpin so much of what is on offer on our screens'.[53] Appearance discrimination punctuates *The Office*, with every statement of good intentions undercut by dense and predatorial judgments.[54]

The pathetic dreams of the men in *The Office* include David Brent's failed musical career, Gareth's twisted relationship with the Territorial Army, Tim's desire for Dawn, Finchy's alcohol dependency and Keith's hopes to be a DJ. They live small lives, with a desperation to be more than they are.

Tim: Thirty is young now anyway. I'm not someone who has specific goals about, you know, having done this or that by my age: 'I should've done this, why haven't I taken that chance?' I just think, well, if you look at life like rolling a dice then my situation now, as it stands, yeah, it may only be a three. If I jack that in now, go for something bigger and better, yeah, I could easily roll a six, no problem. I could roll a six; I could also roll a one, okay? So I think sometimes just leave the dice alone.[55]

Conversely, the women are focused and knowing of their goals: Jennifer is the mini-skirted, ambitious manager, Dawn claims financial security and Donna is sexually aware and demanding. However, the women are isolated from each other. There is no sense that they negotiate and change the workplace as a group with mentoring relationships. Because of this gendered landscape, the multiple and intertwined genres of soap opera, spoof, drama and comedy are mobilized to bring out the plurality of masculinities and femininities. The Christmas episodes push these genres to the extreme, demonstrating what happened to the micro-celebrity men when the cameras were removed.

The brilliance of the masculine negotiations in *The Office* is tethered to two characters: Tim and Gareth. Tim, the sensitive Sales Manager, respects women and continually expresses self-doubt. Gareth, member of the Territorial Army and inflated with (unjustified) masculine confidence, duels with Tim's more complex rendering of the gendered environment. As Tim reflexively admits:

> No I don't talk about my love life for a very good reason, and that reason is I don't have one. Which is very good news for the ladies – I am still available. I'm a heck of a catch, coz, er well look at it. I live in Slough, in a lovely house, with my parents. I have my own room, which I've had since yep, since I was born. That's seen a lot of action I can tell you. Mainly dusting. I went to university for a year as well, before I dropped out, so I'm a quitter. So, er, form an orderly queue, ladies.[56]

Tim is the equivalent of Blackadder or Sid James in the *Carry On* films, using recognition and pathos to move inside and outside the *mise en scene*. Such roles translate a text for an audience. Gareth's interpretation of the relationship between men and women offers an evocative point of contrast. His confidence overwrites Tim's doubt and self-deprecation.

> I can read women. And you've got to know their wants and their needs, and that can be anything from making sure she's got enough money to buy groceries each week to making sure she's gratified sexually after intercourse.[57]

Conservative masculinity is facilitated by the construction of women as suppliant sexual objects, cooks and shoppers. Women buy groceries and are patient enough to wait until after a man's ejaculation to be 'gratified sexually'. Obviously no woman on staff in Slough matches this profile. *The Office*'s men are desperate, clingy, aggressive, demanding and demeaning. The horrifying moment where David Brent is made redundant and then begs for his job back – with tears in his eyes – demonstrates the vulnerability of men, particularly 'the boss'. The smallness of Brent's world is presented in a close-up talking head shot, directly addressing the camera.

> My world does not end with these four walls. Slough's a big place, and when I'm finished with Slough there's Reading, Aldershot, Bracknell, you know, I've got Didcot, Yately, Winnersh, Taplow, you know?[58]

The point is that Slough is not a big place: it is drab and irrelevant. After having left Wernham Hogg to become a sales representative for a cleaning firm which specializes in tampons, he defines his identity through micro-celebrity and personal appearances in sleazy nightclubs. When he returns to his former workplace, which he does with embarrassing regularity, it is clear that the place has not altered. People leave, but the workplace is constant in its crushing uniformity. The polyester suits remain. Only the bodies that fill them change.

Slicing through this overwhelming conformity, *The Office* provides viewers with a final surprise, and gift. In the final few moments of the last episode, David Brent – the archetypal Boss from Hell – is redeemed, not by Finchy, Gareth or even Tim. His saviour is one of the three free consorts sent to him via a dating agency. Brent needed the introduction service in his desperate attempt to appear popular with 'the chicks' and find a date for the office Christmas party. Carol is intelligent, beautiful, funny and understanding of Brent. In short, she is his redeemer, transforming a small white man in an irrelevant job into a person with depth, consciousness and empathy. After all the (reflexive) sexism and racism of the programme, David Brent expresses pride in his meeting with Carol, describing her as intelligent, beautiful and sensual. Redemption is complete when David defends her from hyper-heterosexual abuse. When Finchy calls Carol 'a dog', David Brent does not snicker or laugh at the insult, as he has done in the 13 preceding episodes. Instead, he takes a breath, pauses and tells 'Chris' – rather than the matey label of 'Finchy' – to 'fuck off'.[59] He then walks away from the masculine circle of innuendo and sleaze.

The Office presents a visual, political history of the 2000s that few have talked about and fewer have written in prose. Petty hierarchies pepper the scripts, like our workplaces. As with the best comedies, *The Office* is punctuated by tragedy. Just as *The Goon Show* rewrote the Second World War and Monty Python reframed the swinging sixties, *The Office* attacks the blandness and mediocrity of Blair's Britain. Neither television nor work can provide the patch for masculine identity. Through *The Office*, a first view is offered beyond tropes of masculine crisis and towards negotiating and addressing more important social injustices. If David Brent can be saved by a stranger, an intelligent and beautiful woman, then indeed anything is possible. Suddenly, being on the telly is not as important anymore.

Pree-sen-na kul-cha

One of the great surprises in moving from Australian to British universities is the career goals expressed by students. Being accustomed to the aspirations of prospective journalists, policy gurus, earnest educators, film makers, photographers, librarians and musicians – along with the occasional desire to be captain of the Australian cricket team – one label/career too often spills from the lips of our British first years.

When asked what they wanted to 'be' or 'do' when they leave our campuses, the majority reply using a term that I – at first – did not understand. After their Media degree, they dream of becoming a 'pree-sen-na'. Translating Essex English into Australian English is always a challenge. One linguistic form flattens all sounds by removing the letter 'T' from the alphabet. Australian English clips and cuts consonants with such force that they shatter glass.

After decoding their phraseology, I realized my students want to be a 'presenter'. But I needed further clarification on the function of this role. What did this job description actually involve? Piecing together my students' definitions, a presenter requires (in no particular order for either men or women) big hair, breast implants, being gay, the ability to read an autocue and use a lot of eyeliner, smiling with artificially whitened teeth, crying, wearing designer clothing and revealing a great deal about their 'personality', including failed relationships, challenges with addiction and – most importantly – struggles with weight loss. If the 'pree-sen-na' had an exercise DVD to promote while struggling with sexual 'iss-ews', then the feedback loop is complete: pree-sen-na heaven.

This career description is a problem for those of us who teach in universities because no knowledge – or even skills beyond reading an autocue – is required to fulfill this career. A personality and luck are enough for success, or more precisely, fame. Documenting the micro-traumas of streaking mascara, over-tight trousers and crimes against shoe shopping can fill a talk show with the excitements of the banal. If Richard and Judy could not talk about their children or Fern Britton her weight loss, then how would air time be occupied? The self is sufficient. Identity is enough. A whole suite (sweet?) of 'celebrities' have an ear piece fused to a studio manager's mouth and brain. This wiring is important because someone needs to read more than a press release. These 'managers', 'researchers' or 'assistants' can surreptitiously suggest questions when the dialogue about children, cosmetic surgery and dieting staggers into nonsense.

Pree-sen-nas also have other conversational options, such as parroting innocuous linking statements like 'This is the moment of truth', 'Let's see what the judges say', 'See you after the break', and 'For full terms and conditions, please go to www-dot-bee-bee-see-dot-cow-dot-you-kay-forwardslash-phonevotingripoff'. That blank stare into the autocue, injecting emotion and … and … and … and … pauses to moments of pseudo-tension have put the light into light entertainment, but also assembled barriers for creating professional aspirations in the media.

Pree-sen-nas are deceiving our students. The great lie of celebrity culture is that, behind the frocks, hair and chat, there is a huge community of hard workers in media industries. The future for media, humanities and social science scholars is not constructing an operatic life based on the solitude and loneliness of queuing at Tesco on a Saturday morning. Part of their job will be reporting – not living – these micro-stories. They must operate under the stress of a deadline and summon a deep understanding of how to scan a huge amount of news material, pick an important thread, write copy, verify the copy and deliver it to a diverse range of media platforms.

I realized the scale of this expertise when visiting ITN. I saw postfordist news in action. ITN is responsible for the news broadcasts for ITV, Channel Four and Setanta Sports, but it is their broadband and mobile suite – labelled ITN On – that is most fascinating, creating made-for-mobile news and weather. The room is filled with young men and women in an open-plan office. It is busy, punctuated with multiple screens, telephones and chatter. Adjacent to the newsroom is an alcove containing a camera, autocue and chair. Mark Wood, the CEO of ITN, explained that journalists monitor the feed and footage supplied to all the ITN offices and services, select footage or follow an idea, write copy, feed it to the autocue and record it themselves. This multi-skilled and multi-skilling team are creatively and quickly assembling unique mobile content packages in their own studio. They then release their production to broadband and mobile customers as a video news bulletin. While some current affairs are covered, entertainment and sports news proliferate. The focus for all the ITN operations is to match content with platform and audience. For their mobile business, reporters must have a metaphoric hot desk adjacent to Amy Winehouse's rehab and Britney Spears' custody battle and/or hairdresser.

This ability to move a project from visual feed to idea, and from copy to broadcast, is outside the aspirations of university students' pree-sen-na kul-cha. Our responsibility as educators is to intervene and transform their expectations. Instead of being part of celebrity culture, they must gain the skills and knowledge to report on it. Tabloidization has damaged a generation of media students so that they embrace celebrity not ideas, and personality not argument. We need to (even temporarily) displace the 'me' from 'media'.

Julie Burchill, from the crucible of *The Face*, described the characteristic of 'modern experience' as 'you don't really exist until you see your name in print'.[1] She captures a Thatcherite meritocracy that closed mines but opened Body Shops, and reduced dissent while increasing consumerism. We are now following the trajectory of Burchill's maxim. Currently, our students do not even recognize that they may need to develop an ability in writing to become 'famous'. Instead they are satisfied with 'being themselves'. For Burchill, being famous was about creating an identity through print. In our digitized, compressed and accelerated age, fame only requires being seen on television.

You've got to have a good haircut: *Live Forever* and an end of spin

There is intensity to Liam Gallagher's levity. When the lead singer of Oasis was asked in the Brit Pop documentary *Live Forever*[1] about his androgynous appearance, he repeatedly demanded clarification of the word's meaning. When clearly not grasping the definitions being offered by the interviewers, he finally offered a knight's move answer to his questioner: the basis of his popularity was not 'a feminine side', but a good haircut.

British culture has been rich with doco/mocko/facto-fictional media programming since September 11. Besides *The Office*, Michael Winterbottom's *24 Hour Party People* darted around the simulacrum, playing with punk, acid house, time and narrative. The comedian Steve Coogan (re)created Tony Wilson, the legendary Manchester broadcaster and pop music 'guru', as an edgy amalgam of narrator, character, seer, entrepreneur and King Lear. Similarly Peter Kay, through extraordinary observational skills, has become a leader in comic ethnography. His *Mum Wants a Bungalow Tour*[2] created humour from recognizable situations in family life: the difficulty of finding a working pen when writing a telephone message, the grubby uncle lurking at weddings with ever-ready sleazy comments, and grandmothers obsessed with home security and funerals of people they hardly know. The cringe of recognition comedy is beyond humour: it transgresses the boundaries of self and society, identification and identity. As an explanation for our investment in both the banal and the image, such comedies provide a profound record of our changing relationship between work, family and identity.

Such programmes provide a framework to understand *Live Forever*, the documentary of Brit Pop as told by its survivors. The ghost-like image of a young Tony Blair, before being weighed down by a fruitless search for weapons of mass destruction and the negotiation of a coalition with a willing neo-conservative, remains the haunting image of the film. Like John Harris' *The Last Party*,[3] the film shows the awkward, ambiguous and – in the end – unsuccessful alignment of pop and politics. Tony Blair was never going to be as interested in his hair as Liam Gallagher, and the Prime Minister does know the meaning of androgynous without flicking through *Sexuality for Dummies*. The point made in the documentary, which offers a sharp jolt within the political rumblings of our present, is that the Brit Pop lads attacked and responded to the Americanization of Britain through the 1980s and 1990s. Cool Britannia was as much about claiming cultural space and separation from the United States as offering 'original' music or fashion. With American grammar currently lashing out to punctuate popular culture beyond Canada and South America and throughout the world, the anger of Jarvis Cocker and the Gallagher brothers has found a new resonance and audience.

The documentary is based on interviews with 'above the title' stars of Brit Pop, including not only Liam Gallagher but also his brilliant, but pharmaceutically challenged, brother Noel, bitter and twisted Damon Albarn and coolly distant Jarvis Cocker. Jon Savage, the outstanding style journalist and cultural commentator, provides the spine of the story. Selected news footage, commercials and tacky television splice the narrative, alongside the political destructions and successes of Margaret Thatcher, John Major and Tony Blair. Most usefully, *Live Forever* probes the relationship between Brit Pop and lad culture. The diverse social spaces of Manchester, Colchester and Bristol are evocatively unearthed. 3D from Massive Attack conducted his interview from the passenger seat of a car cruising late-night Bristol. Dub always sounds much better in the dark. Damon Albarn stroked a ukulele in a London pub. Jarvis Cocker reflected upon the past, while propped on a single bed, in a small bed-sit of an upper storey flat. Noel Gallagher held court in a velvet throne-like chair, confirming his status as Brit Pop's king and Tony Blair's favoured consort in spin. Such crafted and intentional use of filmic address increases the irony around Noel Gallagher's critique of the inauthenticity of *Pop Idol* and music in the 2000s. He does not recognize his role in the midst of his own critique. *Live Forever* shows that Brit Pop was preened, spun and spruiked by the music press and news services, and used by Tony Blair. John Dower described the film as 'a savage education in Real Politik'.[4] It is also a tale told by anoraked singers who were fooled by their suited 'representatives'. Innovative menswear was not enough to build a political movement.

The documentary is important for those of us who work in media because it demonstrates how the careful editing of interviews with found footage can build a politically devastating narrative. Further, the evocative use of music creates a palette of popular memory better than any conventional flashback montage. Beyond its structure, *Live Forever* offers a political warning. New Labour and 'new' Brit Pop both dueled with identity. Both lost direction, commitment and popularity. Through the 1980s, the mantle of Greatness was lost from

Britain. By the 1990s, the outsiders returned to visibility, with Massive Attack offering pauses and pulses, the Gallagher brothers spitting expletives and Jarvis Cocker shaking up masculinity and class. It was a temporary energizing of the body politic. Only a few years later, the *Pop Idol* format favoured cover songs, conventional body shapes and rigid commentary for corporeal and fashion dissenters. With pretty and bland pop as the default position for conservative eras, it will be some time before we assess if Brit Pop changed, critiqued or reinforced music, celebrity and politics. *Live Forever* offers an entrée for the commencement of that discussion.

Marginality and deviance are necessary to create popular culture. Brit Pop, in its angry dry retch at 'the system', used popular culture to channel despair and anger into the chasm between aspirations and actuality. Irvine Welsh – while discussing wider political and social movements – also pinpointed the trajectory of Brit Pop as 'you're either right outside society or you're exploited'.[5] Those 'outside' the system, while being materially disadvantaged, actually have the privilege of thinking critically about their surroundings. In the semiotic crunch between *The Office* and *Live Forever*, it is yet to be seen if 'Wonderwall' will outlive 'Handbags and Gladrags'.

Beyond the seducer

Anne Bancroft's death in June 2005 permitted a suite of male baby boomer film critics to nostalgically trot out their adolescent fantasies of older women. They returned to a time – before the reality of their own sagging visage – when satisfying an experienced lover was a greater challenge for the young and eager than arousing a woman with an age below room temperature. In that time capsule of 1967, the sensual Mrs Robinson became the archetype of the demanding and predatory women, the seducer. She was erotic and thrilling.

But Bancroft was much more than a character in a proto-boomer sexcapade. Born in the Bronx in 1931 and trained at the Actors Studio, the role for which she won an Academy Award was as Annie Sullivan, teacher of Helen Keller in *The Miracle Worker*. Her performance captured the epitome of great teaching, balancing empathy with respect. This film confirmed a physical range beyond an action hero and an emotional depth beyond *The Bold and the Beautiful*. It was the absence in the remembering of Bancroft's career that has been most disturbing. *84 Charing Cross Road*, the film for which Bancroft won a BAFTA Best Actress Award, has been left out of her lists of achievements. Released in 1987 and based on a book by Helene Hanff, the narrative tracked the tale of a 20-year correspondence between a rare book dealer and a collector.

This bare narrative captures little of the complexity and subtlety in the film. It is significant because both the main actors are now synonymous with other roles: Anne Bancroft is Mrs Robinson and Anthony Hopkins is Hannibal Lector. Yet dipping into their hidden and shared cinematic history reveals great rewards. Certainly the film is wordy, intelligent and subtle, a relic from an age where intimacy was not reliant on a quick snog before dinner. The cultural reference points are literary, not punched through a backbeat. Bancroft had the scope and experience to capture wit, intelligence and humour.

I admire popular culture that is anchored to the cultural forms it replaces. *84 Charing Cross Road* captures a love for books and pushes it through visual media. Letter writing is uncinematic in the extreme, encouraging excessive voiceover, chronological jumps and a dearth of dialogue. But with a focus on antique books, current events are washed by a more undulating and gentle historical stream. The breadth and scale of the Hanff library, from which her references spring, is extraordinary. I understand bibliomania. It is a comfort to dialogue with the words of the dead, so that they may live in the present. Both the book and film of *84 Charing Cross Road* are obsessive in their validation of reading, writing and thinking. Hanff and Doel read together for 20 years, although they never meet. Their relationship confirms that, when sharing ideas, we also share lives.

Books and bookshops construct frames for thinking pop. Quirky and distinctive comedies have their origins in such spaces. *The Book Group* and *Black Books* are fine examples of how black ink on a parched page can commence drunken televisual discussions about inadequate sex lives, dull work and inelegant words. *84 Charing Cross Road* always raises the issue of intimacy. The desire for contemplation and transcendence, to move beyond the self and experience, is part of the joy of reading. Bancroft delivered one of my favourite lines in film: 'I never can get interested in things that didn't happen to people who never lived.' When I first watched this film in the late 1980s, it was this statement that propelled me into a history degree, not a literature major. So much of my own writing in popular culture and history can be sourced from this single statement. A memory of Bancroft after her death returned this legacy to me. In a time of email, online chatting and text messaging, the 20-year correspondence between a collector and a dealer, separated by religion, nations and experience, is intimate and evocative. It was Bancroft who captured the obsessive New Yorker's desire for English – not American – literature and the sharpness of her brash wit in comparison to the dark desperation of post-war Britain.

The tragedy is that if lovers of the film were to go to the street mentioned in the title, very few bookshops remain. High rents saw the end of Waterstones and Silver Moon, a specialist store featuring works by and for women. While Foyles, Murder One and Al-Hoda remain in the street, the ultimate sadness is that 84 Charing Cross Road no longer sells books at all. The building has transformed into a pub. This touristic disappointment parallels that of Hanff. When she was finally in a position to visit the United Kingdom, the bookshop had already closed.

Through the relentless redundancy of popular culture, we are lucky to be remembered for one role, image or idea. Anne Bancroft has become Mrs Robinson. Near the end of her life, she was exasperated by the fickle nature of this popular cultural memory. In a 2003 interview, she confirmed her surprise that 'with all my work, and some of it is very, very good ... We're talking about Mrs Robinson. I understand the world. I'm just a little dismayed that people aren't beyond it yet.'[1] Indeed, sex has an insistent predictability to it, fuelled by desires unmet by the lunchroom, treadmill or shopping centre. Bancroft's wish to move beyond seduction and the supposed controversy of an older woman shagging a younger man is not yet matched by the journalists who wrote her obituaries.

My hope is that her death is the trigger, not for iPod dipping into Simon and Garfunkel's *Greatest Hits*, but to remember her wider filmic catalogue. *84 Charing Cross Road* is a subtle and important presentation of men, women, intimacy and ideas. The notion that two adults fall in love with words, literature and then each other even though they never touch, is beyond the grasp of the tabloid grab and grope. Here's to you, Ms Bancroft. You captured the complexity of women on film, and the limits of seduction.

I don't believe you. You're a liar

There is a third person in my marriage. His name is Bob Dylan. My husband and I share a love and commitment not only for each other but also for the spectrum of popular culture. Actually, The Pet Shop Boys got us together. But it was always Bob that created tension. This strange man of American culture seemed trapped in an endless 1970s of daggy fashion and shaggy hair. The harmonica wire framing his face looked like a dental brace that had slipped. His voice was out of tune, he stretched vowels over two continents and his political ambivalence and changeability was a tepid leftover and extravagance from a kinder, gentler time. While I banned Bob from the lounge room stereo, every so often I would catch a sonic bleeding from my husband's headphones. He was listening to 'Like a Rolling Stone'. Again. I arrived home from work. As I pulled into the garage, I would hear 'Don't Think Twice, It's Alright' being ripped off the CD player. Again. I didn't mention it. Bob always seemed to be with us.

In 2006, I realized it was me – not Bob or the head-phoned husband – who has the problem. Ironically, it was a film that taught me to revalue and reinterpret Bob, his music and his era. It was only a matter of time before the legendary director Martin Scorsese again returned to documentaries and Dylan. The great chronicler of American music history, his *The Last Waltz*, featuring the final concert of The Band, had Bob as a bit-player in a masterful review of American roots music. Similarly, Scorsese's *The Blues* series shifted our sonic landscape and reshaped and reclaimed archival footage of the early bluesmen. From being the assistant editor on the Woodstock film in 1970, 35 years later *No Direction Home* completed the journey. It is a three-hour, 29-minute documentary that is gripping, horrifying and very funny. Original interviews are featured, including Dylan's review of his own life as told to manager Jeff Rosen. Joan Baez is her usual effervescent and brilliant self. Forty years later, she is still angry at Bob – for either leaving her or not sharing her politics. Passion and principles were entangled and confused. Remember it was the 1960s, man.

Scorsese and Dylan never met to make this documentary.[1] Seemingly, they share enough history to make a conversation irrelevant. They understand New York. They understand the 1960s. They understand the blues. They share a cultural language. That dialogue has created great film making. Both are outsiders – abrasive and difficult – who discover alternative paths through the most conventional subjects. Scorsese was given freedom with the documentary, but with a precise limitation.

> The only rule I was given was that we could do Dylan up until 1966 when he had the motorcycle crash, and it ends with the interesting question of whether the artist should continue to serve society as a political figure.[2]

It is the found footage sourced from the singer's own archive of an impossibly young – and actually handsome – Dylan from 1962 until 1966 that is the gift of the documentary.[3] This journey through time is also a movement through space, from Minnesota to New York. Surrounded by old, rude and profoundly ignorant journalists, Bob handled so much stupidity by the age of 25 that he even foreshadowed his own Buddy Holly-like exit strategy. The most cringing moment of the documentary is when an incompetent and – frankly – embarrassing British photographer asked Bob to 'just suck on your glasses' for a picture. I am glad to report that Dylan did not comply. Instead, he tried to force the arm of his glasses into the photographer's mouth. These press conferences featured dreadful journalists asking dumb questions. While we are accustomed to such patter through the endless stream of talk shows and celebrity interviews, *No Direction Home* is different because Dylan answers back. If he thinks the question is ridiculous, he gives a ridiculous answer. He asks for precise definitions of the journalists' terms, which they cannot provide. My favourite rejoinder is his angry voice howling 'you've got a lot of nerve asking me that'. When watching Dylan handle a press conference, we see what sound bite solutions have done to the standard of debate and argument in our bland, blind age.

Dylan, in describing his first great musical model and mentor Woody Guthrie, realized that 'you could listen to his songs and actually learn how to live'. Bob has held a similar role. He is defiant, uncomfortable and avoids all categorization. He changes his mind and views at a whim, seemingly to stop the precise pigeon-holing of his music, life or views. Dylan does not live the label or role that others have written for him. He is a 'cultural magpie'.[4] The album released after *No Direction Home*, which rejuvenated skiffle and shuffle rhythms, was titled *Modern Times*. In deploying instruments and ideas from the 1930s and 1940s, it is difficult to ascertain if the title is ironic or profoundly historically accurate, continuing Dylan's dialogue with the long project of modernity and the restitching of tradition.

Popular culture – when fresh – is riveting and revelatory. Bob Dylan – somehow – became part of popular culture and changed popular culture. Recognizing this influence, Scorsese did something clever and important. He stopped the documentary at 1966 with the footage of the famous concert at the Free Trade

Hall in Manchester where a distraught folkie – when semiotically electrocuted by a plugged-in Dylan – yelled 'Judas'. The witty reply – 'I don't believe you. You're a liar' – was fully audible to the audience. He then turned to the band and spat a forthright and punchy instruction about the volume of the next song. A heart-starting snare drum erupted from the stage, commencing 'Like a Rolling Stone'. So ends the Scorsese documentary. We as viewers in a very different time must ask why a fine songwriter, who happened to plug his guitar into an amplifier, was booed. If this was the most dreadful – Judas-like – action in these people's lives, then they needed to get out of the Newport Festival and think more about the Vietnam War. Dylan was the figure of cultural displacement in the mid-1960s. It is easy to attack a minstrelling folkie who wanted to get loud, angry and mysterious. It is more difficult to ask why all the folk music in the world allowed a dense and dark injustice to be perpetuated in South-East Asia. When John Lennon made his 'bigger than Jesus' comment, a similar outrage ensued. These men were given too much power, too much influence and too much authority. They *were* bigger than Jesus, but they did not give their fans an opportunity to crucify, mythologize and worship. Instead, they survived, changed, attacked and critiqued their earlier selves. For Lennon the Beatle and Dylan the folkie, there was never going to be a happy or clean ending.

The genre of rock documentary has shadowed rock with aloof respect. Pennebaker's *Dont Look Back*, Albert and David Maysles' *Gimme Shelter* and Scorsese's *The Last Waltz* changed not only rock, but also film making. The convergence of sound and vision was productive and disturbing. *The Last Waltz* was not a straight transmission of a concert, but offered a cinematic history of America. Scorsese started the film with the encore. He sculpted the vision to make it more than a concert, while remaining a concert. Not surprisingly, Scorsese searched for a hook to *No Direction Home*. It is not a biopic. Instead one song – 'Like a Rolling Stone' – becomes the pivot. Everything mentioned – Dylan, folk music, politics and even American history – juts from this track. Such a knight's move selection of an editing imperative ensures that the 'Judas' moment resonates with an intensity only matched by Mickey Jones' pounded opening to the song on his kit.

This documentary has grandeur to it, and there is a justification for Scorsese's attention. Colby Bogie described it as 'probably the most important story in all of American pop music, and possibly the most important in all of American pop culture'.[5] Forty years after the events captured in the documentary, the lesson that both Scorsese and Dylan offer is an affirmation of the right to change, the right to challenge and the right to be different. The best popular culture is created when there is a chance that it may be unpopular. As the young Dylan said to Robbie Robertson, 'It's hard to get in tune when they're booing.' The notion that a documentary offering such an ideology features an Apple logo and a Starbucks tie-in[6] adds complexity to the narrative. The co-production deal was extraordinary. Broadcast rights were presold to the BBC and NHK. Paramount gained the rights to publish the DVD and sell the documentary in 'foreign' markets. Vulcan Productions holds the secondary cable rights. Sony released the soundtrack and Simon & Schuster published the 'scrapbook', including photographs, memorabilia and a CD. Starbucks agreed to sell the CD. Apple was the corporate underwriter.[7] Perhaps such corporate contradictions provide the most effective framework to understand what happened to America after Dylan plugged in. There is something in Scorsese's filmic darkness – marinating *Mean Streets* and *GoodFellas* – that works well choreographing Dylan's face as the surface on which the narrative of corporatization is written. The disintegration of his life appeared on his face in the 1960s and his voice through the subsequent four decades.

A recurring motif of *Thinking Popular Culture* is that we demand too much of our most talented popular cultural icons. Through the documentary, we see a 25-year-old Dylan looking cadavar-jaded. He could have died in that motorcycle accident in 1966 and his fame and talent would be preserved. It would have been a simpler and easier story, and more palatable. As David Knowles realized:

> American popular culture operates within the premises of a tragic contradiction. As a consuming public we demand that our cultural figures embody our feelings, our hopes, our fears, our desires, while at the same time living as their unique creative voice.[8]

Knowles has captured the 'Oprah effect' – the desire to celebrate difference while comfortably knowing that 'they' are really like 'us'. That was the problem for Dylan: he was simply too different. He did not die when the Big Bopper called him home. That he lived and continued to produce fascinating music, with the vocal chords tangled up in blue, is simply a bonus. If a writer, designer, musician or film maker produces one sentence, motif, song or image that changes our world, then that is enough. It is a gift to cherish and remember. Those of us who write (about) pop must avoid 'the Shakespearization of Bob Dylan'.[9] He is part of pop, and transformed pop. That is sufficient.

Dylan changed music, politics, masculinity and fashion between 1962 and 1966. After that time, and the motorcycle accident was merely a synergetic narrative pivot, he stopped being 'Bob Dylan' and would only sample his pop past.[10] To expect such great minds and talents to continue to produce innovation after innovation, revelation after revelation, is unrealistic. It also means that we mortgage our past and present for a cultural future that will never happen.

Bob taught me that. He also taught me that where we start is not our destiny. At his most poetic and ambiguous he confirms that 'I was born very far from where I was supposed to be born, so I'm on my way home'.[11] So are we all. To paraphrase two other volatile critics who also changed culture, we make our own history, but not of our choosing. The choice comes in selecting the sound track for the journey. And – in the end – Bob is a good guide: he knows the direction home.

Bad Wolf

Childhood memories of popular culture trigger the most vivid emotional landscapes. I recall my much bigger big brother introducing me to the world of science fiction; a vista populated by *Outer Limits* aliens, *Twilight Zone* time shifting, *Star Trek* phasers and *Blake 7* bad humour. One programme was always more meaningful than the rest. I remember cowering behind my brother – concurrently frightened, curious and disturbed – watching a man in a flamboyant scarf and his shrieking companions battle cybermen, the Master and pepper pot daleks.

Dr Who fandom has been the metaphoric embarrassing frock in my popular cultural closet. I own the books, the novels, the scarf, the videos, the DVDs and – quite magnificently – 20 miniature daleks. I saw a life-size one in London a few years ago and had to be physically restrained from buying it and taking my chances with excess luggage and Australian customs. I still regret not attempting negotiating it through the authorities. It would have been a great object to remove from the carousel at Perth airport and wheel to the car park.

This unfashionable fandom has created odd and often inappropriate connections with the people I meet. For example, I once had my house burgled. Nothing important was stolen: a cheap video recorder and some compact discs were the only losses. When the policeman arrived to record the details of the crime, he was not terribly interested in me, my house or the video. Instead, he was drawn to the daleks on the shelves and tables. There was something quite disconcerting about seeing an adult male, let alone a policeman, on his hands and knees pushing daleks across my lounge room, appearing to wage a pseudo-invasion of Earth. When I finally extricated him from my plastic pepper pots, he could only say, 'Thank god they only took the video. They could have taken the daleks.'

I understand how he feels. October 2005 saw the release of the DVDs featuring the ninth Doctor, Christopher Eccleston. With this casting, we knew the rebirth of the character was going to be bigger than the simple rebooting of a children's series. Through his extraordinary performances in *Shallow Grave*, *Our Friends in the North*, *Cracker*'s DCI Bilborough and *The Second Coming*, he has the acting range and ability to capture the loneliness, sadness and darkness of the last timelord. He is known for 'his anguished portraits of men in conflict'.[1]

Clad in a battered leather jacket, this Doctor 'doesn't do domestic'.[2] He also remade the Doctor for the knowing Generation X audience. Eccleston was the first Doctor born after the start of the first series and is a believer in television: 'I've always looked for things that don't tie up neatly at the end. TV is basically an art form, but we've lost that ambition.'[3] From such a commitment to the difficult and the excellent, it is no surprise that Eccleston was drawn to the talent and innovation of Russell T. Davies, his words and work.

The other great gift of the show was Davies fulfilling the role as the new scriptwriter. A former fan, he is one of the great writers and enthusiasts of television.

> I remembered when I was a kid. When it was new. All of us would gather round the telly for Doctor Who, all the kids in class, boys and girls, and the teachers and your mum and dad and your nan and people on the bus. Everyone watched it. Everyone loved it. But then they grew up and moved on, and maybe they got a little bit embarrassed about it all. And they forgot. They just forgot. All we had to do to the concept was wake it up, to imagine it again, with all the wit and bravery they'd first had, all the way back in 1963.[4]

He was successful. The fashionable people were suddenly staying home on Saturday nights to watch how Davies had injected imagination and creativity into this old programme. People who would never have been seen dead laughing with Tom Baker's Doctor or screaming with (or at – depending on your perspective) Colin Baker's Doctor, suddenly became born-again Whovians. For those who missed these remarkable 12 Ecclestone episodes or were more enthused by David Tennant's optimistic and energetic Doctor, it is possible to run a science fiction convention for one and play all the DVDs in a day. It is worth the time and effort. This is great television. This is thinking popular culture. No matter who else plays the Doctor or writes the scripts, this season of rebirth will be remembered as the most intelligent, risky and challenging. The reason Eccleston was drawn to the programme was because of the script's intelligence.

> I like a writer as intelligent and rigorous as Russell writing for children, because I think if you can get them young with good stuff as they get older they demand good stuff from their television.[5]

While this ambition was important, everything was working against the new Doctor. It had been 15 years since the series was cancelled. Yet the music (dumb dumb dumb – dumb dumb dumb – dumb dumb dumb – dumb dumb dumb – dumb dumb dumb – dumb dumb dumb – whooo eeeee whooo), the enemies and shoddy special efforts were all landmarks in popular culture. These rose-coloured ray bans of childhood nostalgia did not bode well for the new series. Nothing can compete with childhood myths of fear and fascination.

Then – remarkably – the new series and the new Doctor re-imaged science fiction. He was northern, the dialogue was whippet-fast, quirky and queer, and Eccleston was light, comedic and Cary Grant-charming. He had created a pop miracle: the daggy Doctor became sexy. After living through 40 years, 679 thirty-minute episodes, 15 forty five-minute episodes and a truly dire 90-minute television movie, *Doctor Who* was finally fashionable. It was also critically successful. At the BAFTAs, the programme won best drama series and the audience-voted Pioneer Award. Even more importantly, Russell T. Davies won the Dennis Potter Award for Outstanding Writing for Television.

It was the combination of Eccleston's acting and Davies' writing that remade a memory into even better than the real thing.[6] Perhaps the hardest scriptwriting feat is to refresh old characters with style and make the clunky innovations of the 1960s look contemporary. Through all the talk of creative industries and intellectual capital, Davies has imagination to burn. Best known for *Queer as Folk*, his collaboration with Eccleston was predated by *The Second Coming*, a riveting and disturbing televisual drama where the son of God not only arrived back on Earth, but in Manchester. Miracles were performed at Maine Road, which is more difficult than it would be in any normal football stadium considering the endless cycle of disappointments from Manchester City FC.

This actor and writer were going to 'do' the Doctor with a difference. As always with Davies, he attacks television through television. 'Bad Wolf', the second to last episode of this crucial season, offered sharper commentary on reality television than five years of cultural studies courses have managed. Being broadcast after the conclusion of *The Office*, they were able to enact an even more cutting critique of the genre. Dropping the Doctor into the *Big Brother* house was a ruthless blading of mediocre television programming. Davies created a macabre twist to the conventional tale: instead of being expelled from these shows into a life of micro-celebrity, people were voted off and killed. The prize was to live. Amid such brutality, the Doctor diagnosed the problems of Earth's future, and our present: 'Half the population's too fat. Half the population's too thin and the rest of you just watch television.'

Then after these 12 episodes of speed, energy and laughter, it was over. What an ending they gave us. In 'Parting of the Ways', the war of fundamentalisms that punctuates the 2000s also gutted our future. The daleks survived genocides and holocausts by discovering religion.

The Doctor: You created an army of Daleks. Out of the dead.

Rose: But that makes them … half human.

Emperor Dalek: Those words are blasphemy! …

The Doctor: Since when did the Daleks have a concept of blasphemy?

Emperor Dalek: Since I led them from the wilderness. I am far more than Emperor. I reached into the dirt and made new life. I am the God of all Daleks.

Dalek #1: Worship him!

Dalek #2: Worship him!

The Doctor: They're insane.[7]

Extermination was no longer enough. They quashed all threats of difference with cries of blasphemy. The Doctor was the heathen to be feared and killed.

The most evocative and devastating moment at the end of this new *Doctor Who* did not come from the title character, but his companion, the weeping Rose. On returning to her home – and our time – she was horrified at the pointlessness of life, work, tasteless food and a quiet night in front of the telly. From the bud of this old science fiction show made new, a stark indictment and judgment ruptured our easy acceptance of mediocrity, boredom and stupidity. In remembering the adventure, the challenge and the good fights in the TARDIS, Rose said – on behalf of so many of us – that:

> It was a better life. I don't mean all the travelling and seeing aliens and spaceships and things, that doesn't matter. The Doctor showed me a better way of living your life. You saw him, he showed you too. That you don't just give up. You don't just let things happen. You make a stand. You say no. You have the guts to do the right thing, when everyone else runs away.[8]

Ponder what we have blindingly and blandly accepted in the last decade: detention centres, asylum seekers, war without justification and exhausted sympathy at the horrific waves of tragedy from a tsunami, earthquakes and cyclones. There were so many moments where we should have screamed, raged, scratched, punched, argued, fought, or just said no. Instead we got another glass of wine, immersed ourselves with the fascinations of frittata and feta cheese, and tittered endlessly about celebrities rather than debating about how – precisely – we could ever win a war against fundamentalism with another set of fundamentalisms.

Doctor Who was formed on the most basic of ideas: develop an interesting character and move them through space and time. From this simple premise, the programme has survived the changes of digitization, commodification, colonialism and masculinity. But he always fought the good fight, and was always tortured about the unpredicted consequences of his actions. The Doctor was a talker. He was a traveller. He was also a learner and moved to act by the differences he met.

28.06.42.12

The strange, the gothic, the passionate and the complex: these are the silage of creativity rarely captured within the shuttered enclosures of our cultural life. Genres exist so that critical thought is unnecessary when piecing together ebbs, energies, excesses and excretions. Categories are safe. They create expectations and make us feel like we understand the world. If we confront the caustic light of difference, hybridity and liminality, then our identity bearings corrode. Watching *Donnie Darko* pulls a rip cord into the mental anguish and mediocrity of daily existence.

There are few films that move mind furniture and renovate consciousness. *Blue Velvet, Jubilee, Memento, Alexandra's Project* and *Seven* are a few examples. *Donnie Darko* fits snugly in this list. These films confirm that the most vigorous blading of conservatism comes from cutting up linear time, not gliding effortlessly through space. By (dys)functioning in a Tangent Universe – guided by Roberta Sparrow/Grandma Death – Donnie Darko has agency and is able to repair the patches in the cosmic clock.

It is easy to label an odd and disturbing film a cult classic. This branding is a way to discredit diversity and marginalize critically edged creativity. *Donnie Darko* is more than cult. It is popular culture. Riveting and disturbing, it requires multiple rescreenings, long walks pondering the ending, and a staunch commitment that misunderstanding and confusion add grit, colour and compulsion to our filmic experiences.

Donnie Darko was released in 2001, but is set in October 1988. Directed by Richard Kelly and starring Jake Gyllenhaal, it works between teen flick, satire, horror and science fiction. That the most compassionate character in the film is a medicated schizophrenic who cannot distinguish between high school and a hallucinogenic six-foot rabbit demonstrates the scale to which this hypnotic vision spills beyond concise delineations of real life. *Donnie Darko* changed forever the way I see mirrors, rabbits and old women with shock-white hair.

I always return to *Donnie Darko* each October. The director's cut DVD was released in October 2004, in time for another US presidential election. Odd translations between the filmic and political context were waged. Dukakis was played by Kerry. Bush the elder was replaced by Bush the younger. The best popular culture is able to do this, to move through time and soak up new marinades and remake itself. This film is more poignant and horrifying now than the first time I saw it. That initial viewing was in a trendy cinema, in a trendy suburb with too many coffee shops and not enough primary schools. Its magnetism, pulling between horror, melancholy and banality, meant that I was in shock for much of this initial viewing, and sat in my seat after the ending – too upset to cry, too confused to think straight. The violence and arbitrary power of the establishment was suffocating, medicating the different and isolating the dangerous. There was no rescue for the brave Donnie. His destiny was a deadline, not a timeline.

The music of the film is worth comment on its own. In the year the film was set – 1988 – I was 19 years old. *Donnie Darko* replays this Generation X soundtrack. The music is so cleverly selected that it accurately recaptures the tracks of the time – Tears for Fears, The Church, Echo and the Bunnymen and – extraordinarily – Joy Division. Yet these melodies, harmonies and rhythms have been carried forward on the filmic journey, offering consolation and memories of a time when choosing to wear one or both fingerless gloves was the crucial decision of the day. After watching this great film, it is impossible to think of Echo and the Bunnymen's 'The Killing Moon' without replaying the opening scenes. The remaking of 'Mad World' is a rare and great cover song in *American Idol* times. To celebrate *Donnie Darko* October, I played Tears for Fears' original version to start a first year education lecture. One of my young female students ran to the front of the room and shrieked, 'How dare someone redo this song'. Oh, the folly of youth. Having actually survived the 1980s, we Grandma Deaths move through life with a secret smile. I knew if I lived long enough – and kept returning to that post box – Duran Duran would get back together.

While the music is cyclical, poignant and fresh, *Donnie Darko* will always be about something more: the bunny. The iconography of the film circles around Frank, the punked-up, damaged rabbit who reminds me of a few ex-boyfriends. He is disturbed, provocative and – like Tiresias – blind. As the guide through a tangential universe, a blind seer is always best. Guided by Frank, the pop cultural clock does not reveal predictably, trackable hands of time. The analogue dial, or – even worse – the rigidly digital snap of change, does not convey the warm waves of memory that wash our minds. Our past selves live with us, keeping us company through the dark nights of aloneness, despair and surrender. The greatest challenge of life is to live with less and loss. Like Donnie Darko's journey, there is a peace in accepting our limitations and acknowledging defeats – rather than victories – with dignity, integrity and respect.

Donnie returned to the ides of October to die so that others could live. It is always easier to show courage by accident, to behave well when we did not have time to change our minds. Donnie's courage is mesmerizing in its inevitability.

He looped time and knew what was coming. His death signalled survival, but not for him. In our daily lives – doing the dishes, answering endless emails and remembering to telephone our mother – we rarely have the gothic grandeur of Donnie Darko's life. But every October, I celebrate a popular cultural resurrection that reminds us of time, death and responsibility. Every 2 October, I think about time differently. I know that in 28 days, 6 hours, 42 minutes and 12 seconds, change can happen.

Donnie Darko October reminds us to count the seconds and live life with deliberation, consciousness and agency. Memories matter. They outlive us. If we are lucky, then these moments in time return to illuminate the paths taken and the alternatives denied. Grandma Death whispers to Donnie that 'every living creature dies alone'. The companionship comes through the living.

Life, death and disco

Images flit through the television screen of our minds. An impossibly charismatic Freddy Mercury leading a queer football chant of 'We will rock you'. An implausibly nervous Paul McCartney performing 'Let it Be' after a decade away from the stage. David Bowie, dressed in a smart blue suit that seemed too tight, but was completely appropriate for his sharp performance. There was Midge Ure's grey ghost long coat, flapping through 'Vienna', and the riveting Bob Geldof – arm raised – screaming that the lesson today was how to die. Then Bono and his mullet pulled a girl from the crowd and gently danced through the Edge's screeching guitar.

None of these sepia visions are punctuated by Ethiopian poverty. Charity is like that. It is always more about the giver than the receiver. While the giving of money alleviates individual guilt, it does not create structural change. It is comforting to think that one person can change the world. It lets governments off the hook and deflects us from the scale and scope of global injustice.

We don't want your money – we want you

Nearly a quarter of a century ago – 13 July 1985 – Live Aid made young people feel like they were part of something bigger and better. I was 15 at the time, and it remains one of the great moments of my life.[1] Only in retrospect do we realize that we were karaoke singers to another generation's culture. Queen, David Bowie, The Who, Status Quo and Paul McCartney brought forward 1960s beat groups and 1970s glam rock into the 1980s. It was important to remember who was not present at the concert. Billy Bragg, The Smiths and The Pet Shop Boys, three of the most innovative and politically active acts of their day, did not perform. Dance music was the great unmentionable genre at Live Aid. Madonna was buried in an afternoon performance in Philadelphia. This was a rock concert.

Live Aid was filled with redundant music, but it was nostalgia with a purpose. Britain in 1985 was surviving a civil war through the miner's strike. Significantly, the old working class who had rebelled and lost against Margaret Thatcher was simply cut away from the picture. Paul McCartney reminded us of a simpler, better time when the north produced beat groups not picket lines and rock was fun and quirky, not riddled with class-based rage and stories of disenfranchisement, dispossession and unemployment.

Because this charity was not connected with deeper and wider consciousness, the awareness of Africa dipped after Live Aid. The genocidal deaths in Rwanda seemed expendable as a tide of other global events entered popular consciousness, like the fall of the Berlin Wall in 1989 and the remapping of Europe. The World Wide Web, mobile phones and iPods surpassed the revolutions in compact discs and walkmans. Acid house and techno transformed rhythm. Kurt Cobain's death transformed youth culture.

Twenty years passed. We Generation Xers still held that memory of Live Aid, the buoyant hope that popular music could change the world, even when the evidence weathered that dream. Freddy Mercury died the death that dare not speak its name. The Fairy Princess of the British Empire died with her lover in the back of a black Mercedes. Paula Yates, ever the help-mate of Geldof, found new love, lost it, and collapsed with the tragedy of that loss. The Iron Lady was removed from office by her own party. Her Iron Man, Ronald Reagan, passed on to the cowboy movie in the sky. In their place were men, inappropriately accorded the title of leader, who wanted to be other people. One wanted to be Winston Churchill. The other wanted to be his father. Britain is attempting to live on thin air, which is appropriate considering that the working class is no longer required by the clean and green Labour Party.

From charity to justice

In such a time, Live 8 seemed appropriate. Money was not the issue. In the hyped-up, cashed-up, text messaging credit card economy, asking people to consume less and give more is about as likely as asking the Easter Bunny to dinner for Christmas. Consciousness of inequality would have to suffice. In our displacement economy of debt and dysfunction, we now have a fully functional displacement culture. Instead of contributing to charity, we now contribute guilt to eight men who have been given (by us) too much power and significance.

Live 8 showed that politics has morphed. Live Earth would only perpetuate this transformation. There has been a movement from philanthropy and charity to consciousness and awareness. At first glance, it appeared that music had not changed between Live Aid and Live 8. But book-ended by the old rock acts – Paul McCartney, U2, The Who and Pink Floyd – there were surprises and new edgy pop that jutted through the wrinkles. Once more, the Philadelphia concert was a disappointment. Unlike 20 years ago, there were some remarkable American performances. Fascinatingly, none of them performed in America.

The Scissor Sisters put the party back into politics at Hyde Park. Green Day howled their rage in Berlin, the stage of thrash. 'American Idiot' became the unofficial anthem for European anger at the state of the world. Just as the miner's strike was not mentioned in 1985, so was the Iraq War the great silence at the later musical banquet. In fact, leaders of the demonstration on Edinburgh urged protesters to stay 'on message' and, like Basil Fawlty, 'don't mention the war'. There must be no critique of capitalism.[2] So the goal was to make poverty history, yet provide not cause, context or reasons for its existence. In other words, to make poverty history, we have to forget that history makes poverty. It was almost as if Bono and Geldof invented the anti-poverty movement, rather than Tom Paine in England and Antoine-Nicolas de Condorcet in France. These great visionaries disconnected poverty from divine retribution, and made it a man-made inequality, with man-made solutions. This realization was made at the end of the eighteenth century, and it required a dense understanding of politics and context.[3] Bono and Geldof got rid of this dignified history of protest. It is history with the history left out. Live 8 was like that. The past of pop was summoned without explanation. It was like a zombie movie, but without the graveyard scene.

The long walk

Some of the 1980s still lived. Duran Duran looked like guest stars from Miami Vice when performing in Rome. Madonna, white and like a virgin, outdiva-ed Mariah Carey. Poor Mariah appeared to be wearing an overstuffed football as a dress and the silliest stilettos in show business. In a scrag fight with Madonna, it is always important to wear sensible shoes.

Through the divas and bitchiness, there were passionate moments that I cherish. Without a doubt the emotional highlight was The Pet Shop Boys' performance in Moscow of 'Go West'. Cutting through the symbols of Stalin and czars, communism and autocracy, the crowd bounced in the air with joy. The irony, humour and disquiet of Neil Tennant and Chris Lowe in being part of such a global event captured my own ambivalent belief and dense longing that the world could actually become more like a dance track. PSB, who closed Live 8 in Moscow, have deployed Russian history throughout their musical career. It seemed appropriate to repay the favour and play (in) Russia.

End poverty now

In the British press, the absence of African performers from the main stages roused disquiet. In another age, white men speaking (and singing) on behalf of black peoples used to be called colonization. In our postcolonial age, such judgments may seem harsh. There was an uncomfortable moment when Birhan Woldu was on the stage with Madonna, but no one escorted her from the stage. Unable to understand English, she held hands with Madonna, but then became like a shadow, a totem around which Madonna danced. In an age of global inequalities, such decisions about performers from Geldof certainly seemed inappropriate. Not surprisingly, *The Guardian* poked and probed.

> They say the message is justice and not charity, trade not aid, but that's not what we saw on our screens. Show not tell, guys, as any novice novelist knows. You could have shown us the talent, the experience, the beauty, the variety. 'Africa' is not just one tiddly little homogenous place, you know. Mali is not Uganda, Zambia is not Nigeria, and there is one thing that Africa is not short of, it is outstanding musical talent. But the image we were given, the non-verbal message coming out loud and clear, was this; African people – starving, dying, grateful, in the background; white people, generous, sympathetic, pleased with themselves, showing off.[4]

If the goal was consciousness and not charity, then there must be an affirmation that consciousness starts at home. If there is a desire to reveal the New Africa without debt but with fairer trade, then such a project starts in popular culture.

Not surprisingly, it was Billy Bragg – who was absent from both Live Aid and Live 8 – who expressed the disquiet and confusion. He asked within the progressivist womb of the *New Statesman*, 'can we save the world with songs?'[5] He had the credentials to ask such a question through his service to the Red Wedge. In writing of Glastonbury and Live 8, he also remembered The Clash's commitment to Rock Against Racism. The man who sang – with or without irony – about the revolution being a t-shirt away, offers a more definitive connection between pop and politics.

> We use music to attract an audience that we hope to engage in a political dialogue, which will inspire these fans to activism themselves.[6]

The language is telling: engage, dialogue and inspire, not probe and change. Yet he remains aware of his own problem: 'how do we translate the audience's willingness to create a better world into a movement capable of achieving that goal?'[7] There are songs that have tethered to political change. 'Free Nelson Mandela' and Bob Dylan's 'The Hurricane' are examples where 'awareness' did move into political transformation.

The seed of change for Africa and for all of us is not with eight men in a room, but in the disposable trash of a culture. We value and validate the words of old white men too much in this world. It makes them feel self-righteous and self-important. They must not be encouraged. All of us can change the face of popular culture, by shifting our expectations of truth, beauty, fashion and desire. Live 8 did not do that. Safraz Manzoor described it best: 'Live 8 resembled nothing so much as the live incarnation of the contents of a Mojo-reading Radio 2 listening i-Pod.'[8]

After Live 8, Bono and Geldof confirmed that their issue-based politics did not bleed into broader social transformation. Bob Geldof became part of the Conservative Party's working group on poverty. He justified this decision by stating that the party he chooses does not matter, 'so long as I can help steer the policy towards those that are dying'.[9] Dear me. Bono was similarly superficial in his political programme, stating that George W. Bush 'deserves a place in history for turning the fate of the continent around'.[10] Bianca Jagger reminded Bono that the United States is actually the lowest aid donor in the industrial world, providing only 0.16 per cent of their Gross National Product. Jagger, who bears the name of a rock star but has earned a credibility beyond her marriage and divorce, realized that:

> The mutual admiration club between Bono, Geldof, Blair and Bush – rock stars and men who would love to be them – has been the abiding symbol of the G8. It is deeply disturbing.[11]

Also, thought must be given to Paul McCartney's place in the culture. Certainly he is the embodiment of the benefits of vegetarianism. He appears younger every time he steps into public. As Martin Kelner – tongue in journalistic cheek – affirmed:

> I am ready to sign up to whatever is needed in the way of prosthetics, bio-technology, macrobiotic food, wacky yogic wisdom, and deals with the devil, in order to keep ageing rock stars alive long enough to save the planet. I mean, who else is going to do it.[12]

We also have to ponder what is gained from Brian Wilson's continued presence in popular culture. It is hard to know what is more disturbing: seeing *Smile* given such attention outside of the 1960s or watching Wilson's hand puppet choreography on stage.

The other great difference between the live music concerts separated by 20 years was the use of language. Text messaging had entered mainstream politics. The mobile posters above the stage were like situationist mantras meeting Crazy Frog. The result was an ever-changing suite of slogans on the digital banner that were concurrently powerful, pithy and disturbing. Participation, agency and involvement continued this digital feast. The goal was to create a text list of global citizens to present to the G8. Viewers used their phones to confirm e-democracy and e-resistance. It was unsettling. This messaging community was global in spread, but virtual in the many meanings of that word.

Still, there was emotion, that overwhelming sense – even in spite of ourselves – that the world could change, and we could be involved in it. Euan Ferguson captured this belief best.

> We're here, aren't we, really here, today. Something is happening, and we're part of it. Precisely what is happening is going to be harder to pin down, and terribly reliant on events of the next few days. But the remarkable thing about yesterday's Live 8 concerts was the speed … [of] cynicism.[13]

There was an eeriness to Ferguson's prediction. The next few days would be destructive beyond words. So quickly, it was over. It had been a long Australian night in front of the television. In a timely reward for leading a new type of politics and consciousness, the Olympic Games were granted to London. It was a prize for the grand old city that had been the core of Empire and seemed to rebirth as the focus of mobile politics.

There was a sense that maybe life and justice would be different this time. Through all the squishy rock politics of U2, The Who and Bob Geldof, I felt a bit like that 15-year old girl again. I wanted to believe in a big community that could change the world. Geldof, standing with Bono and Midge Ure at the conclusion of the final 6 July 2005 concert in Edinburgh, exclaimed 'How can they ignore us now?'[14] At that time and on that day – bubbling with hope – he seemed right. But through his effusive affirmations of change, his hopes were not only crushed, but erased from pop cultural history.

One voice can make poverty history

Suddenly 'our' moment was wiped clean. Bombs burst through the London Underground. The old world, the old violence, cut through the steel and concrete, the hair gel and the text messaging like milky clay. Tears of happiness and connectivity were washed with blood and fear. My own husband was on the British train system on that dreadful day, travelling between Brighton and London. We couldn't find him for hours. Unlike the Live 8ers, we do not believe in mobile phones. Thankfully he was uninjured, but unnerved. I was literally half a world away, and that space was filled with bodies and pain and doubt and loss. Simply, I will never recover from those few hours. Yet the many that lost friends and lovers will hold that horror forever. I acknowledge the pain of those who have lost, and those who mourn. I can never grasp what they feel. But I feel the fear.

Live 8. G8. Be Great

We want to believe in virtual collectivity, that our virtual community can bring justice. The reality of bombs and bodies tortures the truths of texting. Live 8 asked us – and the G8 – to Be Great. Perhaps the poignant realization of that long day – and the subsequent week that erased its lasting influence – is that this is not our time. It is a bittersweet symphony suffocating a cacophony of poverty, inequality and rage.

Winds of change

The greatest social and political challenge of our time is not global warming, debt in the developing world or terrorism. The most profound problem is emotional and intellectual disconnection from any issue, topic or idea that does not have immediate personal relevance. Karl Marx and Frederick Engels predicted this disengagement when trying to understand how and why exploited workers accepted the dense injustices of the early industrial revolution. They realized that 'life is not determined by consciousness but consciousness by life'.[1] The profound difficulty in making empowered citizens of the world aware of the reasons for environmental damage, the consequences of colonialism or the history of the Middle East is explained through their maxim. If a life is filled with four-wheel drives, plasma screen televisions, sun-dried tomatoes and Kate Moss maxi dresses, then a consciousness of pains, pleasures and problems beyond these trivialities is – frankly – impossible to develop.

The first decade of the twenty-first century was filled with concerts, some in an attempt to raise consciousness, like Live 8, some in a mark of commemoration, and some – in the case of Glastonbury – to celebrate muddy music and revive 1960s idealism. The strangest concerts, particularly in terms of the press commentary, were The Concert for Diana and Live Earth. Both demonstrated that popular music is dead as a unifying force between people of diverse ages. The audience for Genesis is distinct from the fans of Metallica. The middle-aged screamers for Duran Duran occupy a different social positioning from the supporters of Nellie Furtado. We hope that the iPodification of musical tastes through the infinite downloading of iTunes will widen pop literacies. These concerts demonstrate, not the success of the 'long tail' and the diversification of sonic literacies, but the fragmentation of music markets. Perhaps the greatest example of this unproductive proliferation was during the Diana concert to 'commemorate' ten years since her death in that Parisian tunnel, when Tom Jones performed a cover of the Arctic Monkeys' 'I Bet You Look Good on the Dancefloor'. The older, mostly female audience did not recognize the track, wanting to hear 'It's Not Unusual'. Clearly Tom is ahead of his audience by a wide margin.

However, I remain most interested in why Live Earth received one third the televisual audience of the Diana Concert, even though it was held the following weekend. Why is a consciousness-raising event for an issue that is effecting the world seen to have less relevance than a slightly morbid event 'celebrating' a woman who did some earnest charity work, lived a fairy tale wedding and survived its more depressing aftermath, but has been dead for ten years? Similarly, I have been asking myself not only why the BBC coverage was so poor for Live Earth, but also why all the complaints to both the public broadcaster and the regulator OfCom focused on musicians swearing.[2] Really, is the most important issue facing public discourse at the moment the fact that Phil Collins swears? While language is important, actions matter much more.

Absent from the complaints about BBC coverage was their extraordinary excising of indigenous peoples from the broadcast. While indigenous performers opened the concert in Sydney, it was not shown on the BBC except through the morning news. Replicating nineteenth-century structures, where indigenous peoples were reported as a curiosity rather than a source of knowledge, they were shown in a dancing sound bite rather than offering a voice and view on global warming. Even more offensive was the coverage of the Live Earth event in Washington. The presenters 'filled in' until Al Gore spoke. What they 'filled in' (or over) was the space where indigenous Americans spoke about the importance of the environment to first peoples and the importance of protecting the landscape for future generations. It is not helpful to British citizenship or consciousness to continue to actively forget and ignore colonization and the consequences of the British Empire, British law and British institutions on the rest of the world.

Indeed, there was a significant indigenous story to tell in Live Earth. Al Gore had originally wished the concert to be held in Washington, with the Capitol grounds being a possible location. The Republicans, led by Senator James Inhofe, blocked this opportunity. Therefore, the organizers based the American performance in Giants Stadium in New Jersey. However, the day before the event, Gore announced that a concert would be held in Washington, at the National Museum of the American Indian. Tom Johnson, the acting director of the Museum and descendant of the Mohawk tribe, confirmed that 'there is no more important matter before us than the question of how to live sustainably on the Earth'. Gore expressed his appreciation to the organization in a way that was both historically and politically appropriate. He stated that: 'The cavalry didn't come riding to the rescue; the American Indians did.' This was not only a socially generous comment, but an act of tactical historical revisioning. The BBC did not grasp the scale and importance of the gesture from the National Museum of the American Indian, nor the social and symbolic function of indigenous peoples more generally in understanding environment politics with both rigour and respect.

Since the concert, I have continued to be unsettled and unhappy with the BBC coverage. It involved the flattening of politics, the shrinking of history and the disconnection between our daily behaviour and a consciousness of the consequences of our choices on others. Indigenous peoples remain the seers of our future, but they are also a corporeal reminder of our past and the long-term and unpredictable costs of 'discovery' and 'progress'. Listening to the views of indigenous peoples reminds those of us implicated in the other side of the colonial equation that there are other ways of living, thinking and being. We need to remember, and we need to think.

None of the songs or performers in Live Earth – not Madonna, Crowded House or even Duran Duran – could ease my disquiet. Instead, I have been drawn to one song: 'Four Strong Winds'. The best known version is probably included on Neil Young's 1978 album *Comes a Time*, which he performed not only at Live 8[3] but also in his recent documentary concert *Heart of Gold*. Featuring the extraordinary harmony of Emmylou Harris, it has become a folk standard. 'Four Strong Winds' is a rare song that seems small and insignificant, but is deceptively expansive in its panorama. Although seemingly 'about' the life of transient farm workers, it metaphorically captures the fleeting nature of personal relationships and the realization that every transitory moment of happiness is undercut by knowledge that it will not last. This song encapsulates the profound link between our search for happiness and the unrecognized costs of this journey on others.

The history of this extraordinary song is intricate, convoluted and multiple, moving through both space and time. Its origins resonate within the intertwined colonial and musical histories of Canada. It was written by Ian Tyson in 1961. Music was his second career, having learnt how to play guitar while recovering from injuries as a rodeo rider. Meeting his future wife Sylvia in folk clubs in Toronto, they later moved to New York, were assisted by Bob Dylan's manager Albert Grossman and recorded for Vanguard Records. But it was their second album, titled *Four Strong Winds*, that ensured their fame by recording this extraordinary song of gentle change and marked consequences. While they recorded many albums, their popular cultural gift was this exceptional song that would continually be reinvented for new times and places. Yet it propels a sonic shard of Canada into the world. Even in 2005, CBC Radio One listeners voted 'Four Strong Winds' the greatest Canadian song of all time, and it is still sung on the last night of the Edmonton Folk Music Festival each August.

We learn much about our digitized iTunes age that Ian and Sylvia's version is not available to download. Many of the 50 covers are available for purchase – from Johnny Cash to John Denver and Bobby Bare – but not the original. As with the BBC coverage of Live Earth, the denial of the original, the indigenous, the first, blocks our careful reflection on time, life and politics.

'Four Strong Winds' is part of a select few songs that resonate in the space between a real and imagined landscape – myth and history – pushing listeners to prise open the gap between self-congratulatory nationalism and self-aware postcolonialism. The Triffids' 'Wide Open Road', Icehouse's 'Great Southern Land' and Christine Anu's 'My Island Home' perform a similar function in Australia. The Muttonbirds' 'Dominion Road', The Front Lawn's 'Andy' and Split Enz's 'Six Months in a Leaky Boat' navigate the ideological expanse between Aotearoa and New Zealand. Live Earth needed more songs to track these spaces of disquiet, contradiction, paradox and confusion. No matter how well Madonna played guitar or Sting trashed Police songs with jazzy excesses, we are left with an uncomfortable discord between expectations and experience, our life and our consciousness.

Conclusion: Cut Elvis

Woody Guthrie's guitar not only killed fascists, but its owner's proclamation of his premature mortality was eerily accurate. Guthrie still 'ain't dead'.[1] He lives in every singer who picks up an acoustic guitar and tries to intervene in the injustices they see. The key attribute of politically effective popular culture is to quarry the past in a careful and contextualized fashion, so as to create a resonance with the present.[2] John Clarke, the great scholar of labour, leisure and culture, addressed the consequence of hyper-consumerism on determinations of class.

> The 'affluence' debate raised issues that are important but largely unrecognized and unresolved. They are not issues that can be answered by a 'lazy' Marxism: by a ritualistic defence of the category of class itself, by the demonstration of the continued polarity of labour and capital, or by insisting that we still stand within the epochal structure of the capitalist mode of production. The answers lie at a lower level of abstraction: they concern, for the most part, more specific, short-run historical movements which cannot be grasped fully at the level of generality.[3]

Clarke's realization is pivotal. In this book, I have worked through his 'specific, short-run historical movements', through the lens of popular culture. The sharpness and clarity of these ephemeral visions have revealed much about power and social justice. The reorganization of class, work and leisure has invested the word 'lifestyle' with almost mystical power. The invention of new forms of community – gated housing estates, blog spots and reality television voters unified through text messaging – have a goal in making us forget about alternatives, to trade debates about ideas for wardrobe makeovers. Therefore the strategic function of popular culture in mobilizing the resources of citizens to provoke and question must not be underestimated or undermined. In using what we have, rather than whining about what we lack, a thinking popular culture can emerge.

Most writing about popular culture is nostalgic. Such a perspective is ironic considering that popular culture itself sucks at the marrow of its time with ruthless intensity. Because particular songs, films, fashions and ideas embed themselves so deeply into our lives, through narratives of love, loss, rage and confusion, it is difficult for us to move on from our personal database of pop's greatest hits. Like a delicate and intricate weave, popular culture has given our lives depth, texture and warmth.

Such fixations can be dangerous. In January 2006, a woman stabbed her partner with scissors. While such an act may not seem unusual – or too unusual – in itself, the cause of her scissor-rage was distinctive. She was enflamed because her partner repeatedly played Elvis Presley's 'Burning Love'. As in, 'hunka hunka'. Police charged her with unlawful wounding. However, she remains a freedom fighter for thinking pop. Any man who believes – and wants the world to know – that he is 'a hunka hunka burning love' needs to be put out of his misery. He was lucky it was scissors. I would have poisoned him. Meanwhile, the real Scissor Sister remained in police custody while 'hunka' was treated for wounds to his head, back and legs.[4]

This is a funny story, in a violent Freddy Krueger kind of way, but it does confirm that popular culture matters a great deal. The most trivial of music, fashion or television can drill deeply into the love, loss and confusions in our lives. 'Burning Love' was released in 1972 and reached number two in the American charts, but for this man in 2006, the song narrated masculinity, love and sex. Now, it has new meanings cutting into the lyric for him to replay at his leisure.

In this time of war, torture, injustice and hollow ambivalence, there is popular culture that is hot and fiery. Bad times produce attacking, probing and angry culture. The memory and legacy of punk has peppered these pages more than I expected, showing that Johnny Rotten's rage howls through to our present. Outsiders – from Dylan to Cash, from Saville to Bancroft – make us think and feel more, giving us courage to live with both respect and responsibility. This book commenced with Hanif Kureishi's empowered use of difference to make a difference. It is appropriate for the project of this book that the greatest commentary on George W. Bush emerged, not from CNN or BBC World, but from Green Day.[5] *American Idiot* was brilliant in the way that The Clash were brilliant, moving punk beyond the 'I can't play, I can't sing, I don't care' ideology and into a thrashed and thrashing assault on the establishment. The single, 'American Idiot', captured the rage. 'Wake me up when September ends' was a song of mourning. 'Boulevard of Broken Dreams' is the masterpiece. Perhaps it is the experience of listening to it on an iPod while walking (alone) down darkened streets, but the melody, the relentless and melancholic guitar, and the incisor sharp lyrics confirm why we will remember the first decade of the twenty-first century with repulsion and shame at our complacency, consumerism and clutter. Naomi Klein diagnosed this time as under the rule of 'the shock doctrine'.

Believers in the shock doctrine are convinced that only a great rupture – a flood, a war, a terrorist attack – can generate the kind of vast, clean canvases they crave. It is in these malleable moments, when we are psychologically unmoored and physically uprooted, that these artists of the real plunge in their hands and begin their work of remaking the world.[6]

I have always believed through my adult life that the most radical decision we can make is to live in the present. I have changed my mind. After September 11, our priority is to read and remember history, to prevent the shock of war, terrorism and injustice from bleaching our responsibility and respect for the differences and dissent of others. Antonio Gramsci, the political campaigner and writer who was imprisoned by Benito Mussolini, despairingly demanded that all of us 'turn your face violently towards things as they exist now'.[7] Popular culture occupies the present, but it must also act in a journalistic way, capturing the present moment at speed to permit later reflection.

Thinking Popular Culture, at its best, does not allow us to wallow in our iPod isolation, but demands that we hear, see, speak, learn and connect. So much American popular culture is implicated in war, bombing and destruction. We must continue Margaret Cho's directive: choose to stay and fight. Like Christopher Eccleston's Doctor, we must demand good writing and fine television. Remembering Johnny Cash, we must see a problem and speak out. Following Dylan, we must have the right to be brilliant and political but also to change. Most importantly, each of us must temper our individual emotion and experience to use popular culture to build bridges to walk over and through to a new type of community.

Selected Bibliography

Anderson, C. *The Long Tail* (New York: Random, 2007).

Arnove, A. *The Essential Chomsky Reader* (New York: The New York Press, 2008).

Butler, J. *Precarious Life: The Powers of Mourning and Violence* (London: Verso, 2004).

Carey, J. *What Good Are the Arts?* (London: Faber, 2005).

Faludi, S. *The Terror Dream: What 9/11 Revealed about America* (New York: Atlantic Books, 2007).

Fukuyama, F. *After the NeoCons: America at the Crossroads* (London: Profile, 2006).

Gladwell, M. *The Tipping Point* (New York: Abacas, 2002).

Gladwell, M. *Blink: The Power of Thinking Without Thinking* (London: Little Brown and Company, 2005).

Gray, J. *Al Qaeda and What it Means to be Modern* (London: Penguin, 2007).

Gomez, J. *Print is Dead* (London: Macmillan, 2008).

Jenkins, H. *Convergence Culture* (New York: New York University Press, 2006).

Jenkins, H. *Fans, Bloggers and Gamers* (New York: New York University Press, 2006).

Klein, N. *The Shock Doctrine* (London: Penguin, 2007).

Kureishi, H. *The Word and the Bomb* (London: Faber, 2005).

Leadbeater, C. *We-Think* (London: Profile, 2008).

McGuigan, J. *Cultural Populism* (London: Routledge, 1992).

Miller, D. and Slater, D. *The Internet: An Ethnographic Approach* (Oxford: Berg, 2000).

Redhead, S. *The Clubcultures Reader* (Oxford: Blackwell, 1997).

Surowiecki, J. *The Wisdom of Crowds: Why the Many are Smarter than the Few* (New York: Abacas, 2005).

Zinn, H. *On War* (New York: Seven Stories, 2001).

Notes

Introduction: Interventions in/denial

1   I. Welsh, 'Foreword', in P. Vasili, *The First Black Footballer* (London: Frank Cass, 1998), p. xii.
2   Welsh, 'Foreword', p. xii.
3   I. Welsh, 'Post-punk junk', in S. Redhead, *Repetitive Beat Generation* (Edinburgh: Rebel Inc, 2000), p. 145.
4   I also note Barry Schwartz's analysis in *The Paradox of Choice* (New York: Harper Collins, 2004). He stated that 'The "success" of modernity turns out to be bittersweet, and everywhere we look it appears that a significant contributing factor is the overabundance of choice. Having too many choices produces psychological distress, especially when combined with regret, concern about status, adaptation, social comparison, and perhaps most important, the desire to have the best of everything – to maximize' (p. 221).
5   Welsh in Redhead, p. 138.
6   Susan Faludi's third book, *The Terror Dream: What 9/11 Revealed about America* (New York: Atlantic Books, 2007) offered a pathway through this history. Describing her project, she stated that 'the media and the rest of popular culture weren't recording people's reactions to 9/11; they were forcing made-up reactions down people's throats', in D. Aitkenhead, '9/11 ripped the bandage off US culture', *The Guardian*, 18 February 2008, p. 8.
7   J. Butler, *Precarious Life: The Powers of Mourning and Violence* (London: Verso, 2004), p. xi.
8   A strong suite of articles have analysed Michael Moore's impact on popular culture. Please refer to G. Watson, 'The documentary films of citizen activist Michael Moore', *Cineaction*, 22 June 2006; A. Misiak, 'Not a stupid white man', *Journal of Popular Film and Television*, Vol. 33, Fall 2005; P. Wilshire, 'Michael Moore's Fahrenheit 9/11 and the US election', *Australian Screen Education*, No. 39, September 2005; S. Feldman, 'Canadian social documentary in the age of Michael Moore', *Cineaction*, Vol. 65, 2004; R. Economou, 'Documentaries raise questions journalists should ask themselves', *Nieman Reports*, Fall 2004; R. Ordonez-Jasis and P. Jasis, 'Bowling for Columbine', *Social Justice*, Vol. 30, No. 3, 2003.

9   A documentary on Howard Zinn's life – after his autobiography – is titled *You Can't Be Neutral on a Moving Train* (First Run Features, 2004). A pacifist, in 2001, he released *On War* (New York: Seven Stories Press, 2001) and then *A Power Governments Cannot Suppress* (San Francisco: City Lights Press, 2007).

10 While there are many points and nodes of debate and discussion to be made with Chomsky's analysis of the media, his role as a public intellectual asking the difficult questions is almost unequalled, particularly after the death of E.P. Thompson and Edward Said. Significantly, he never excludes himself from blame, guilt, culpability and complicity. When he evaluates the United States' foreign policy, Chomsky is quick to place himself as 'us' against 'them'. For example, in a lecture at Harvard University, he stated, 'So when I say "we," I mean ... to include myself in "we" because I have never proposed that our leaders be subjected to the kinds of punishment that I have recommended for enemies. So that is hypocrisy. So if there are people who escape it I really don't know them and have not come across them', *Distorted Morality* (Plug Music and Silent Films, 2002). For an overview of his writings, please refer to the Anthony Arnove-edited, *The Essential Chomsky* (New York: The New Press, 2008). Significantly, Michael Moore also confirms how he is implicated in American policy. When confronted by a naval officer who said that the film maker did not send him to Iraq, Moore replied, 'But I didn't find the right words to convince enough people. I am, in part, responsible. And I helped to pay for it. I pay my taxes, so that means I continue to foot the bill. I am responsible', *Will They Ever Trust Us Again?* (London: Penguin, 2004), p. 2.

11 A. Slaughter, 'Beware the trumpets of war', *Harvard Journal of Law and Public Policy*, Vol. 25, No. 3, Summer 2002.

12 The most overt example of this ideological linkage is made by Charles Leadbeater. He stated that 'broadband access is our most potent way to promote democracy', 'People power transforms the web in the next online revolution', *The Observer*, 9 March 2008, p. 26.

13 Paul Gilroy argued that 'the declaration of "war against terror" allows minimal scope for active dissent', *Postcolonial Melancholia* (New York: Columbia University Press, 2005).

14 J. Carey, *What Good Are the Arts?* (London: Faber, 2005), p. x.

15 Richard Eyre realized that 'it's no longer possible to pretend that "civilisation" means what it meant to a "man of culture" in the 1960s – and it almost invariably was a man. Culture is about what we think, what we do, what we buy, how we behave, how we entertain ourselves, our "lifestyle," if you must. Culture is by definition an inclusive concept; art, however, is not. The word "art" is not neutral. To talk of "art" is to imply a sense of values, of taste, of standards, and – because of educational disadvantages – the word is inevitably shadowed by the spectre of class', in 'The great divide', *The Guardian*, 15 December 2007, p. 3.

16   G. Orwell, 'Charles Dickens', *George Orwell* <http://orwell.ru/library/reviews/dickens/english/e_chd>. The essay can be found in his collected essays, with a Bernard Crick introduction, *George Orwell: Essays* (London: Penguin, 2000).

17   D. Birch, 'Publishing Populism', *Cultural Studies*, Vol. 1, No. 1, 1987, p. 127.

18   *Ibid.*, p. 135.

19   George Bush stated that 'I'm a war president. I make decisions here in the Oval Office in foreign-policy matters with war on my mind. Again, I wish it wasn't true, but it is true. And the American people need to know they got a president who sees the world the way it is. And I see dangers that exist, and it's important for us to deal with them', from *Meet the Press*, MSNBC, MSNBC.com, 8 February 2004 <http://www.msnbc.msn.com/id/4179618>.

20   This great story was retold in Jaroslav Pelikan's *The Idea of the University: A Reexamination* (New Haven: Yale University Press, 1992), p. 137.

21   H. Kureishi, *The Word and the Bomb* (London: Faber, 2005), pp. 3–4.

22   This alternative mode of distribution is important. Peter Hughes confirmed that 'rarely commented upon but usually evident in discussion of documentary, is an implicit assumption that documentaries are produced for a theatrical audience, a single, autonomous text. The medium of exhibition is assumed to be largely transparent and irrelevant', in 'Strangely compelling', *Media International Australia*, No. 82, November 1996, p. 48.

23   R. Greenwald, *The Robert Greenwald Documentary Collection Bonus Disc* (New York: Disinformation, 2005).

24   Henry Jenkins in particular has assumed international leadership in theorizing the relationship between popular culture and digitization. Please refer to H. Jenkins, 'Confessions of an aca/fan' <http://www.henryjenkins.org/aboutme.html>; H. Jenkins, 'Confronting the challenges of participatory culture', *Occasional Paper on Digital Media and Learning*, 2006 <http://digitallearning.macfound.org/atf/cf/{7E45C7E0-A3E0-4B89-AC9C-E807E1B0AE4E}/JENKINS_WHITE_PAPER.PDF>; and H. Jenkins, 'Interactive audience?' *MIT Publications* <http://web.mit.edu/cms/People/henry3/collective%20intelligence.html>.

25   J. Street-Porter, 'Illiterate school kids?' *The Independent on Sunday*, 27 August 2006 <http://comment.independent.co.uk/columnists_m_z/janet_street_porter/article1222083.ece>.

26   J. Gray, *Al Qaeda and What It Means to be Modern* (London: Faber, 2003), p. 1.

27   A. Keen, in D. Smith, 'Enough! The Briton who is challenging the web's "endless cacophony"', *The Guardian*, 29 April 2007, p. 3.

28   P. Gilroy, *Postcolonial Melancholia* (New York: Columbia University Press, 2005), p. 1. This book was published in the United Kingdom under the title *After Empire* (Oxfordshire: Routledge, 2004).

29 This book unsettles the assumptions about the United States of America offered by Ray Browne and Pat Browne in their 'The generalities of cultures', in R. Browne (ed.), *Profiles of Popular Culture: A Reader* (Madison: University of Wisconsin Press, 2005). They state that, 'popular culture is the way in which and by which most people in any society live. In a democracy like the United States, it is the voice of the people – their practices, likes, and dislikes – the lifeblood of their daily existence, a way of life. The popular culture is the voice of democracy, speaking and acting, the seedbed in which democracy grows' (pp. 6–7). This is a problematic statement as it conflates popular culture and democracy, popular culture and the United States, democracy and the United States. Not only does such a matrix encourage inwardness and a lack of reflexivity, but it fails to probe how the ideologies of 'Americanness' travel around the world. Popular culture is not intrinsically democratic, resistive, liberationist or radical. It is often conservative, xenophobic, racist and militarist. *Thinking Popular Culture* does not continue the assumption that popular culture is democratic or the font of political struggle. It may hold this function, but requires considered attention to context and history. Significantly, Browne's book was published in 2005 and there is no chapter included on the topics of terrorism, September 11 or the war in Iraq. A better study was Neil Campbell, Jude Davies and George McKay (eds), *Issues in Americanisation and Culture* (Edinburgh: Edinburgh University Press, 2004).

30 M. Cho, *I Have Chosen to Stay and Fight* (New York: Riverhead, 2005), p. 206.

31 An example of their programming is *Indecision 2004: The Daily Show with Jon Stewart* (Comedy Partners, 2005).

32 J. Stewart, *America (The Book): A Citizen's Guide to Democracy Inaction* (New York: Warner, 2004).

33 *Crossfire*, CNN, YouTube <http://www.youtube.com/watch?v=vmj6JADOZ-8>.

34 T. Goetz and J. Stewart, 'Reinventing television', *Wired*, September 2005, p. 104.

35 'Hillary on Jon Stewart's *Daily Show*', YouTube <http://www.youtube.com/watch?v=Y-J9FaukWbw>.

36 F. Fukuyama, *After the NeoCons: America at the Crossroads* (London: Profile, 2006).

37 J. Gray, *Al Qaeda and What It Means to be Modern* (London: Faber, 2003).

38 For example, John Howard, the former Prime Minister of Australia who was in power on September 11 and part of the Coalition of the Willing, stated on radio on 20 April 2006 that 'I mean we all understand it's necessary to be able to be literate and coherent … and we also understand there's high quality literature and there's rubbish, and we need a curriculum that encourages an understanding of the high quality literature and not the rubbish', cited in R. King, 'Howard blasts OBE as rubbish', *The West Australian*, 21 April 2006, p. 1.

Google is white bread for the mind

1   J. Grappone and G. Couzin, *Search Engine Optimization: An Hour a Day* (London: John Wiley, 2006).

2   M. Gladwell, *The Tipping Point* (New York: Abacas, 2002).

3   J. Surowiecki, *The Wisdom of Crowds: Why the Many are Smarter than the Few* (New York: Abacas, 2005).

4   C. Anderson, *The Long Tail* (New York: Random, 2007).

5   *Ibid.*

6   M. Gladwell, *Blink: The Power of Thinking Without Thinking* (London: Little Brown and Company, 2005).

7   J. Gomez, *Print is Dead* (London: Macmillan, 2008).

8   *Ibid.*, p. 7.

9   *Ibid.*, p. 4.

10   *Ibid.*, p. 57.

11   *Ibid.*, p. 40.

12   *Ibid.*

13   Examples of this literature include A. Ip, I. Morrison and J. Mason, 'Managing online resources for teaching and learning', Sixth Australian World Wide Web Conference, 2000 <http://ausweb.scu.edu.au/aw2k/papers/ip/paper.html>; A. Bundy, 'One essential direction: information literacy, information technology fluency', *Journal of eLiteracy*, Vol. 1, 2004, pp. 7–22; D. Leu and C. Kinzer, *Theoretical Models and Processes of Reading* (International Reading Association, 2004); 'Quality information checklist', *Quick.org.uk* <http://www.quick.org.uk/menu.htm>; B. Dalton and D. Grisham, 'Taking a position on integrating literacy and technology in the curriculum', *Reading Online*, March 2001 <http://www.readingonline. org/editorial/edit_index.asp?HREF=/editorial/march2002/index.html>; M. Hagood, 'New media and online literacies: no age left behind', *New Directions in Research*, Vol. 38, No. 3, July/August/September 2003; H. Nixon, 'New research literacies for contemporary research into literacy and new media', *New Directions in Research*, Vol. 38, No. 3, July/August/September 2003; K. Leander, 'Writing travelers' tales on New Literacyscapes', *Reading Research Quarterly*, Vol. 38, No. 3, July/August/September 2003; C. Beavis, 'Magic or Mayhem? New texts and new literacies in technological times', paper presented at the Annual Conference of the Australian Association for Research in Education, Melbourne, 28 November–2 December 1999 <http://www.aare.edu.au/99pap/bea99689.htm>.

14   W. Richardson, *Blogs, Wikis, Podcasts and Other Powerful Web Tools for Classrooms* (Thousand Oaks: Corwin Press, 2006), p. xiii.

15   Andrew Keen's *The Cult of the Amateur* features a homicidal subtitle: 'how today's internet is killing our culture'. Keen offers a critique of the 'wisdom of the crowd'

and the excessive egotism of social networking sites. While some of the arguments offered are important, it is a superficial analysis that is confusing a critique of banality, mediocrity and professionalism with an attack on 'our' cultural standards and moral values. As the book continues, Keen becomes fixated on 'anonymous sexual predators and pedophiles'. He completes the Salvation Army crusade by also attacking online gambling. With 'the moral fabric of our society ... being unraveled by Web 2.0', the new folk devils of identity thieves, paedophiles, online gamblers, digi-plagiarists and peer-to-peer music sharing copyright violators are the source of all that is wrong with the world. While the trading of sex, luck and music may be the basis of his moral crusade, such a campaign is based on a single error: he is confusing morality with intelligence. He states that, 'democratization, despite its lofty idealization, is undermining truth, souring civic discourse, and belittling expertise, experience, and talent' (p. 7). Democracy and democratization are not the problem. It must be valued and validated at every opportunity. Keen has confused elitism and expertise, morality and argument. Web 2.0 should be assessed as a symptom of what has happened to our democratic institutions through the post-war period, not an excuse to return to nineteenth-century categorizations of cultural value.

16   T. Brabazon, 'The Google Effect', *Libri*, Vol. 56, No. 3, September 2006, pp. 157–67 <http://www.librijournal.org/pdf/2006-3pp157-167.pdf>.

17   T. Brabazon, *The University of Google* (Aldershot: Ashgate, 2007).

18   An ironically titled article adds weight to my generalization. Lynn Schofield Clark published 'When the University went "Pop": exploring cultural studies, sociology of culture, and the rising interest in the study of popular culture', *Sociology Compass*, Vol. 2, No. 1, 2008, pp. 16–33. This title suggests a booming field. However, there is a radical disconnection between the argument and references. For example, she stated, 'the prominence for the study of culture, and of popular culture within it, is suggestive of the ways in which scholars in various fields have explored through the prism of popular culture a variety of issues related to the economy, social movements, family life, urban and rural geographies, and differences of race, gender, socioeconomic status, nationality, and sexual orientation, among other things'. To make this case she references her own text, (Clark 2005b). This citation refers to her article 'Globalizing Popular Communication Audience Research', in *Popular Communication*, Vol. 3, 2005, pp. 153–66. The connection between this argument and reference is unclear. Further, she mobilized the argument that 'In large part, this transformation of the view of popular culture came about through the work of feminists within cultural studies. Feminist scholars pointed out that popular culture itself had been delegitimated because its purchase and consumption often occurred in relation to the home, which was considered the domain of women' (p. 17). She then cites *Women Take Issue* from 1978 and Andreas

Huyssen's *After the Great Divide* from 1986. Clark then draws the generalization that 'as a result of these and related efforts, researchers are now taking as a starting point the fact that, for better or worse, most people are immersed in a media-saturated environment in their everyday lives' (p. 18). The academic literature about popular culture, the media and everyday life, while it does overlap, is more frequently distinct and certainly deploys a diverse array of research materials and methods from the social sciences and humanities.

19   S. Frith and J. Savage, 'Pearls and Swine', *New Left Review*, Issue 198, March–April 1993.

20   S. Redhead (ed.), *The Clubcultures Reader* (Oxford: Blackwell, 1997).

21   The Google Scholar results for the Frith and Savage article are located at <http://scholar.google.co.uk/scholar?hl=en&lr=&cites=16141108415650349249>.

22   J. McGuigan, *Cultural Populism* (London: Routledge, 1992).

23   J. Fiske, *Reading the Popular* (London: Routledge, 1989); and *Understanding Popular Culture* (London: Routledge, 1989).

24   H. Jenkins, *Textual Poaching* (London: Routledge, 1992).

25   H. Jenkins, *Convergence Culture* (New York: New York University Press, 2006); and *Fans, Bloggers and Gamers* (New York: New York University Press, 2006).

26   S. Frith and J. Savage, 'Pearls and swine: intellectuals and the mass media', in S. Redhead (ed.), *The Clubcultures Reader* (Oxford: Blackwell, 1997), p. 7.

27   *Ibid.*, p. 8.

28   *Ibid.*, p. 8.

29   *Ibid.*, p. 8.

30   One example of this digitized pleasure not leading to social change in the market economy was the battle over the Christmas number one single in 2007. In an attempt to block Leon Jackson, a reality television winner, from topping the charts, a Facebook group was formed that described itself as 'A group to try and get a proper Christmas song to number 1 for Christmas instead of the stupid X-Factor Winner' <http://brighton.facebook.com/group.php?gid=20778141304>. They instigated a campaign to make Shane MacGowan and Kirsty MacColl's 'Fairytale of New York' the Christmas number one. The first chance that this type of action was possible was in 2007. As no physical release was required for a track to enter the charts, downloads were sufficient to propel a song into the number one position. In response, Facebook was able to organize a challenge. But besides agitating Simon Cowell and disturbing the X Factor brand, this impetus to intervene in the Christmas number one did not signify a great social change. N. Caine, 'Downloads have saved the Christmas number one', *MSN Money*, 19 December 2007 <http://money.uk.msn.com/guides/christmasmoney/article.aspx?cp-documentid=7029743>.

31 'Tristan und Isolde: The trouble with Tristan', *Daily Telegraph*, 13 December 2007 <http://www.telegraph.co.uk/arts/main.jhtml?view=DETAILS&grid=&xml=/arts/2007/12/13/bmstorey113.xml>.

32 S. Hall, 'Notes on deconstructing "the popular"', in R. Samuel (ed.), *People's History and Socialist Theory* (London: Kegan Paul, 1981), p. 239.

33 'Wikipedia: no original research', Wikipedia <http://en.wikipedia.org/wiki/Wikipedia:No_original_research>.

34 'Wikipedia: neutral point of view', Wikipedia <http://en.wikipedia.org/wiki/Wikipedia:Neutral_point_of_view>.

35 An example of this search result is when entering the search term 'terrorism' into Google. On 21 March 2008, the result of this search saw Wikipedia as the first return, with the UK-based Metropolitan Police as the sponsored link <http://www.google.co.uk/search?hl=en&q=terrorism&meta=>.

36 Because creative industries initiatives, strategies and policies are inflected by 'third way' labour ideologies, it means that there is a movement away from the 'big government/big business/big union' nexus. For a discussion of this change, please refer to Steve Redhead's 'Creative Modernity: the cultural state', *MIA*, No. 112, August 2004 <http://www.emsah.uq.edu.au/mia/issues/miacp112.html#redhead>. In this environment of change in the political economy, small businesses – often called 'independents' – are being rebranded as the engine of 'the new economy'. Importantly, theories of the state and public institutions are underwritten in the creative industries literature, with attention placed on reducing regulation, 'red tape' and government intervention. For example, please refer to Charles Leadbeater's texts in the field: *Living on Thin Air* (London: Viking, 1999); (with Kate Oakley) *The Independents* (London: Demos, 1999); *Up the Down Escalator* (London: Penguin, 2004); and *We-Think* (London: Profile, 2008). It is significant to note in Leadbeater's writing on the creative industries that he moves from technological-scepticism to techno-enthusiasm when enabled by wiki-led media. The key book in understanding this transition is *The Pro-Am Revolution* (London: Demos, 2004).

37 Louis Althusser reached his peak of influence in media and cultural studies in the 1970s. By the late 1970s, Foucault's influence increased. However, the trajectory of Althusser's scholarly fame is tethered to his murder of his wife in 1980. He remained in an asylum until his death in 1990. His late scholarly works include *The Future Lasts a Long Time* (London: Verso, 1994) and *Philosophy of the Encounter* (London: Verso, 2006).

38 A discussion of Poulantzas' influence on the left is found in an article written at the time of his death. Please refer to Stuart Hall, 'Nicos Poulantzas: State, Power, Socialism', *New Left Review*, Issue 119, January/February 1980. To see his theories of the state, refer to the Stuart Hall-introduced *State, Power, Socialism* (London:

Verso, 2000) and *The Poulantzas Reader: Marxism, Law, and the State* (London: Verso, 2008). To view the impact of Poulantzas' death and Althusser's confinement, please refer to Andy Merrifield, *Metromarxism* (London: Routledge, 2002), particularly page 198.

39   Although Michel Foucault's *Discipline and Punish* appeared in English in 1977, there is no doubt that the intellectual vacuum created by the death of Poulantzas and the confinement of Althusser increased his presence and influence. As an arbitrary but repeatable trace of influence, the first two pages (twenty titles) from Google Scholar for the four mentioned in this passage showed the following citation results: Bourdieu (28,696), Foucault (26,631), Althusser (5,016) and Poulantzas (2,285).

40   To explore Pierre Bourdieu's theorization of cultural capital, please refer to *Distinction* (London: Routledge, 1986); and *The Field of Cultural Production* (London: Polity, 1993).

41   Frith and Savage, p. 16.

42   The archetype of this argument is that Leadbeater, on the first page of his book, states, 'thanks to the web, more people than ever can exercise their right to free speech, reviving democracy where it is tired and inspiring its emergence in authoritarian societies, from Burma to Vietnam and China' (p. 1). Significantly, in March 2008, less than one month after Leadbeater published his book, the Chinese authorities ruthlessly crushed Tibetan resistance. The confusion of 'awareness' and 'activism', 'blogging' and 'social change' is corroding the – often analogue – development of social movements.

43   'Demographics', Internet and American Life Project <http://www.pewinternet.org/PPF/c/2/topics.asp>.

44   OfCom Media Literacy <http://www.ofcom.org.uk/advice/media_literacy/>.

45   V.I. Lenin, *What Is To Be Done?* (London: Penguin, 1989).

46   The remarkable analogue history of The Byrds is Johnny Rogan's *Timeless Flight: Definitive Biography of the Byrds* (London: Scorpion, 1980).

47   *No Direction Home* (Paramount Home Entertainment, 2005).

48   There are many collections of Peter, Paul and Mary songs. One which features their hit singles is *The Very Best of Peter, Paul and Mary* (Rhino Records, 2005). Their songs are also well represented on iTunes and commercial downloading services. Their best known covers of Bob Dylan songs are 'The Times They Are A-Changin'' and 'Blowin' in the Wind'.

49   H. Blaine and Mr Bonzai, *Hal Blaine and the Wrecking Crew: The Story of the World's Most Recorded Musician* (Alma, Michigan: Rebeats Publications, 2007).

50   The Band, 'The Weight', *Songs from Big Pink* (EMI 2001), track 5.

51   The Band, 'Up on Cripple Creek', *The Band* (Brown Album) (EMI, 2000), track 16.

52   E. Clapton, *Layla: Remastered Twentieth Century Edition* (Universal, 2001), track 13.

53   J. Hendrix, *Experience Hendrix* (Universal, 2000), track 5.

54   There were technical innovations in this Rickenbacker 12-string guitar. Firstly, the headstock design features both a solid peghead and a slotted groove for half of the strings. It also reverses the ordering of the octave course of the strings, ensuring the sustaining ring of the high string after playing the bass side.

55   The phrase 'jingle jangle' is derived from Bob Dylan's lyric in 'Mr Tambourine Man', with reference to 'a jingle jangle morning'.

56   John Ryan and Richard Peterson explored the impact of this guitar in 'The guitar as artifact and icon', in the remarkable *Guitar Cultures* (Oxford: Berg, 2001), edited by Andy Bennett and Kevin Dawe. They stated: 'In 1989 I saw an advertisement for a new Rickenbaker model: the 370-12 RM. This was a limited edition Roger McGuinn signature model. McGuinn helped design the guitar, basically a 370-12 like the one he used to play but with additional on-board electronics to capture the sound of his twelve-string on those original studio recordings. Hand made from the finest materials, only 1,000 were manufactured. They listed for $1,399 each, at the time a lot of money for a new electric guitar. My wife surprised me with one for my fortieth birthday. I've used the guitar some in home recording, but mainly I have been learning Byrds' songs note for note – I'm not sure why but it has nothing to do with recording or making it in the music business. I know it's a thrill to play these songs I've loved so much on an instrument that I've admired for so long. I guess when I play it I feel like Roger McGuinn. Oh, if you can find one for sale, it will now cost you about $4,000. I'll never sell mine. Not just because of the associations with McGuinn and The Byrds, although that is important; it's also because it is such a beautiful instrument to hold' (p. 96).

57   ByrdHouse, *I Feel Possessed* (Capital, 1989).

58   One song's lyric expressed the impact of The Byrds' success on McGuinn's post-Byrds' career. Titled 'Same Old Sound', it was included on the *Peace on You* album, which was released by Columbia in 1974.

59   Roger McGuinn, *The Folk Den* <http://www.ibiblio.org/jimmy/folkden/php/search/>.

60   A fine article on 'disruptive' platforms is by Robert Godwin-Jones, 'Emerging technologies: skype and podcasting – disruptive technologies for language learning', *Language Learning & Technology*, Vol. 9, No. 3, September 2005, pp. 9–12.

61   An early article tracking the impact of podcasting on radio is Xeni Jardin's 'Podcasting killed the radio star', *Wired*, 27 April 2005 <http://www.wired.com/entertainment/music/news/2005/04/67344>.

62   While Radiohead gained much publicity for *In Rainbows*, they were affiliated with a record label. More courageous was Trent Reznor of Nine Inch Nails. Working without any record company, on 3 March 2008, he released the new 'album' *Ghosts*

1–IV. Using the plurality and diversity of the new musical environment, it is a two-hour, 36-track 'album'. Volume 1 was made available for free. All 36 tracks were downloadable for US$5. Please refer to www.nin.com.

63 Roger McGuinn Testimony, 'Music on the Internet: is there an upside to downloading', Senate Judiciary Committee, 11 July 2000 <http://judiciary.senate.gov/testimony.cfm?id=195&wit_id=253>.

64 *Ibid*.

65 Another example of this new environment for popular music that cuts away conventional record companies is Sellaband (www.sellaband.com). Unsigned bands upload music to the site and listeners can then buy US$10 shares in the performers. Once the band has attracted US$50,000, they gain studio time. No record company is involved in the process.

66 R. McGuinn, *Treasures from the Folk Den booklet* (West Chester: Appleseed, 2001), p. 1.

67 Appleseed Recordings <http://www.appleseedrec.com/>.

68 This software has now been upgraded to Adobe Audition 3 <http://www.rm.com/HE/Products/Product.asp?cref=PD168239>.

69 *Roger McGuinn's Basic Folk Guitar* (Homespun video, 2003).

70 *Roger McGuinn's 12-string guitar* (Homespun video, 2003).

71 *Roger McGuinn's guide to home recording on a computer* (Homespun video, 2004).

72 McGuinn is also conscious that he is creating a more equitable relationship between performers and record companies. He states that home recording equipment 'really levels the playing field for artists these days. You don't have to sell out to the record company. You don't have to get five hundred thousand dollars, or whatever, and pay them back for the rest of your life to record a record. Now, you can just get a laptop, get some software, put a microphone on it and make a record. You have to know how to do it. It does help if you've had 35 or 40 years of experience in the studio. But, it still levels the playing field so artists can record their own stuff', in Rick Lander's 'Roger McGuinn Interview', *Modern Guitars Magazine*, 15 February 2006 <http://www.modernguitars.com/archives/001633.html>.

73 E. Said, *On Late Style* (London: Bloomsbury, 2007).

74 B. Agger, *Fast Capitalism* <http://www.fastcapitalism.com/>.

75 G. Coulter, *International Journal of Baudrillard Studies* <http://www.ubishops.ca/BaudrillardStudies/contents.htm>.

76 P. Stortz, *History of Intellectual Culture* <www.ucalgary.ca/hic/>.

77 S. Habib, *Nebula* <http://www.nobleworld.biz/journalhome.html>.

78 Google Scholar <http://scholar.google.co.uk/>.

79 Directory of Open Access Journals <http://www.doaj.org/>.

80 Public Knowledge Project <http://pkp.sfu.ca/>.

81 A. McRobbie, 'Post-Marxism and Cultural Studies', in L. Grossberg, C. Nelson and P. Treichler (eds), *Cultural Studies* (New York: Routledge, 1991), p. 721.

82 H. Giroux and S. Aronowitz, *Education Still Under Siege* (New York: Bergin and Garvey, 1993), p. 149.

83 Jimmy Wales and Tim O'Reilly proposed guidelines for bloggers in 2007 and confronted a remarkable backlash. Please refer to 'Web gurus want blog etiquette despite backlash', *Reuters.com*, 11 April 2007 <http://www.reuters.com/article/gc08/idUSN1042471620070411>; and Ed Pilkington, 'Howls of protest as web gurus attempt to banish bad behaviour from blogosphere', *The Guardian*, 10 April 2007, p. 17.

84 This lyric is from Marianne Faithful's cover of 'The Ballad of Lucy Jordan', from *The Ballad of Lucy Jordan* (London: Island, 1979). Originally it had been written by Shel Silverstein for Dennis Locorriere of Dr Hook.

85 To use the *Daily Mail* as an example, here are a few of the featured headlines: 'Reid wins battle to stem flood of migrant workers', 4 October 2006 <http://www.dailymail.co.uk/pages/live/articles/news/news.html?in_article_id=412264&in_page_id=1770>; 'Four out of five migrants "take more from economy than they put back"', 29 August 2006 <http://www.dailymail.co.uk/pages/live/articles/news/news.html?in_article_id=402607&in_page_id=1770>; 'Half a million migrants pour into Britain in a year, but 200,000 leave', 16 November 2007 <http://www.dailymail.co.uk/pages/live/articles/news/news.html?in_article_id=494235&in_page_id=1770>; '80% of new jobs have gone to migrants since Labour came to power', 11 December 2007 <http://www.dailymail.co.uk/pages/live/articles/news/news.html?in_article_id=501128&in_page_id=1770>; 'Number of Britons in work falls by 270,000 – because migrants get most new jobs', 1 November 2007 <http://www.dailymail.co.uk/pages/live/articles/news/news.html?in_article_id=491223&in_page_id=1770>; 'Migrants put billions on council tax', 1 November 2007 <http://www.dailymail.co.uk/pages/live/articles/news/news.html?in_article_id=490992&in_page_id=1770>; and 'Britons unconvinced over migrants', 19 February 2007 <http://www.dailymail.co.uk/pages/live/articles/news/news.html?in_article_id=437024&in_page_id=1770>.

86 R. Williams, 'Culture is ordinary', in B. Levinson (ed.), *Schooling the Symbolic Animal: Social and Cultural Dimensions of Education* (New York: Rowman & Littlefield, 2000).

87 E.P. Thompson, in B. Palmer, *E.P. Thompson: Objections and Oppositions* (London: Verso, 2004), p. 67.

Stop crying – start thinking

1   Paul Harris captures the impact of these women in his article, 'Sex, drink, drugs, jail: we're all hooked on the antics of Hollywood's bad girls', *The Observer*, 29 July 2007, p. 21.

2   Bono, in 'How to get ahead in politics', *Word*, No. 21, November 2004, p. 24.

3   John Hartley, for example, coined the term 'democratainment', in *The Uses of Television* (London: Routledge, 1999).

4   G. Turner, *Understanding Celebrity* (London: SAGE, 2004).

5   G. Turner, 'The mass production of celebrity: "Celetoids", reality TV and the "demotic turn"', *International Journal of Cultural Studies*, Vol. 9, No. 2, 2006, p. 154.

6   Ironically, Germaine Greer summoned *Friends* to offer a critique of university education, particularly the worthlessness of lectures, and affirm the value of popular culture. She wrote in *The Guardian* that '*Friends* was the standard text for one of the brightest groups of students at Warwick University. They were the ones who ran the bar, organized protests, made movies and videos and did OK in their exams. They also studied *Friends*, watching DVDs of the series over and over again, learning how to construct social interaction in their peer group, how to avoid turning into a prat. Sure, as one of their teachers, I might have wanted them to know the works of Aphra Behn as well as they knew *Friends* but, as it turned out, *Friends* has been of more use to them. Two are now scriptwriters for the country's best-loved soaps', in G. Greer, 'Another hard day in the Library', *The Guardian*, 1 February 2006, p. 7.

7   The ambivalent relationship between sexual 'freedom', feminism and popular culture is displayed in J. Gerhard, 'Sex and the city', *Feminist Media Studies*, Vol. 5, Issue 1, March 2005, pp. 37–49; L. Kim, 'Sex and the Single Girl', *Television New Media, Vol. 2*, 2001, pp. 319–34.

Coalition of the guilty

1   M. Cho, *Assassin* (Cho Taussig Productions, 2005).

2   'Tsunami: Ground Zero', *Discovery Channel* <http://www.discoverychannel.co.uk/earth/ground_zero/introduction/index.shtml>.

3   B. Wickens, 'Waves of mass destruction', *Macleans*, 10 January 2005 <http://www.macleans.ca/article.jsp?content=20050110_97208_97208>.

4   *Human Development Report*, United Nations Food and Agricultural Organization, New York, 2001, p. 9.

5   J. Lawson, in L. Fleeson, 'Bureau of missing bureaus', *American Journalism Review*, October/November 2003, p. 35.

6   M. Fisher, 'The metamorphosis', *American Journalism Review*, November 2002, p. 22.

7   Please refer to S. Redhead's *Paul Virilio: Theorist for an Accelerated Culture* (Edinburgh: Edinburgh University Press, 2004).

8   J. Vidal and J. Borger, 'Will the world walk away', *The Guardian*, 30 December 2004 <http://www.guardian.co.uk/world/2004/dec/30/internationalaidanddevelopment. tsunami20041>.

9   T. McFadyen, 'The big issue: Iraq five years on', *The Observer*, 23 March 2008, p. 36.

The eighth deadly sin

1   D. Ben-Ami, 'Why people hate fat Americans', *Spiked*, 9 September 2005 <http:// www.spiked-online.co.uk/Articles/0000000CAD43.htm>.

When Paris became a celebrity, not a city

1   K. Glynn, *Tabloid Culture: Trash Taste, Popular Power and the Transformation of American Culture* (Durham: Duke University Press, 2000).

2   S. Elizabeth Bird, 'Trash talk', *Cultural Studies*, Vol. 19, No. 1, January 2005, p. 128.

3   E. Cashmore, 'I'm an MP, get me into the red-tops', *The Times Higher*, 11 August 2006, p. 14.

Free wiki (but what is the cost?)

1   'Wikipedia: neutral point of view', Wikipedia <http://en.wikipedia.org/wiki/ Wikipedia:Neutral_point_of_view>.

2   'Wikipedia: no original research', Wikipedia <http://en.wikipedia.org/wiki/ Wikipedia:No_original_research>.

3   B. Agger (ed.), *There is a Gunman on Campus* (Lanham: Rowman and Littlefield, 2008).

4   The URL confirming the redirection from the Virginia Tech shootings to massacre is <http://en.wikipedia.org/w/index.php?title=Virginia_Tech_ shootings&redirect=no>.

5   One solution – and a great comedic intervention – in Wikipedia's vandalism is 'Every topic in the universe except chickens' <http://www. everytopicintheuniverseexceptchickens.com/>. This site recommends that all the Wikipedia vandals focus their attention on the 'Chicken' entry.

6   Oddly, Nicholas Baker saw the errors and flaws as an advantage. He states, 'It just feels good to find something there – even, or especially, when the article you find is a little clumsily written. Any inelegance, or typo, or relic of vandalism reminds you that this gigantic encyclopedia is not a commercial product', *The Guardian*, 10 April 2008, p. 5.

7   This search was performed on 23 February 2008. Obviously the nature of the 'we edit' culture is that lengths and priorities are changeable; however, the tendency of Wikipedia entries is that the entries lengthen rather than shorten. This practice has been labelled by Johnny 'DocEvil' Titanium as 'The Art of Wikigroaning', *Something Awful*, 5 June 2007 <http://www.somethingawful.com/d/news/wikigroaning.php>.

8   Significantly, in 2006, the 'freedom' of Wikipedia – where 'anyone' can edit a page – was lost. As Nicholas Carr – a digi-utopian enthusiast – reported, 'Where once we had a commitment to open democracy, we now have a commitment to "making sure things are not excessively semi-protected." Where once we had a commune, we now have a gated community, "policed" by "good editors." So let's pause and shed a tear for the old Wikipedia, the true Wikipedia. Rest in peace, dear child. You are now beyond the reach of vandals', *Rough Type*, 24 May 2006 <http://www.roughtype.com/archives/2006/05/the_death_of_wi.php>.

9   D. Pink, *A Whole New Mind* (New York: Riverhead, 2006).

10   As one example of the systematic attack on migration within journalism, Julia Hartley-Brewer stated that, 'what's really scandalous is that Labour decided in 1997 to launch a social revolution on an unprecedented scale by opening up Britain's borders to virtually unlimited immigration without ever once bothering to tell the rest of us. The problem with Labour ministers, and the political classes in general, is that they think mass immigration is good because, for them, it means cheaper cleaners and nannies. They neither understand nor care about the huge impact that the arrival of vast numbers of foreign workers can have on the lives of ordinary working people in this country. We have a massive housing shortage, a chronic traffic problem, desperate hospital waiting lists, too few teachers and millions of people on the dole. So what's Labour's solution? To encourage a few million more people to come to our shores', *Sunday Express*, 4 November 2007, p. 29.

It's only food, dude

1   C. Cadwalladr, 'TV chefs may be the new evangelists', *The Observer Magazine*, 20 January 2008, p. 5.

2   *Slow Food Manifesto*, 1989 <http://www.slowfoodludlow.org.uk/docs/manifesto.html>.

3   C. Petrini and G. Padovani stated that, 'by 1982, politics have already begun
     to move to the right, and many on the left have abandoned activism for other
     goals. Some have left politics entirely. Others have focused on environmentalism.
     And one small group has made a seemingly innocent discovery: food and wine.
     They explore their local wine cellars, get to know small wine producers, and end
     up preaching – with an almost political zeal – the cause of conviviality and its
     pleasures'," *Slow Food Revolution* (New York: Rizzoli, 2005), p. 2.
4   *Ibid.*, p. 7.
5   B. Disraeli, *Sybil, or the Two Nations*, Project Gutenburg, e-text number 3760
     <http://www.gutenberg.org/etext/3760>.
6   R. Patel, *Stuffed and Starved* (London: Portobello, 2007), p. 286.
7   Cadwalladr, p. 5.
8   G. Browning, 'How to … poach an egg', *The Guardian Weekend*, 5 April 2005,
     p. 10.

Crazy Frog capitalism

1   A. Goodwin, *Dancing in the Distraction Factory* (Minneapolis: University of Minnesota
     Press, 1992).
2   N. Maycroft, 'Cultural consumption and the myth of life-style', *Capital and Class*,
     Winter 2004, pp. 61–76.
3   M. Bunting, *Willing Slaves: How the Overwork Culture Is Ruling Our Lives* (London:
     HarperCollins, 2004).
4   K. Marx, *Economic and Philosophical Manuscripts* <http://www.marxists.org/archive/
     marx/works/1844/manuscripts/preface.htm>.

What are the young people wearing?

1   This paragraph is not facetious. Charles Leadbeater stated that, 'in 2020 the British
     Library will still be a building on London's Euston Road, although by then it might
     be known as perhaps the Cisco British Library. The Library will prosper only by
     making available a much larger range of material in digital form, much of it stored
     on computers owned by other people and organized by communities of users
     working with librarians. The library of the future will be a platform for participation
     and collaboration, with users increasingly sharing information among themselves
     as well as drawing on the library's resources', *We-Think* (London: Profile, 2008), p.
     145.
2   G. McGovern, 'New thinking in the digital age', *New Thinking*, 19 July 1998
     <http://www.marketing-magic.biz/archives/archive-internet-marketing/new-
     thinking-in-the-digital-age.htm>.

3   B. Thompson, 'End of the innocence for Mac fans', *BBC News*, 6 November 2007 <http://news.bbc.co.uk/go/pr/fr/-/1/hi/technology/7079777.stm>.

4   'School leavers "lacking three Rs"', *BBC News* 24, 21 August 2005 <http://news.bbc.co.uk/1/hi/education/4170336.stm>.

5   I. Aja-Nwachuku, in K. Bevan, 'Are One Laptop Per Child sales living up to expectations?' *The Guardian*, 29 November 2007.

6   K. Seeley, 'A Little Sleuthing Unmasks Writer of Wikipedia Prank', *New York Times*, 11 December 2005 <http://www.nytimes.com/2005/12/11/business/media/11web.html>.

7   A. Coleman, 'Students "should use Wikipedia"', *BBC News*, 7 December 2007 <http://news.bbc.co.uk/1/hi/technology/7130325.stm>.

8   J. Wales, in A. Coleman, *ibid.*

9   Jimmy Wales has a degree in finance and made a career as a futures trader. Please refer to R. Blakely, *The Times*, 30 December 2005 <http://business.timesonline.co.uk/tol/business/industry_sectors/media/article782970.ece>.

10   J. Schofield, 'Where Wikipedia works', *The Guardian*, 13 August 2007 <http://www.guardian.co.uk/technology/2007/aug/13/wikipedia/print>. The Wikipedia relationship with the Klingon language is extraordinary. The site that confirms 62 articles in Klingon is found at <http://meta.wikimedia.org/wiki/List_of_Wikipedias>. In 2005, the Wikipedia leadership made these links between Wikipedia and the Klingon articles 'read only'. Most of these articles have been migrated to <http://klingon.wikia.com/wiki/ghItlh%27a%27>. The now variable status of Klingon in the Wikipedia discourse is discussed at the following site <http://en.wikipedia.org/wiki/Category:Klingon_languages>. Again, the democratic 'anyone can edit' culture betrays the more feudal reality.

You've been Jaded

1   P. Bazalgette, in O. Gibson, 'So was it a tipping point in race relations … or just ratings Viagra', *The Guardian*, 20 January 2007, p. 6.

2   T. Kirby referred to Goody as 'the architect of her own demise', in 'Jade's evicted – and so are the crowds as Channel 4 acts to avoid a celebrity lynching', *The Independent*, 20 January 2007, p. 3.

3   D. Evans, 'Bully Dani is ditched by Teddy', *News of the World*, 21 January 2007, p. 5.

4   These comments were recorded live from *Big Brother Live* on Channel 4 and reprinted in Cole Moreton's 'Look back in Ongar', *The Independent on Sunday*, 21 January 2007, pp. 4–5.

5   J. Goody, 'It was racist. I am a bully', *News of the World*, 21 January 2007, p. 1.

6   T. Lott, 'The witches of Endemol', *The Independent on Sunday*, 21 January 2007, p. 36.

7   A. Duncan, in T. Kirby, 'Police launch investigation of Big Brother "racism" as sponsors desert contestants', *The Independent*, 19 January 2007, p. 7.

8   G. Spivak, 'Can the subaltern speak?' in L. Grossberg and C. Nelson (eds), *Marxism and the Interpretations of Culture* (Urbana: University of Illinois Press, 1988).

9   E. Balibar, 'Is there a "neo-racism"', in E. Balibar and I. Wallerstein (eds), *Race, Nation and Class* (London: Verso, 1991).

10   H. Bhabha, 'The other question', in R. Ferguson, M. Gever, T. Minh-ha and C. West (eds), *Out There* (New York: MIT Press, 1990).

11   Lott, p. 36.

12   M. Collins, *The Likes of Us* (London: Granta, 2005).

13   A. Chancellor, 'Is the Big Brother row really about race – or is it more to do with old-fashioned class hatred?' *The Guardian*, 19 January 2007, p. 9.

14   T. Kirby, 'Police launch investigation of Big Brother "racism" as sponsors desert contestants', *The Independent*, 19 January 2007, p. 7.

15   R. Gervais, S. Merritt, 'Portrait of the artist as himself', *The Guardian*, 14 January 2007 <http://arts.guardian.co.uk/reviews/observer/story/0,,1989784,00.html>.

16   K. Flett, 'Are you sitting uncomfortably?' *The Observer*, 14 January 2007, p. 2.

17   N. Morris and A. McSmith, 'Meanwhile, these are the realities of racism in Britain', *The Independent*, 18 January 2007, p. 2.

18   J. Huggler and S. Shah, 'Mass appeal of a star said to have "the best body in Bollywood"', *The Independent*, 18 January 2007, p. 3.

19   A. Johnson, in R. Garner, 'Schools must teach British values to beat "Big Brother"-style bigotry, says minister', *The Independent on Sunday*, 21 January 2007, p. 7.

20   The Mayor of London recognized the possible cost of this publicity. When Jade Goody was voted out of the *Big Brother* House, he stated, 'I think everyone is delighted that we got the result we did … otherwise the image of Britain across India, which is the second biggest investor in London after American now, would have been really damaged and it would have done a lot of harm to jobs', in C. Moreton, 'Look back in Ongar', *The Independent on Sunday*, 21 January 2007, p. 4.

21   T. Phillips, in T. Kirby, 'Jade's evicted – and so are the crowds as Channel 4 acts to avoid a celebrity lynching', *The Independent*, 20 January 2007, p. 3.

22   T. Brabazon, 'Mobile learning: the ipodification of Universities', *Nebula*, Vol. 4, No. 1, March 2007 <http://nobleworld.biz/images/Brabazon.pdf>.

23   B. Read, 'What's happening to our tolerant nation?' *Daily Mirror*, 18 January 2007, p. 19.

24   G. Pascoe-Watson, 'The Dim Reaper', *The Sun*, 18 January 2007, p. 1.

25   E. Cox, 'BB Bitch', *The Sun*, 1 January 2007, p. 7.

The last punk

1   P. Saville, in R. Poynor, 'Post-Los Angeles' <http://www.btinternet.com/ ~comme6/saville/interview.htm>.

2   *Ibid.*

3   The importance of this degree in his first years of designing is often underestimated. When describing his 'early style' on the Factory Sampler, he stated that, 'I was twenty two and in my last weeks at college, and becoming aware of the great tradition of Twentieth century graphics, as well as certain schools such as the Russian constructivists, the Bauhaus and De Stijl. I was really into Jan Tschichold and Die Neue Typographie of the 1930s, which was exclusively typography and graphics and reflected in the mood of the time. Thus my first studies were reflected in the sleeves of my first records', from an interview with James Nice, 'Perfect stylistic attitude' <http://www.btinternet.com/~comme6/saville/interviewpsa. htm>.

4   He confirmed, in 'In Camera SHOWstudio', when asked about his favourite album sleeves, 'All time: Autobahn Andy Warhol's Velvet Underground Fear of Music The White Album Another Time Another Place' <http://www.btinternet. com/~comme6/saville/interviewshowstudio.htm>.

5   Saville, in Poynor.

6   Paul Morley described the impact of this music for *The Observer*: 'Over a hundred years after the Industrial Revolution, which seemed destined to crush the area into dust and isolation as the world it inspired moved Manchester out of the way, an Emotional Revolution happened that would push Manchester into the 21st Century', *OMM*, May 2006, p. 7.

7   Saville, in Poynor.

8   The two-disc set of Michael Winterbottom's *24 Hour Party People* featured a large segment on Peter Saville, with him offering an auditory commentary on his Factory 'gallery'. Please refer to disc two, Madman Entertainment, 2002.

9   P. Saville, in C. Wilson, 'Interview with Peter Saville', P. Saville, *Designed by Peter Saville* (London: frieze, 2003), p. 34.

10 Wilson and Saville, p. 30.

11 The Factory designs feature in a book by Matthew Robertson, *Factory Records: The Complete Graphic Album* (London: Thames & Hudson, 2006).

12 P. Saville, 'Peter Saville In Camera SHOWstudio', *Artwork*, Spring/Summer 2003 <http://www.btinternet.com/~comme6/saville/interviewshowstudio.htm>.

13 P. Saville, in Sean O'Toole's 'Design Indaba' <http://www.btinternet.com/ ~comme6/saville/interview5.htm>.

14 As Andrew O'Hagan remembers, 'most of the people I grew up with had never worn designer clothes, but they could tell a Peter Saville album cover at a hundred

yards', *London Review of Books*, 19 June 2003 <http://www.lrb.co.uk/v25/n12/ohag01_.html>.

15   'Be careful what you wish for: the graphic design of Peter Saville' <http://www.btinternet.com/~comme6/saville/interview4.htm>.

16   Adrian Shaughnessy stated that, 'to promote their rejuvenated city, Manchester City Council turned to the branding experts. A body called Marketing Manchester was handed the task of turning Manchester into a "brand"', in 'Peter Saville: Creative Director of Manchester', *Voice*, 6 May 2004 <http://www.aiga.org/content.cfm/peter-saville-creative-director-of-manchester>.

17   P. Saville, from 'Factory Outlet', October 2007 <http://www.btinternet.com/~comme6/saville/interview6.htm>.

18   Rick Poynor, in 'The graphic design of Peter Saville', described how he stands against contemporary trends: 'one by one the proselytes of style have recanted, repented and re-dedicated themselves to the pursuit of content and the responsibilities of communication', in *Peter Saville's Pentagram for the Nineties* <http://www.btinternet.com/~comme6/saville/pentagram.htm>.

19   As Andrew O'Hagan realized, 'I think it likely – or slightly more than likely – that Peter Saville is the only English graphic artist to have had an actor play him in a major motion picture', in 'At the Design Museum', *London Review of Books,* 19 June 2003 <http://www.lrb.co.uk/v25/n12/ohag01_.html>.

Handbag nation

1   T. Cox, 'Would you sleep with a guy for an expensive handbag?' *Cosmopolitan*, September 2003, No. 363, p. 58.

A game you play with your brain: Philosophy Football

1   Clive Hamilton and Richard Denniss, in *Affluenza* (Sydney: Allen and Unwin, 2005), believed that 'Australians today feel materially deprived, even though they are richer than ever before; a pervasive discontent is continually reinforced by consumer culture. This cultivation of a sense of deprivation in the midst of plenty is essential to the reproduction of consumerism. For people infected by affluenza, more is never enough, yet they fail to understand that more consumption will not allay their feeling of discontent' (p. 179).

2   Mark Perryman has also published books continuing the principles of the company. In *Philosophy Football: The Team that Plays with Strength In Depth* (Edinburgh: Mainstream, 1999), he stated that 'the idea behind this book is delightfully simple. Take eleven of the world's greatest minds then imagine how they would have turned out if their brains had been in their boots instead of their heads' (p. 13).

3   D. Allirajah, 'Offside', *Spiked*, 26 April 2002 <http://www.spiked-online.com/Articles/00000006D8B9.htm>.

4   M. Perryman, 'Hooligan Wars', in M. Perryman (ed.), *Hooligan Wars: Causes and Effects of Football Violence* (Edinburgh: Mainstream, 2001), p. 19.

5   P. Gilroy, *Postcolonial Melancholia* (New York: Columbia University Press, 2005), p. 1.

6   Perryman, 'Hooligan Wars', p. 33.

7   B. Bragg, 'Two world wars and one world cup', in M. Perryman (ed.), *The Ingerland Factor* (Edinburgh: Mainstream, 1999), p. 42.

Punking yoga

1   M. Erben, 'Biography and research method', in N. Erben (ed.), *Biography and Education: A Reader* (London: Falmer, 1998), p. 12.

2   M. Rimel, personal email, 25 May 2006.

3   B. Beal, 'Disqualifying the official: an exploration of social resistance through the subculture of skateboarding', *Sociology of Sport Journal*, Vol. 12, No. 3, 1995, p. 252.

4   *Ibid.*, p. 253.

5   D. Hebdige, *Subculture: The Meaning of Style* (London: Routledge, 1987), p. 79.

6   Richard Butsch confirmed the value of this model because 'it allowed resistance to such domination, but also for co-optation (i.e., incorporation) of such resistance', in 'Considering resistance and incorporation', *Leisure Sciences*, Vol. 23, 2001, p. 71.

7   Subcultures were described by Robert Wood as comprising 'sets of norms, values, and beliefs, along with networks of individuals, objectives, and relationships designed for the purpose of sub cultural boundary communication and maintenance', in 'Threat transcendence, ideological articulation, and frame of reference reconstruction: preliminary concepts for a theory of subcultural schism', *Deviant Behavior*, Vol. 21, 2000, p. 26.

8   Stuart Hall captured this 'crisis of class' – in terms of both language and positioning – through his book, *The Hard Road to Renewal: Thatcherism and the Crisis of the Left* (London: Verso, 1988).

9   This argument was best captured in the title of the Birmingham Centre for Contemporary Cultural Studies' monograph, edited by Stuart Hall and Tony Jefferson, *Resistance through Rituals* (London: Hutchinson, 1976).

10   H. Beazley, 'Voices from the margins: street children's subcultures in Indonesia', *Children's Geographies*, Vol. 1, No. 2, 2003, p. 183.

11   Women's Studies Group, *Women Take Issue: Aspects of Women's Subordination* (London: Hutchinson in association with the CCCS, 1978).

12   P. Gilroy, *There Ain't No Black in The Union Jack* (London: Hutchinson, 1987).

13   M. Rimel, from 'Yoga gets punky', *Sunday Telegraph*, February 2006, retexted on <http://yogurtactiveculture.blogspot.com/>.

14   'Yoga is going punk rock' was the description by Alle Hall in "Hey ho, let's om!" in *Bust Magazine*, April/May 2006, retexted on <http://yogurtactiveculture.blogspot.com/>.

15   Within an American article, Morgwn Rimel and Gaylee Bulter are described as 'Australian yogis-cum-e-tailers', in Alle Hall, *op. cit.*

16   'Poser' <http://www.Yogurtactiveculture.com/womens/womens.htm>.

17   'Rock hard core'<http://www.Yogurtactiveculture.com/womens/womens.htm>.

18   In this way, Yogurt Activewear is perpetuating many of the standards and values of the fashion industry. Jan Wright stated that 'the dominance of particular sets of values and beliefs over others is maintained through the practices of individuals and groups. For instance, media images, the fashion industry, aerobics instructors, physical educators who constantly promote thin bodies as the ideal for women provide messages about valued expressions of femininity', in 'Changing gendered practices in physical education: working with teachers', *European Physical Education Review*, Vol. 5, No. 3, 1999, p. 184.

19   A.C. Sparkes, 'Exploring body narratives', *Sport, Education and Society*, Vol. 4, No. 1, 1999, pp. 17–30.

20   'Men's   Proactive-Wear'   <http://www.yogurtactiveculture.com/mens/mens.htm>.

21   'Empower   tools'   <http://www.yogurtactiveculture.com/tools/images/Wmpower_tools_text.jpg>.

22   'God save the yogi, it's anarchy in the ashram', *National Post*, 25 December 2005 <http://yogurtactiveculture.blogspot.com/>.

23   M. Perez, 'Hardcore Asana Gear', *Venuszine.com*, May 2006, retexted on <http://yogurtactiveculture.blogspot.com/>.

24   Robin Boudette confirmed that – for her patients – yoga had been a successful 'medication'. She stated that 'Yoga … enables patients to experience their bodies in a new way. Living in a society that values how you look more than how you feel, eating disorder patients often relate to the body as an ornament; they suffer from a disconnection from the body, feelings, appetites, and inner experience', in 'How can the practice of yoga be helpful in recovery from an eating disorder?' *Eating Disorders*, Vol. 14, 2006, p. 168.

24   Jens Granath, Sara Ingvarsson, Ulrica von Thiele and Ulf Lundberg stated that 'stress-related health problems, such as chronic fatigue, muscular pain and burnout, have increased dramatically in modern societies in recent years … Yoga is an ancient Indian practice focusing on breathing and physical exercises, thereby combining muscle relaxation, meditation and physical workout', in 'Stress management: a

randomized study of cognitive behavioural therapy and yoga', *Cognitive Behaviour Therapy*, Vol. 35, No. 1, 2006, p. 3.

26   B. D'Mello, 'Reebok and the global footwear sweatshop', *Monthly Review*, February 2003, p. 26.

27   *Ibid.*

28   *Ibid.*, p. 32.

29   S. Strauss, 'Adapt, adjust, accommodate: the production of yoga in a transnational world', *History and Anthropology*, Vol. 13, No. 3, 2002, p. 248.

30   G. Wythes, 'Who owns yoga?' *Australian Yoga Life*, Issue 14, March–July 2006, pp. 6–10.

31   *Ibid.*, p. 7.

32   *Ibid.*

33   C. Leadbeater, *Living on Thin Air: The New Economy* (London: Penguin, 2000).

34   This case is outlined on the OSYU website <http://www.yogaunity.org>.

35   Wythes, *op. cit.*, p. 7.

36   K. Desikachar, in *ibid.*, p. 7.

37   S. Hasselle-Newcombe, 'Spirituality and "mystical religion" in contemporary society: a case study of British Practitioners of the Iyengar Method of yoga', *Journal of Contemporary Religion*, Vol. 20, No. 3, 2005, p. 306.

38   R. Bishop, 'Stealing the signs: a semiotic analysis of the changing nature of professional sports logos', *Social Semiotics*, Vol. 11, No. 1, 2002, p. 37.

39   V. Carducci, 'The aura of the brand', *Radical Society*, Vol. 30, Nos 3–4, 2003, pp. 43–4.

40   M. Rimel, in Perez, *op. cit.*

41   Jacqueline Lunn, 'Downward dog adopts a rebellious pose', *The Sydney Morning Herald*, 8–9 April 2006, retexted on <http://yogurtactiveculture.blogspot.com/>.

42   'Pose off', *Slimming & Health*, April 2005, retexted on <http://yogurtactiveculture.blogspot.com/>.

43   C. Hamilton and R. Denniss, *Affluenza* (Crows Nest: Allen and Unwin, 2005), p. 7.

44   R. Butsch, 'Considering resistance and incorporation', *Leisure Sciences*, Vol. 23, 2001, p. 78.

Kindle surprise

1   A strong compendium on the history of the book is David Finkelstein and Alistair McCleery (eds), *The Book History Reader* (London: Routledge, 2002).

2   N. Patel, 'Kindle sells out in 5.5 hours', *Engadget*, 21 November 2007 <http://www.engadget.com/2007/11/21/kindle-sells-out-in-two-days/>; and 'Jeff Bezos posts Kindle apology on Amazon's front page', *Engadget*, 20 March 2008 <http://

www.engadget.com/2008/03/20/jeff-bezos-posts-kindle-apology-on-amazons-front-page/>.

3 A. Pressman, 'Buy Amazon – Kindle is the iPod of books', *Business Week*, 19 November 2007 <http://www.businessweek.com/investing/insights/blog/archives/2007/11/buy_amazon_-_ki.html>.

4 Significantly, and incorrectly I believe, 'Bob' stated that 'there is a big target market difference between the iPod and the Kindle. Everyone likes music, regardless of their IQ or education. Kids at Harvard and kids at XYZ community college are plugged into iPods. Not everyone likes books. With the dumming [sic] down of America, the target market for the Kindle is limited to the more educated and motivated in our society', comments to Pressman <http://www.businessweek.com/investing/insights/blog/archives/2007/11/buy_amazon_-_ki.html>. We need more research conducted on the ethnography of reading, particularly between analogue and digital platforms. The impact of dumbing down – or even 'dumming down' – may or may not be a classed, gendered, raced or generational formation. However, the complexity and size of the contemporary publishing – let alone writing – environment suggests that many audiences are deploying diverse literacies through multiple reading and writing contexts.

5 Poetry faces particular problems in terms of intellectual property rights and copyright. Wendy Cope confirmed that 'a poem is very easy to copy, whereas nobody is going to photocopy or download a whole novel or work of non-fiction. Therefore poets are especially at risk if people do not know and respect copyright law … My poems are all over the internet. I've managed to get them removed from one or two sites that were major offenders but there are dozens, if not hundreds of sites displaying poems without permission. If I Google the title of one of my poems, it is almost always there somewhere, and I can download it and print it out. I'm sure that this must affect sales of my books', from 'You like my poems? So pay for them!' *ALCS News*, Spring 2008, p. 4.

Two bars

1 'Scissor Sisters triumph at Brits', *BBC News*, 10 February 2005 <http://news.bbc.co.uk/1/h1/entertertainment/music/4249031.stm>.

2 N. Hornby, *31 Songs* (London: Penguin, 2003).

3 N. Hornby, *Fever Pitch* (London: Penguin, 2000).

4 P. Morley, *Words and Music* (London: Bloomsbury, 2004).

5 This obsessional quality of fandom was also captured by another journalist who started in the music papers but moved to the broadsheets. Julie Burchill stated that 'I'm such an indiscriminating lover of dance music that I'll have eight versions of Sweet Harmony by Liquid and happily buy a compilation with 39 tracks I've

already got to get the one I haven't', interviewed by Andrew Harrison, 'When was the last time Julie Burchill took cocaine?' *Word*, No. 21, November 2004, p. 36.

6 P. Morley, *Joy Division Piece by Piece: Writing about Joy Division 1977–2007* (London: Plexus, 2008).

7 The two remarkable biographies of Ian Curtis are Deborah Curtis' *Touching from a Distance* (London: Faber, 1995); and Mick Middles and Lindsay Reade, *Torn Apart: The Life of Ian Curtis* (London: Omnibus, 2006).

8 Mick Middles produced the important book on this transition: *From Joy Division to New Order: The Factory Story* (London: Virgin, 1996).

As cool as The Crickets

1 'Live in Brighton', from *We Are Scissor Sisters and So Are You* (Polydor, 2004).

It's not easy being Johnny Cash

1 M. Haggard, 'Half a Mile a Day', from *Johnny Cash: The Anthology* (Hallway Group, 2001).

2 G. Bush, 'Address to a joint session of Congress and the American people', The White House website <http://www.whitehouse.gov/news/releases/2001/09/20010920-8.html>.

3 Cash loaned his name and songs to an album for victims of AIDS. Titled *'Til Things Are Brighter*, the proceeds went to the Terrence Higgins Trust.

4 J. Phoenix, 'I'm too busy for love', *NW*, 12 June 2006, p. 79.

5 S. Miller, *Johnny Cash: The Life of an American Icon* (London: Omnibus, 2003), p. viii.

6 The Tennessee Two, Marshall Grant and Luther Perkins, deserve much credit in establishing 'the Cash sound'. The tightness of the relationship, formed when Cash was an appliance salesman and Grant and Perkins were mechanics, survived from their meeting in 1954 through to Perkins' death in 1968 – a few months after the Folsom concert. Grant remained performing with Cash through to the 1980s.

7 'I Walk the Line' was later recorded by more than 100 other performers. Please refer to Todd Leopold, '"Man in Black" Johnny Cash dead at 71', CNN.com, 12 September 2003 <http://cnn.entertainment.printthis.clickability.com/pt/cpt?action=cpt&title=CNN.com>.

8 M. Streissguth, *Johnny Cash at Folsom Prison: The Making of a Masterpiece* (New York: Da Capo, 2004).

9 *Ibid.*, p. 13.

10 Leopold, *op. cit.*

11 Cash stated that 'The lyrics came as fast as I could write', in Miller, *op. cit.*, p. 62.

12   It was this complexity that made James Mangold, director of *Walk the Line*, choose Joaquin Phoenix. He stated that 'Joaq has the same thing. His face is complicated, and it's hard to find someone who can communicate complication', in J. Tyrangiel, 'Fade to black', *Time*, No. 166, 31 October 2005, p. 76.

13   J. Cash, in S. Turner, *The Man Called Cash* (London: Bloomsbury, 2005), p. 246.

14   R. Rubin, in Miller, *op. cit.*, p. 329.

15   Bono, in Turner, *op. cit.*, p. 190.

16   To view the video for 'Hurt', please refer to <http://www.losthighwayrecords. com/e/cash11403.html>.

17   'Johnny Cash', Toptown.com <http://www.toptown.com/hp/66/cash.html>.

18   Teresa Ortega built upon this ideology of transgression in her article, 'My name is Sue! How do you do: Johnny Cash as lesbian icon', *The South Atlantic Quarterly*, Vol. 94, No. 1, 1995, pp. 259–72.

19   Tom Morello of Audioslave stated that 'there is something in the soul of the music of Johnny Cash that has something very much in common with Bob Marley and Joe Strummer. Though they are artists from different continents and completely different genres of music, there's an honesty and an integrity to the music that they make. I think that if Johnny Cash had been born in Jamaica, he could have been Bob Marley', in 'Johnny Cash: original gangsta', MTV News.com <http://www. mtv.com/bands/c/cash_johnny/news_vma_feature/index4.jhtml>.

20   Cash stated that 'I always wanted a hit gospel song, but God game me "A Boy Named Sue" instead and I'm happy with it', in Turner, *op. cit.*, p. 242.

21   'Joaquin Phoenix', *Star*, 26 April 2006, p. 11.

22   'Beautiful Screen Duos: Reese & Joaquin', *Who*, 1 May 2006, pp. 100–101.

23   'Johnny Cash: original gangsta', *op. cit.*

Play 'Great Leap Forward', you bastard

1   J. Peel, 'The Ingerland factor playlist: can you hear the English sing?' in M. Perryman (ed.), *The Ingerland Factor* (Edinburgh: Mainstream, 1999), p. 35.

2   B. Bragg, in A. Collins, *Still Suitable for Miners* (London: Virgin, 1998).

Singing a city

1   S. Hall, 'Minimal Selves', in H. Baker, M. Diawara and R. Lindeborg (eds), *Black British Cultural Studies: A Reader* (Chicago: University of Chicago Press, 1996), p. 115.

2   *Thunderstruck* (Sunset Home Entertainment, 2005)

3   To hear this tissue of connectiveness, compare The Stone Roses' 'Waterfall' from 1989 with The Panics' 'Don't Be Kind' from 2003.

4   J. Robb, 'Louder than Bombs: Happy Mondays', in C. Hutton and R. Kurt (eds), *Don't Look Back in Anger: Growing Up with Oasis* (London: Simon and Schuster, 1997), p. 215.

5   J. Robb, *The Stone Roses and the Resurrection of British Pop* (London: Ebury Press, 1997), p. 137.

6   J. Laffer, in J. Tompkin, 'The Panics the last Laffer', *X Press*, No. 860, 7 August 2003, p. 34.

7   The Panics, *Cruel Guards* (Dew Process/Universal, 2007).

8   J. Laffer, 'Cruel Guards', The Panics <http://www.thepanics.com.au/disco. cfm>.

9   Hall, *op. cit.*, p. 114.

Downloading democracy

1   There have also been opportunities for remixers to create new texts in old forms. James Rutledge, for example, has constructed a four-hour remix of Radiohead's 'Videotape', the final track from the *In Rainbows* album. This remix is only for sale on a 240-minute VHS video cassette, with visual accompaniment by Philip M. Lane. Rutledge realized that 'there was a certain irony in making an undownloadable version of a track from an album that was originally only available as a download', in J. Clay, 'Straight to video', *The Guardian – The Guide*, 5–11 April 2008, p. 12.

2   D. McAleer, *The Downloader's Music Source Book* (London: Carlton Publishing Group, 2005).

3   N. Caine, 'Downloads have saved Christmas number one', MSN Money, 19 December 2007 <http://money.uk.msn.com/guides/christmasmoney/article. aspx?cp-documentid=7029743>.

I know I won't be leaving here with the Archduke

1   'Brit nominee to headline The Edinburgh Lectures', 13 January 2005 <http:// www.edinburghlectures.org/edinburghlectures/130105/13jan05.html>.

2   For a discussion of their Mercury Award and how their prize money was to be spent, please refer to 'Ferdinand win Mercury Music Price', *BBC News*, 9 August 2004 <http://newsvote.bbc.co.uk/mpapps/pagetools/print/news.bbc.co.uk/1/ hi/entertainment/>.

3   Ben Granger described Franz Ferdinand's ability to create a place 'where the smart are cool and the cool are smart', in 'Believe The Hype', *Spike Magazine*, June 2004 <http://www.spikemagazine.com/0604franzferdinand.php>.

4   'Sound of 2004: Franz Ferdinand', *BBC News*, 1 August 2004 <http://newsvote. bbc.co.uk/mpapps/pagetools/print/news.bbc.co.uk/1/hi/entertainment/>.

5   Alex Kapranos encouraged such governmental initiatives in his Edinburgh Lecture. He stated that 'Without infrastructure, a nation collapses. Without roads, healthcare, rail, emergency services, a civilisation would collapse. Likewise, a cultural infrastructure is essential. We should think of funding for popular music more in the way we should fund other parts of industry and an investment that will bring both cultural and financial returns', in 'February Music Lecture features Franz Ferdinand Frontman', *The University of Edinburgh News & Events*, 17 January 2005 <http://wwwed.ac.uk/news/050117edlecture.html>.

6   M. Arnold, *Culture and Anarchy* (Oxford: Oxford University Press, 2006).

7   *Ibid.*

I'm with stupid

1   Later, I found out that this famous coat was designed by Stephen Linard.

2   The 'sexuality' of The Pet Shop Boys through much of their career has been textually and publicly ambivalent. Neil Tennant 'came out' in a 1994 magazine, in the article 'Honestly', *Attitude*, Vol. 1, No. 4, 1994. While the tabloids – and indeed the magazine article itself – made his 'declaration' of much greater significance than was needed either musically or politically, when reading his quotations at the time, his own 'theory' of sexuality – and indeed popular music – emerged. He stated, 'I never wanted to be a part of this separate gay world. I know a lot of people will not appreciate hearing me say that. But when people talk about the gay community in London, for instance, what do they really mean by that? There is a community of interests, particularly around the health issue, but beyond that what is there, really? There's nightclubs, music, drugs, shopping … Well I'm sorry, but that really isn't how I define myself. I don't want to belong to some narrow group or ghetto. And I think, if they're really honest, a lot of gay people would say they felt like that as well' (p. 68).

3   While *Release* suffered from the critics, Johnny Marr's musical influence and impact on this album is both undermined and underestimated. He had earlier provided a subtle and intricate guitar line on 'My October Symphony', on *Behaviour*.

4   Peter Robinson wrote that 'In 2003, the Pet Shop Boys' career retrospective *PopArt* – arguably the best British pop collection of the past 30 years – limped its way to No. 30 in the charts. It was an uncomfortable sight following the previous year's *Release*, a foray into non-electronica for which the term "lukewarm reception" might have been invented. Would anybody care if the Pet Shop Boys never released another album?' *OMM*, May 2006, p. 65.

5   The Pet Shop Boys were aware of this Pop/Art relationship before their critics. Andrew Harrison stated that 'The Pet Shop Boys take pop music seriously enough to be frivolous with it … For this they're usually characterized as ironic,

and I suppose it is somewhat ironic that a gay-themed disco duo can sing more convincingly about straight relationships than most of our guitar-thwacking real men and writhing sexpots. For all it matters, most of the Pet Shop Boys enthusiasts I know are heterosexual', *The Word*, Issue 38, April 2006, p. 100.

6 An example of this fan influence is seen on a stream of websites. For example, Martin Aguilar of Mexico City, in response to *Fundamental*, stated: 'Pet Shop Boys, my religion I love you guys an[d] I think you are the best', in T. Kraines, 'Fundamental', *BBC Music*, 22 May 2006 <http://www.bbc.co.uk/music/pop/reviews/petshop_fundamental.shtml>.

7 A. Petridis, 'Pet Shop Boys, Fundamental', *The Guardian*, 19 May 2006 <http://arts.guardian.co.uk/print/0,,329483458-117421,00.html>.

8 Andy, in Kraines, *op. cit.*

9 L. Turner, 'Fundamental', *Playlouder*, 23 May 2006 <http://www.playlouder.com/review/+fundamental/>, accessed on 27 May 2006.

10 Petridis, *op.cit.*

11 E. Said, *On Late Style* (London: Bloomsbury, 2007).

12 A. Gill, 'Album: Pet Shop Boys, Fundamental', *The Independent*, 19 May 2006 <http://enjoyment.independent.co.uk/music/reviews/article496551.ece>.

What have you ever done on the telly?

1 'Slough stationers beat New York's finest', *The Guardian*, 26 January 2004 <http://media.guardian.co.uk/broadcast/story/0,7493,1131304,00.html>.

2 R. Gervais, 'Talk', *The Guardian*, 25 October 2002 <http://mediatalk.guardian.co.uk/WebX?50@@.3ba76720>.

3 S. Moss, 'The Office', in A. Merullo and N. Wenborn (eds), *British Comedy Greats* (London: Cassell Illustrated, 2003), p. 132.

4 'Two nights at *The Office* for Ricky Gervais', *Manchester Online* <http://www.manchesteronline.co.uk/entertainment/comedy/stories/Detail_LinkStory>.

5 BBC 2 has a great history for commissioning innovative comedy. Both *The Royle Family* and *Absolutely Fabulous* appeared on BBC 2 and then moved to BBC 1. *The Office*'s first two seasons were broadcast on BBC 2, with the Christmas episodes screened on BBC 1. Significantly BBC 3 is increasingly fulfilling this function, with both *Pulling* and *Gavin and Stacey* playing on this channel.

6 There are many reasons that could explain the incredible success of *The Office* in its rescreening. One interesting possibility revolves around The Stereophonics releasing a cover of the programme's theme song: 'Handbags and Gladrags', which was originally sung by the paint-stripping voice of Chris Farlowe. This cover version reached number one, increasing general awareness of the programme.

7   4.6 million people watched the first episode of the second series. Only the second episode dipped with the audience, losing viewers (appropriately) to the Channel 4 programme, *A Man's Best Friend*, which investigated a man's relationship with his penis.

8   A. Burton, 'When was Britain? Nostalgia for the nation at the end of the "American Century"', *The Journal of Modern History*, Vol. 75, June 2003, p. 373.

9   Tim, in *The Office*, Series One, Episode Six, in Ricky Gervais and Stephen Merchant, *The Office: The Scripts Series 1* (London: BBC Books, 2002), p. 266.

10   David, *The Office*, Christmas Episode One, 26 December 2003, BBC.

11   Simon Hoggart stated that 'Ricky Gervais ought to copy John Cleese and find fresh worlds to conquer, leaving behind a dozen near-perfect little comedies, and our memory of Gareth, his haircut a pudding bowl mounted on a bog brush', in 'Farewell, Ricky', *The Spectator*, 9 November 2002, p. 98.

12   The level of reflexivity is increased in these final two programmes of *The Office*, by leaving in the interviewer's questions to the talking heads. In the previous two series, the views of the staff are seamlessly spliced. However, by leaving the disembodied questions on the soundtrack, it adds to the reflection on the reality television genre and the celebrity process.

13   S. Redhead, *Paul Virilio: Theorist for an Accelerated Culture* (Edinburgh: Edinburgh University Press), p. 51.

14   David, *The Office*, Christmas Episode One, BBC.

15   S. Wollaston, 'Last night's TV', *The Guardian*, 15 September 2006, p. 28.

16   John Smithson, co-producer of *Touching The Void*, argued that the changes to television have been one of the causes for the increasing popularity of documentary film-making. He stated that 'the schedules are increasingly filling up with reality and make-over shows … Particularly at times when people are watching, there is less and less room for anything long and serious', in Mark Ellen, 'You couldn't make it up', *Word*, No. 21, November 2004, p. 73.

17   D. Potter, 'What new reality?' *American Journalism Review*, January 2002, p. 60.

18   Emma Brockes recognized the consequences of the changing formations of news to critical thinking and interpretation. In response to the wars in Afghanistan, Iraq and Lebanon, she stated: 'we are accustomed, as sophisticated consumers of the 24-hour news media, to take a rolling approach to disaster, which means never regarding a story as finite, which means pretending that nothing has ultimate consequences, which means, if you want to go the whole philosophical hog, existing in a constant state of denial about death. Anyway. In news as in life, the way we deal with disturbing events is to wrap them in analytical packaging, an evasion that makes us feel more in control. If you don't have a position on war in the Middle East, you at least have an appreciation for the range of positions at your disposal and as long as Sky News keeps booking the experts and loading the

graphics, there is no catastrophe too great or too strange to absorb', in 'Oh God (redux)', *The Guardian*, 5 August 2006, p. 27.

19   Tim, *The Office*, Christmas Episode Two, 27 December 2003, BBC.

20   G. Noble, 'Everyday work', in F. Martin (ed.), *Interpreting Everyday Culture* (London: Hodder Headline, 2003), p. 88.

21   S. Aronowitz, D. Esposito, W. DiFazio and M. Yard, 'The post-work manifesto', in S. Aronowitz and J. Cutler (eds), *Post-work* (London: New Fetter Lane, 1998), p. 64.

22   Tim, *The Office*, Series One, Episode Six, BBC.

23   Tim, *The Office*, Series Two, Episode Three, in Ricky Gervais and Stephen Merchant, *The Office: The Scripts Series 2* (London: BBC Books, 2003), p. 103.

24   M. Poster, 'Workers as cyborgs: labor and networked computers', *Journal of Labor Research*, Vol. 23, No. 3, Summer 2002, p. 347.

25   Anthony Townsend and James Bennett investigated this economic, social and educational shift in 'Information technology and employment law', *Journal of Labor Research*, Vol. 24, No. 3, Summer 2003, pp. 425–35.

26   D. Ezzy, 'A simulacrum of workplace community', *Sociology*, Vol. 35, No. 3, p. 633.

27   K. Healy, 'What's new for culture in the new economy?' *The Journal of Arts Management, Law and Society*, Vol. 32, No. 2, Summer 2002, p. 90.

28   D. Bell, *The Coming of Post-Industrial Society: A Venture in Social Forecasting* (New York: Basic Books, 1976).

29   David and Donna, *The Office*, Series One, Episode Two, in *The Office: The Scripts Series 1, op. cit.*, p. 69.

30   Keith, *The Office*, Series One, Episode Four, *ibid.*, p. 167.

31   Dawn, *ibid.*, p. 178.

32   Tim, *ibid.*, p. 187.

33   A. Greenspan, in Diane Coyle, 'How not to get into education: the information age workforce', *Critical Quarterly*, Vol. 43, No. 1, 2003, p. 47.

34   Dawn, *The Office*, Series Two, Episode Two, in *The Office: The Scripts Series 2, op. cit.*, p. 60.

35   J. Wajcman and B. Martin stated that 'Women have worked for slightly more companies than men in the first decade of their careers and they are much more likely to have worked across sector boundaries', in 'Narratives of identity in modern management', *Sociology*, Vol. 36, No. 4, 2002, p. 989.

36   A considered analysis of women's relationship with the workplace is Sigal Alon, Debra Donahoe and Marta Tienda, 'The effects of early work experience on young women's labor force attachment', *Social Forces*, Vol. 79, No. 3, March 2001, pp. 1005–34.

37   Noz2, 'Talk', *The Guardian*, *op. cit.*

38   Juicy Pip, *ibid.*

39   K. Farrell, *Post-Trauma Culture: Injury and Interpretation in the Nineties* (Baltimore: Johns Hopkins University Press, 1998).

40   I. Hunter referred to these films as 'The celluloid cubicle', *The Journal of American Culture*, Vol. 26, No. 2, March 2003.

41   Tim, *The Office*, Christmas Episode Two, 27 December 2003, BBC.

42   Andrew Tolson, *The Limits of Masculinity* (London: Tavistock, 1985).

43   Michael S. Kimmel argued that 'if men are changing at all … it is not because they have stumbled upon the limits of traditional masculinity all of themselves. For at least two decades, the women's movement … has suggested that the traditional enactments of masculinity were in desperate need of overhaul', in 'Rethinking masculinity', in M. Kimmel (ed.), *Changing Men: New Directions in Research on Men and Masculinity* (Newbury Park: SAGE, 1987), p. 9.

44   S. Faludi, *Stiffed* (London: Chatto and Windus, 1999), p. 61.

45   E. Probyn, 'The masculine mystique', *The Australian*, 11 July 2001, p. 37.

46   A. Walzer, 'Narratives of contemporary male crisis', *The Journal of Men's Studies*, Vol. 10, No. 2, Winter 2002, p. 210.

47   The Promise Keepers and Christian churches have facilitated this type of conservative model of masculinity, based on being a better husband, father and Christian. For a discussion of these movements, please refer to A. Singleton's 'Men getting real', *Journal of Sociology*, Vol. 39, No. 2, 2003.

48   A discussion of the relationship between masculinity and consumerism is J.M. Clark's 'Faludi, Fight Club and phallic masculinity', *The Journal of Men's Studies*, Vol. 11, No. 1, Fall 2002.

49   Chris Finch, *The Office*, Series One, Episode Two, BBC.

50   Gareth, *The Office*, Series One, Episode Three, BBC.

51   David, *The Office*, Series One, Episode Three, BBC.

52   Brenda, Gareth, Tim, *The Office*, Series Two, Episode Five, in *The Office: The Scripts Series 2*, *op. cit.*, pp. 183–4.

53   A. McClimens, 'Disability on the box', *Learning Disability Practice*, Vol. 6, No. 6, July 2003, p. 27.

54   Ricky Gervais has built on his politicized critique of disability policy in society, by featuring in an advertising campaign to challenge discrimination against disabled people. He wrote, directed and starred in a cinematic commercial. He plays a factory worker who lists the reasons why people with disabilities would not fit into the workplace. The slogan of the advertisements concludes his performance: 'Is ugly a disability?' This advertisement was described by Julia Day in 'Fact! Gervais stars in disability ad', *The Guardian*, Wednesday 27 November 2002 <http://media. guardian.co.uk/print/0,3858,4555551-105235,00.html>.

55 Tim, *The Office*, Series Two, Episode Six, in *The Office: The Scripts Series 2*, *op. cit.*, p. 229.

56 Tim, *The Office*, Series Two, Episode Three, BBC.

57 Gareth, *The Office*, Series Two, Episode Two, BBC.

58 David, *The Office*, Series Two, Episode Six, in *The Office: The Scripts Series 2*, *op. cit.*, p. 216.

59 David, *The Office*, Christmas Episode Two, 27 December 2003, BBC.

Pree-sen-na kul-cha

1 J. Burchill, *Sex and Sensibility* (London: Grafton, 1992), p. 245.

You've got to have a good haircut

1 *Live Forever*, written and directed by John Dower (Passion Pictures, 2003).

2 Peter Kay, *Mum Wants a Bungalow Tour* (Universal, 2003).

3 J. Harris, *The Last Party: Britpop, Blair and the Demise of English Rock* (London: Fourth Estate, 2003).

4 J. Dawson, 'Real politic meets rock and roll', 7 February 2004 <http://www.amazon.co.uk/exec/obidos/ASIN/B00009B0RO/026-3164820-4318820>.

5 I. Welsh, 'Post-punk junk', in S. Redhead, *Repetitive Beat Generation* (Edinburgh: Rebel Inc, 2000), p. 144.

Beyond the seducer

1 A. Bancroft, 'Graduate star Anne Bancroft dies', *BBC News*, 8 June 2005 <http://news.bbc.co.uk/1/hi/entertainment/film/4071734.stm>.

I don't believe you. You're a liar

1 P. Gallo, 'Love song to Dylan', *Variety*, 18 September 2005, p. 59.

2 M. Scorsese, in K. Aftab, 'His direction home', *The Independent*, 18 November 2005, p. 8.

3 The role of Scorsese in this picture has attracted commentary. Erik Moe stated that 'the film is billed as "A Martin Scorsese Picture", but the interviews were mostly conducted and approved by Dylan's inner circle well before Scorsese came on board in 2001. Other filmmakers began doing the footwork for "No Direction Home" as early as 1995 (which explains the new interview with poet Allen Ginsberg, who died in 1997). Despite the micromanaging of source material, the

editing makes it clear that this is a serious work of art from Scorsese the auteur', in 'No direction home: Bob Dylan – A Martin Scorsese Picture', About.com <http://documentaries.about.com/od/reviews/fr/no_direction.htm>.

4   A. Hornaday, '"No Direction": Scorsese points the way to Dylan', *Washington Post*, 26 September 2005 <http://www.washingtonpost.com/wp-dyn/content/article/2005/09/25/AR200509250124>.

5   C. Bogie, 'Movie review: No direction home', *Harvard Independent*, 20 October 2005 <http://www.harvardindependent.com/media/paper369/news/2005/10/20/Arts/Movie.Review>.

6   The complex commodification of *No Direction Home* was investigated by David Yaffe in 'The last temptation of Dylan', *Slate*, 23 September 2005 <http://www.slate.com/id/2126752/>.

7   Karen Everhart explored these tie-in and licensing rights in 'Scorsese and Dylan waltz again for PBS', *Current.org*, 25 July 2005 <http://www.current.org/music/music0514dylan.shtml>.

8   D. Knowles, 'Scorsese documents Dylan on No Direction Home,' *The Miscellany News*, 30 September 2005, accessed on 6 November 2005.

9   F. Capers, 'No direction home', *Metaphilm*, 6 October 2005 <http://metaphilm.com/philm.php?id=451_0_2_0_M>.

10   Richard Corliss described his career after the accident as 'the past four decades have been a fascinating coda to the brief musical miracle this documentary captures', in 'When he was on his own', *Time*, Vol. 166, No. 12, 19 September 2005, p. 71.

11   Bob Dylan, from M. Scorsese, *No Direction Home* (Paramount Home Entertainment, 2005).

Bad Wolf

1   'Home truths', *The Guardian*, 15 January 2000 <http://film.guardian.co.uk/Feature_Story/interview/0,5365,122551,00.html>.

2   C. Eccleston, 'Doctor Who Confidential', *Doctor Who: The Complete First Series* (BBC WorldWide, 2005), Disc Five.

3   C. Eccleston, in L. Hoggard, 'You've got to laugh', *The Independent*, 2 November 2002 <http://www.findarticles.com/p/articles/mi_qn4158/is_20021102/ai_n12650558/print>.

4   R. Davies, 'Foreword', *The Shooting Scripts* (London: BBC Books, 2005), p. 5.

5   C. Eccleston, *The Complete First Series*, *op. cit.*

6   Justin Richards stated that, 'despite only staying for a year in the role of the Doctor, Christopher Eccleston is now inextricably linked with the role. He will be remembered for all time as the talented actor who brought the Doctor back to

life and resurrected a screen legend', in *Doctor Who: The Legend Continues* (London: BBC, 2005), p. 391.

7   'The Parting of the Ways', script written by Russell T. Davies, *The Shooting Scripts*, *op. cit.*, pp. 480–81.

8   Rose, 'The Parting of the Ways', *op. cit.*, p. 492.

Life, death and disco

1   It was also a moment that changed the positioning of music in the daily news. Mark Ellen confirmed that 'prior to Live Aid it took the assassination of a Beatle for pop music to make the front pages. After Live Aid its commercial power jogged the needle right across the fourth estate and all bar the broadsheets carried new pop gossip sections to ensure rock stars were a daily fixture. On July 14 Live Aid was even the lead story on the television news. Finally music appeared to have achieved what it had failed to do at The Concert for Bangladesh. It had reached out way beyond its constituency to mobilise those who cared about the famine even if they didn't care about seeing 20 minutes of George Thorogood And The Destroyers', from 'The Longest Day', *Word*, No. 21, November 2004, p. 85.

2   Rachel Shabi explored the consequences of 'protesting' in this environment. Please refer to 'The war on dissent', *The Guardian*, Saturday 2 July 2005, p. 19.

3   Please refer to Gareth Stedman Jones, 'A history of ending poverty', *The Guardian*, 2 July 2005, p. 19.

4   L. Young, 'Bob you really blew it', *The Guardian*, 3 July 2005 <http://www.guardian.co.uk/arts/live8/story/0,16066,1520476,00.html>.

5   B. Bragg, 'Can we save the world with songs? Glastonbury holds a lesson for Bob Geldof about pop and politics', *New Statesman*, 4 July 2005, Vol. 134, No. 4747, p. 31.

6   *Ibid.*

7   *Ibid.*

8   S. Manzoor, 'T-shirts shout allegiances but even warring stars reunite for this cause', *The Observer*, 3 July 2005, p. 3.

9   B. Geldof in C. Brown, 'Geldof defends link with Tories', *The Independent*, 29 December 2005.

10   Bono, in B. Jagger, 'Why I don't trust them, or sleeping with the enemy' <http://www.wagingpeace.org.articles/2005/07/11_jagger_don't_trust_them>.

11   Jagger, *ibid.*

12   M. Kelner, 'Caught between the devil and the deep red sea', *The Guardian*, 4 July 2005.

13   E. Ferguson, 'We don't want charity, what we want is justice', *The Observer*, 3 July 2005, pp. 1–2.

14   B. Geldof, *Live 8* (EMI, 2005) disc four.

Winds of change

1   K. Marx, *The German Ideology* <http://www.marxists.org/archive/marx/works/1845/german-ideology/ch01a.htm>.

2   L. Haines, 'OfCom slaps BBC for Live Earth Swearing', *The Register*, 9 April 2008 <http://www.theregister.co.uk/2008/04/09/live_earth_ruling/>.

3   Peggy and Neil Young, 'Four Strong Winds', *YouTube* <http://www.youtube.com/watch?v=wzcH87Yxjok>.

Conclusion: Cut Elvis

1   'Biography', *Woodyguthrie.org* <http://www.woodyguthrie.org/biography/biography9.htm>.

2   Trevor Blackwell and Jeremy Seabrook, in assessing two centuries of labour history, termed this desire *The Politics of Hope* (London: Faber, 1988).

3   J. Clarke, 'Capital and culture: the post-war working class revisited', in J. Clarke, C. Critcher and R. Johnson (eds), *Working Class Culture: Studies in History and Theory* (London: Hutchinson and Co., 1979), p. 238.

4   'Woman charged over alleged song stabbing', *Sydney Morning Herald*, 10 January 2006 <http://www.smh.com.au/articles/2006/01/10/1136863227203.html>.

5   The risk faced by Green Day in releasing *American Idiot* was realized by Michael Odell in 'Three Kings', *Q*, No. 225, May 2005. He stated: 'Two years ago he was up the road at Green Day's Studio 880 rehearsing a record which he feared would take his band back to having a fan base of "about 50". Now he's touted as the spokesman for a generation … *American Idiot* isn't just another 12 songs but a highly charged concept album on the state of Bush's neo-conservative America. When Bruce Springsteen or Michael Stipe tried to muster dissent they sounded either oblique or world-weary. Armstrong went for the jugular' (p. 70).

6   N. Klein, *The Shock Doctrine* (London: Penguin, 2007), p. 21.

7   A. Gramsci, 'Antonio Gramsci' <http://individual.utoronto.ca/bmclean/hermeneutics/gramsci_dir.htm>.

Index

INDEX